Partial Memories

Sketches from an Improbable Life

Ernst von Glasersfeld

imprint-academic.com

Published in the UK by Imprint Academic
PO Box 200, Exeter EX5 5YX, UK

Published in the USA by Imprint Academic
Philosophy Documentation Center
PO Box 7147, Charlottesville, VA 22906-7147, USA

ISBN 9 781845 401863

A CIP catalogue record for this book is available from the
British Library and US Library of Congress

In memory of my parents

who never worried about what "people" might say

and gave me the courage to follow my own ideas.

Contents

List of Photographs

Preface

Memories are a personal affair. They are what comes to mind when you think back, not what might in fact have happened at that earlier time in your life. You can no longer be certain of what seemed important then, because you are now looking at the past with today's eyes. The Italian philosopher Giambattista Vico had that insight three hundred years ago: When we think of things that lie in the past, we see them in terms of the concepts we have now.

Neurophysiologists and science in general have no idea of how we manage to remember. Memory is still a miracle, no less than our capability of becoming aware of experiences.

I have at times returned to places where I had been fifty years earlier. I can say that my memories always contained a core that was compatible with the later experience; but they also had features that now seemed distorted or downright wrong. The discrepancies concerned not only visual impressions, landscapes, cities, houses, and the appearance of people, but also events, conversations, feelings, and the relationships with others.

I therefore have to stress that these sketches are sketches. They are not an autobiography and they make no claim to be objectively "true". I recount what I manage to reconstruct and know full well that this may not be the way I experienced it at the time. I call my reminiscences "partial", because on the one hand they are incomplete and on the other biased by my likes and dislikes.

People who are no longer alive I mention for the most part by the names they had when I knew them. To the living I have given other names, because I should hate to cause anyone embarrassment.

I sincerely thank Lisa Nelson for helpful suggestions, Marie Larochelle and Danielle Lochhead for proofreading, Jack Lochhead for his unfaltering support and Josef Mitterer for constant encouragement and spotting contradictions in my dating of events. I am grateful to Anthony Freeman of Imprint Academic for his exceptional patience and expert advice.

About Translation

When I decided that it was time to review and collect such sketches of the past as I had occasionally written my friend Josef Mitterer, who had read some of them, felt sure that they could be published in German. He found a publisher in Vienna who produced a little volume with 57 of them.[1] More than half of them had been written in English and needed to be translated. I do not know what determined the language I wrote them in, but it probably was the mood in which I happened to remember what then seemed worth recounting.

If you translate memories that are in fact your own, it happens that searching for ways to formulate them in this second language brings forth expressions that seem more appropriate than those you chose in the first. It may also remind you of details you had left out in your first account. So the translation sometimes led to an alteration of the original. This seemed to me a valuable process and I decided to translate the German originals into English. I know full well that the meaning of the two versions could never be the same—the fact that I had grown up with more than one language had taught me that; but the very task of formulating them in the other language sometimes showed possibilities of broadening the picture. Given that I do not consider myself a native speaker of either German or English, it does not worry me that readers of both languages may find my way with words a little foreign. That is as it should be. I have always striven to remain a foreigner no matter where I happened to be living.

E.v.G.
Amherst/Leverett, October 2008

---

1   *Unverbindliche Erinnerungen*, Folio Verlag, Vienna, 2008

'One must remember that truth itself is always halved in utterance.'

— Lawrence Durrell (*Balthazar*)

Chapter One

1917–1936

My Parents

Not having become pregnant after seven years of marriage, my mother began to worry that she or her husband might be sterile. So they both went to see a doctor. He found nothing wrong with either of them and told them to go on trying. Spurred by the good news, they were soon successful. Fortunately this was long before fertility drugs were invented. I should not have liked being one of a litter of five or six.

I suppose children always find it difficult to imagine their parents conceiving them. I certainly could never visualize my father doing it. When I was a small boy, he still played tennis every now and then, not as a sport but for his health. Being moderate in everything, he decided that twenty minutes of exertion was about right. When he came to play with my mother or her sister—both were tournament players—he brought a large alarm clock and set it for twenty minutes. When it rang, he finished the game, thanked them for their trouble, and bicycled home to a hot bath. Much later, when I had been told how babies were made, I sometimes wondered whether he had followed the same pattern in his marital activities and, during the first seven years, had set the alarm too early.

* * *

Being pregnant did not stop my mother from continuing her sports. She played tennis and went skiing until well after the sixth month, and I remember her proudly recounting that right up to my birth she was able to put on her stockings standing on one leg. It was a picture that came to

my mind at various occasions during my later life. There was always
something of a "Lausbub" in my mother ("brat" is probably the best
translation, provided one thinks of it with a hint of affection).

At boarding school I had spent weeks learning to whistle through my
teeth, that shrill ear-splitting whistle that is louder than anything you
could produce by putting fingers in your mouth. My jaw was hurting and
my face threatened to stay permanently out of shape when at last the first
piercing whistle came forth. It was during a history class and the appalled
teacher could think of nothing better than to send me out of the room. This
was no serious punishment because I was not very keen on history anyway; besides, I was so elated with my success that any punishment
seemed a picnic. It allowed me immediately to solidify the technique.

When I came home for the summer holiday and my mother heard my
new whistle, she tilted her head and said in her most innocent voice:

"Could you teach me?"

I said, I thought I could, but it would take a long time, it would be painful, and she might even get cramps in her jaw.

"Will you do it, if I double your pocket money?"

It was a challenge I could not resist. My mother, of course was a perfect
student, fanatical almost. Whenever she was alone or when there was no
one but me in sight, she practiced. The trouble is that it takes a long time to
get comfortable pushing your lower jaw as far out in front of the upper
one as you can; and it's only when that position is easy to hold, that you
can begin to try for a sound. It took all the holiday but in the end my
mother got it. She found it useful when she was driving her open roadster
and a cyclist was not keeping to his side. It's more effective than the horn,
she would say. But she used it also in more uncommon situations. Once
we were going out to meet friends of hers for lunch. She was wearing a
rather elegant dress and had put on a hat, which she rarely did. On the
way to the restaurant she wanted to buy a pair of gloves and we went into
a big shop. There was no one else in it and two sales girls were gossiping
at the other end of the counter. My mother waited a moment for one of
them to come, but they didn't move. So my mother pushed her jaw forward and produced a marrow-curdling whistle. It hit the girls like an electric shock and they came scampering across. My mother smiled and said:

"Thank you for your attention, I'd like a pair of black gloves."

* * *

The most salient memories of my mother, however, are from the times she
took me skiing. I must have been about seven when she decided I was
good enough to come with her on excursions. There were no ski lifts or

cable cars in those days and if you wanted to ski, you first had to walk up. You put strips of sealskin on the soles of your skis. The hair on them is fairly stiff, it lies flat in one direction, and stops your skis from sliding back when you walk uphill. One of the first trips my mother took me on was in the Dolomites. It was a three-day hike from the Val Gardena over three passes to Cortina. Each day you climbed up to a pass, a climb of about three hours, and then you skied down to the valley on the other side and stayed over night in the first village. There was not a track of another skier anywhere, just deep powder snow wherever you went.

Of course, I hated the walking up, but my mother was wonderfully patient and coaxed me along until we could finally take off the sealskins and start going down. And that I enjoyed enormously.

In Cortina my mother met some of her friends at an international jumping competition. The Norwegians were then the unbeatable masters in that discipline, but they had never practiced downhill skiing. After the competition, a few of the jumpers decided to try the run down from Pocol, which was then the top station of one of the first cable cars in the Alps. My mother took me along and I had a great time. There happened to be the worst kind of snow for skiing, the kind that is called "breakable crust". It has an icy crust that is just not strong enough to carry the skier. It breaks along the edge of the skis and holds them as in rails. The only way to change direction is to jump right out of it. But not if you are as light as an eight-year-old. I sailed down on top of the crust, making all the turns I wanted to make and trying not to laugh at the clumsy adults who were struggling in the most inelegant fashion.

* * *

Of my father, too, I have only pleasant memories. Once I had learned to respect his privacy he was the gentlest of friends. He never forced himself upon me, but whenever I went to him with a question, he was ready to help. He was good with his hands and early on he showed me how to use tools. Only once did he show annoyance. I was five or six years old and we had just moved into the house he had had built for us in Meran (an old spa in the South Tyrol, the part of Austria that became Italy after the First World War). He had bought a number of tools and showed them to me. Among them was a small stone chisel that fascinated me because I had never seen one before. He showed me how to hold it at an angle so that it would not jar your hand when you hit it with the hammer. I remembered this the next morning and wanted to try it out. By the time he came to see what I was hammering on the balcony, I had made a sizeable hole into the brand new wall of the house. The way he picked up the hammer and grabbed the chisel out of my hand left no doubt that he was very angry. But all he said was:

"You go up to your room and stay there!"

It may be that he was so controlled because *his* father was something of a tyrant and tended to lose his temper. As far as I know, this grandfather, who died long before I was born, did only one good thing for my father. He wanted him to be a military man, too, and in a cavalry regiment that he admired. So he sent him to the best riding school, which, he rightly thought, was the circus. I think it was the only pleasant memory my father had from his childhood. Unlike Thomas Mann's hero Felix Krull, what my father saw at the circus did not launch him on an impostor's career. What he got from it was a great deal of skill with horses, some skill in juggling with three or four balls, and infinite equanimity with regard to the strangeness of other people. The last served him throughout his life: When people did things he did not like, he simply kept out of their way. I was able to learn some of that attitude from him and am as grateful for it as I am for the love of fun and the passion for snow and mountains that my mother instilled into me with unfaltering patience.

Boarding School 1928

It was a long drive that for the first time took me to Neubeuern, the boarding school my parents had chosen. It also was a silent drive. I was about eleven years old and had no conception of what it would be like to be away from home; but I was frightened. I did not know why, but I knew it would be awful. In the past my parents had sometimes gone on trips and left me at home, early on with the *Kinderfräulein*, and more recently I had been considered old enough to stay by myself with only the housekeeper. But what was ahead, I knew, would be altogether different — unimaginable and frightful. I was desperately hoping for something to happen, so that we would never get there.

My mother, too, was obviously depressed. The night before, when she was packing my things, I noticed that she was crying. Let's not go, I said. But she merely shook her head and so I, too, began to cry. It all seemed different from anything that had happened before — incomprehensible and unspeakably ominous.

I was sitting in the back of the car and stared straight ahead without see-ing. When I caught my mother looking at me in the rearview mirror, I turned my head away. I knew she was worried, and I could not understand it. Why had she decided to do this, when she did not like it? Was it to punish me? I had not been told that I had done anything wrong. I simply could not find an answer.

My mother was also worried that I was worrying. At one point she said: "You know, we are going to see Konrad … that will be nice, won't it?"

I did not answer. It seemed totally beside the point to me. It was true, I liked Konrad a lot, but what did that have to do with my being sent to boarding school?

Konrad, who was about my mother's age, was an engineer with a passion for cars. It was he who had taught my mother not only to drive but also all about ignition and carburetors and gears, and he had accompanied her on her first long drives. You don't learn to drive in a couple of weeks, he said, it takes at least 5000 kilometers.

Cars in those days differed a great deal and almost every new model incorporated some novel solution to a problem. Konrad kept up with them all by reading technical journals; but what he liked best was to see them for himself. When we went for walks together — which seemed to happen quite often when my parents and I came to Munich, where Konrad lived — he might stop dead in his tracks and point to a car coming out of some street:

"Look, look! That is the new Delage — it has four-wheel brakes!"

And we would try to follow the car, hoping that it would stop and we could look at it more closely. If we were lucky and got there before the owner had disappeared, Konrad would raise his hat and say:

"Excuse me, Sir, could you possibly let us see the engine? This is the first Delage *Gran Sport* that has come our way."

And the owners of new cars were often only too happy to show them off and talk about them. So I learned a good many things about cars.

At some time, Konrad had also given driving lessons to my father, but my father was not really interested. He never went for the test to take out the required license. He loved to be driven and he trusted my mother. He left everything to do with the car to her — its choice when a new one had to be bought, its maintenance and the repairs on the road (which were not infrequent in those days), and above all the driving. He hardly ever looked at the road ahead but scanned the landscape on either side for the things that interested him: peasant houses, flowers, old trees, and the mountains that formed the background to most of our drives. He never showed any nervousness and never commented on what my mother was doing or not doing. As in many other realms of living, he was a perfect passenger, a little silent perhaps, but also forever uncomplaining. That is, with one exception. When another car was driving ahead of us, my father became restless and after a while he would say: If you can't pass him, let him get further away — I cannot stand the smell.

My mother was a spirited driver and she especially enjoyed going up mountain passes as fast as the car would go. They were all dirt roads then, and she was an expert in judging just how much skidding was useful in the hairpin turns. As a result we often caught up with the dust of slower drivers. That was when my father complained.

"Well, I can't stop right here," my mother would say, "and it's bad for the engine to pull uphill slowly."

Occasionally my father, who in time had picked up quite a lot about cars, would gently ask:

"But couldn't you go in a lower gear?"

My mother would sigh and pull up abruptly as soon as the road was wide enough for another car to pass.

"I need to stretch my legs anyway," my father would say, and amble into the landscape. Sensing my mother's displeasure, I would follow him. Often the slopes were wooded, with little clearings here and there, where one could look down at the villages in the valley. There were hardly ever people to be seen, but we did not miss them. My father would point out mushrooms and explain what they were, or he would turn over stones with his walking stick and talk about the beetles that had hidden underneath. If we were already above the tree line, he would carefully move the alpine flowers with his stick without hurting them and talk at length about the ones he liked best. It was not that I had a burning interest in those things, but the affection with which he spoke of them was somehow contagious and I often ran ahead to point specimens out to him. Much later I realized that I had learned a lot during those walks; useless knowledge, from a mundane point of view, but endlessly rewarding the moment you stepped into a forest or an Alpine meadow.

But on this drive the mountains and the Alpine flowers were far away. All that, I felt, had come to an end. I was going to be stuck in school, immeasurably far from everything I liked, without my parents, without cars, without forests and meadows, and without the electric railway, which, I think, was my main interest at the time.

As I had been afraid all along, the drive came to an end. The road climbed up a steep hill that stood like a forepost of the Alps where they merged into the Bavarian plain south of Munich — and there it was, dark and ominous: Neubeuern, the large, thick-walled, rambling castle that had been turned into a boarding school.

As we got out of the car, I think, I must have begun to tremble. I was about to break into tears.

"Look," my mother said, "you can see the Wendelstein!"

She pointed to a peak in the serrated skyline of the Alps, far away at the horizon. It was a mountain we had skied on the year before, and for a moment the memory distracted me. Then we trotted to the director's office and I felt too numb to cry. Herr Rieder was a very big man with a large, perfectly round hairless head and a soft, noncommittal voice. I don't remember hearing anything that was said, but I have never forgotten his double-breasted suit that enveloped his bulging stomach like a cylindrical tent. It must have been this first sight that generated my life-long aversion against double-breasted suits.

What I remember of the director's office is that it was somber, smelt of cigar smoke, and I wanted to get out. This impression was reinforced later, because the director's office was where you were brought when you had done something wrong.

My parents' interview was cut short. There was a knock on the door, the Director said "Herein!", and a middle-aged man—probably one of the teachers—tiptoed towards him and whispered something in his ear. The director turned to my parents and said:

"A visitor has arrived for you; he is waiting in the courtyard."

I suppose my parents, though for different reasons, did not feel any more comfortable than I during the interview and were quite happy to end it.

"It's a friend of the family," my mother said apologetically, and we trooped out of the office. I had no idea who it could be, but as we came out through the big door into the courtyard, I saw Konrad unloading a bicycle from the roof of his little car.

One of the things I had been told the first time boarding school was mentioned, was that I would get a new bicycle. I had had one for several years, but it was now a little battered and too small. I don't think the promise diminished the fear and forebodings I felt at the prospect of being sent away, but a new bicycle was an attractive idea and I dwelt on it quite a lot. I had a very clear picture of what I wanted. It had to be one of those light, fragile looking ones, bright blue or silver, with narrow rims and caliper brakes and a handlebar like a racer.

The thing that Konrad was now wheeling towards us left me dumbfounded. Had I been able to verbalize my impression, I would have said, it looks like a hearse. It was the opposite of my dream. It was black and heavy, with thick tires and clumsy mudguards, and if you put a big basket behind the saddle it would have been the image of the bicycle that every morning brought bread and groceries to our house in Meran.

At the age of ten years, there are many things you feel but do not articulate conceptually, let alone in words. They are dark, amorphous masses in your world, and every now and then they push you into a corner, relentlessly and incomprehensibly. I did not say to myself: How could they do this? But I knew that I had to say "Thank you" for a surprise that was not just a disappointment but something like an insult.

I have few recollections of the rest of the day. My mother was crying again when they said Good Bye, and I do not remember my father. Much later, when I got to know and like him as a person, I realized that he must have been almost as uncomfortable that day as I was.

I was shown to the room I was to share with three others, and the trunk that had come with me was brought up. There were four narrow wardrobes and the empty one, I was told, was mine. Left alone, I started unpacking and it quickly became clear that there was not nearly enough room for all my things. The wardrobe was about 18 inches wide, with one shelf on top, two at the bottom, and a space to hang clothes in between. My mother had packed my clothes and helped me select the toys to bring, a tiny fraction of what I would have liked to take. I now carefully arranged them on the bottom shelves. They were not really toys, but a few small things with which I was used to spending time—a pathfinder's compass, a paper weight one could shake to create a snow storm, a small camera with a couple of rolls of film, some puzzles with rings and hooks, a few picture books, and two stuffed animals. The biggest item was a large box with old alarm clocks in various stages of deconstruction and small pliers and screw drivers. The year before I had caught German measles and was confined to bed and dimmed light for three or four weeks. To keep me happy, my mother had a brilliant idea. She went to a watchmaker and came back with an assortment of broken clocks. As she anticipated, the challenge to get one of them to work again turned the days in bed into a thrilling adventure and I returned to my clock collection many times after I had got well.

I managed to stuff shoes, socks, and pullovers on the top shelf, but the trunk was still more than half full with clothes and underwear, ski boots and gloves, a box of pencils and a writing pad, and a framed photograph of my parents which my mother had slipped in. I looked round the room for other possibilities, but there were four beds and four chairs and that was it.

I was sitting on one of the beds, when the door opened and in came a large woman in a dark grey skirt and blouse that had small white buttons all the way up to her chin.

"Ah," she said cheerfully, "you are von Glasersfeld, the new boy!"

I got up and stared at her. No one had ever called me by that name. Even if I had had another, she left me no time to say so.

"Good! You have been unpacking."

She looked at the open wardrobe and knitted her brows in an ominous frown. But then she turned to me with the same smile she had worn when she came in and said:

"I'm afraid we'll have to organize your things differently — this is not like home. You understand, don't you?"

I am sure I had less experience of the world than many others at that age, but I had learned to recognize and to dislike the expression of spurious friendliness and concern. It was part of that ominous conspiracy of strange adults.

My introduction into the life of the school began at dinner time. There were ten or twelve long tables in the dining room for about a dozen inmates each. Someone showed me to a free place and said:

"This is von Glasersfeld."

The boys who were sitting there seemed to be amused. One of them asked:

"Does this mean the field of the Glaser or the Glaser of the field?"

They all laughed, and it did not matter that I would not have known how to answer. Then the teacher at the head of the table turned to me:

"What class are you coming into, von Glasersfeld?"

I said that I was to enter the second.

"Where did you do the first?"

"I had private lessons."

"Ah, that is interesting — I hope you learned some Latin, because that is what I teach!"

Everybody laughed, and it was the end of the conversation as far as I was concerned. The soup was served, and as I raised the first spoonful to my mouth, the boy on my right pushed my elbow, and it spilled. Again, all the others laughed. The teacher uttered a mild reprimand, but it was not clear to me whether it was aimed at the boy who had pushed me or at me. Much later, when I saw it happen to other new boys, I realized that it was part of a ritual.

Indeed, the initiation rites are what I remember best of that first and fortunately short boarding school experience. When the lights had gone out and I was lying in the strange bed with three others in the room, the weight of it all became too much for me and I started crying, softly and desperately.

"Don't cry," one of them said, "you'll get used to it."

I don't remember all they did to console me, but for the sake of humanity I want to say that they did a lot. They asked me where I came from, and then some questions that I could not answer. For instance, Why had I been sent there? And then there was a question that I did not understand: Have you been *aufgeklärt?* — the German word means "enlightened".

Aufklärung is the German term for the eighteenth-century period called "The Enlightenment". The fact that I didn't know what they were referring to delighted them no end. For a long time, that night, they continued to explore just how much I didn't know; especially about sex.

My mother had explained to me that, before being born, I was in her tummy. It never struck me to ask how I got there. My ignorance was therefore total in the area that most occupied my new schoolmates. They enjoyed their advantage over me enormously, but after one more night of flaunting it, they could not resist telling me all about it. So they began to enlighten me. My reaction exhilarated them, because I flatly refused to believe what they described in very simple terms. It seemed utterly absurd to me. My reluctance eked them on to present more and more graphic details and to recount what older brothers had told them. A few days later, when my first religion lesson had supplied me with a bible, they took the trouble to show me several passages which they took to be evidence for what they had told me, and after a while I began to consider that they were probably right.

Many years later, when I told my mother the story of my enlightenment, she was taken aback.

"Good God," she said, "I should have told you—but it never occurred to me, it somehow never came up. But don't worry about not believing it at first. Frank Wedekind, whom we saw a few times when we lived in Munich, once remarked that as long as babies are made the way we make them, nothing about the human species can surprise him."

In time I got used to the regimented life in school, to the horrible electric bells that shrieked through the castle and regulated our day, and to the strange customs that governed the interactions among the boys. But every now and then something happened that shook me so much that I wrote about it in my letters home.

Two of the teachers had the name Müller; Karl Müller, a gentle, easy man who taught geography and was referred to as "Herr K-Müller"; and Otto Müller, called "Herr O-Müller", the Latin teacher, who walked like a ram rod with a limp and frequently reminded us that he had defended the fatherland on the western front throughout the four years of the First World War. He was subject to uncontrollable fits of rage and had a particular, nasty way of pulling up your head by your ear before slapping your face. On the days when he was supervising the upper floor, where our bedrooms were, everybody tried to remain as invisible as possible.

One afternoon I forgot that it was O-Müller's day and was sitting on my bed when he burst into the room. Perhaps he had been displeased by the look of some rooms where he found no one to blame. He was obviously boiling with rage. He went straight to the four wardrobes and tore them open.

"Is this how you manage your quarters?" he shouted as he turned to me. He took one step and reached for my ear — but I was closer to the door than he. I made a dash for it and ran down the corridor at full speed, O-Müller after me. Just before I reached the staircase, a boy coming out of his room opened a door just in front of me, and I crashed into it.

The boy helped me pick myself up and suddenly said in a shocked voice:

"You are bleeding!"

I began to cry, and Herr O-Müller, who was staring at the cut in my forehead, was immobilized by a fit of trembling that shook all of his stiff body.

I saw the blood on my hand after I had touched my face, and I suppose it was this that gave me courage. I firmly held on to the other boy, who was much older than I, and said, I want to go to the Director. What happened? asked the boy on the way to the office.

"He looked at our wardrobes — and he was going to hit me ..."

"He's mad, you know, he thinks he's still at the front."

When we stood before the Director's desk, I was sobbing and couldn't speak. So the older boy explained what had happened.

"Take him to the infirmary," said the Director.

They sewed up my cut with a couple of stitches, and for the next few days I was treated like a hero by my colleagues. Then I was called to the Director's office. He patiently explained it all to me. Herr O-Müller had been in the terrible battle against the French at Verdun and he had been wounded and buried by a shell. When they dug him out, he had shell shock. But he recovered quickly and could go on fighting the war. Some after effects, of course, remain from such a terrible adventure. We must be understanding and forgiving with the men who served the fatherland so bravely.

I wrote some of this to my parents, and it was then, I think, that they began to change their mind about Neubeuern. The second event came some months later.

Every second Saturday evening there was a concert or a lecture by an invited speaker. On an evening shortly before the end of the fall term, there was a lecture on the Treaty of Versailles and its injustice to Germany. With great passion the speaker focused on the tragedy of "having lost the South Tyrol" and on the atrocities the Italians were committing there. After the lecture, some of the boys collected round me and a classmate of mine whose home was also in Meran. It must be terrible to live there, they said, with all these horrors going on. I looked at my class mate and he was just as puzzled as I was. We had both been living in Meran with our German-speaking parents, had been in bilingual elementary schools, and were friends with Italian children. We had never heard of any horrors and we said so.

"But what about all the mountain peasants," the others asked, "the speaker tonight said the Italians put them in chains and took them to prisons in Trient?"

My class mate was obviously better informed politically than I was. He answered with an assurance that I found enormously admirable:

"Well, they arrested some people who demonstrated against the Italian government and they didn't treat them very well. But they were not mountain peasants. One of them, I remember, was a German—because my father said, What the hell is he doing here? This was Austria before the war, not Germany!"

Somehow the Director must have come to hear of what we said. A day or two later we were called to his office. He told us it was impertinent for us to contradict what Herr so-and-so had said. Herr so-and-so was an authority on the shameful Treaty of Versailles, and we knew nothing about politics and the tragedy that the South Tyrol had been lost to Italy.

I was thoroughly bewildered and it bothered me. So I wrote something about it in my next letter home. I did not understand why we had been called to the Director for a reprimand. I had no idea that it would be a matter of importance to my parents, but I got an immediate answer: I was to be taken out of Neubeuern at end of the term and would go to a much nicer boarding school in Switzerland. My parents wrote their decision at once to the school, and the Director, apparently did not keep it to himself. A week or so later, Herr O-Müller caught me at the end of his class and said:

"Your mother seems to think that the wardrobes in Switzerland are larger than ours! Ha, ha!—You'll never become a good soldier."

And he was right on both counts.

Moonlight Skiing 1931

When my parents took me out of Neubeuern it was late autumn. Around the middle of January, I was to start at my new boarding school in Switzerland. The school was at Zuoz in the upper Engadine, one of the most beautiful valleys in the Alps. I was looking forward to it because I felt sure it would be much better than the Bavarian castle.

I was not disappointed. There was an altogether different mood at Zuoz. You were treated like a human individual rather than like a numbered inmate. It was still an institution where you had to toe the line in every respect, but as institutions go, the general atmosphere was closer to that of a hotel than of a prison.

The school comprised two buildings, the Small House, for boys up to fifteen years of age, and the Big House, for the last three grades of high school. When I arrived, I quickly realized that I could not have chosen a better time of the year. New boys are usually given a hard time in boarding schools, until they somehow manage to establish a place for themselves in the peculiar unofficial hierarchy that rules most interactions among the population. The initiation was not as savage at Zuoz as the "hazing" customary in some fraternities at American universities, but for a young teen-ager the first few months were usually stressful and sometimes downright cruel. But this time I was spared all that. The fact that I was far more at home on skis than the others, gave me an instant reputation, and when, at the beginning of February, I won the slalom race of the "Small House", my social standing was established once and for all.

When the snow had melted and land hockey became the dominant sport, I did quite well and soon was playing in the team that represented the Small House, a status-enhancing activity during the summer months.

This relative ease of gaining the respect of my schoolmates, no doubt gave me the surplus of confidence that led me to embark on a very questionable adventure two winters later. Our skiing on Saturdays and Sundays was free, in that we could choose from some five or six points to which we were allowed to climb and we had to write on a list where we were going. There were no ski lifts or other mechanical devices in those days, and you first had to climb up if you wanted to ski down. But skiing was for the weekends.

Ice hockey was the team game during the winter. On terraces below the school, there were three ice hockey rinks covering what during the summer were tennis courts. When frost settled in, sometime during November, the tennis courts had to be sprayed at night and from then on, whenever it snowed, the rinks had to be cleared and sprayed again to create a new layer of ice.

As it usually snowed rather thickly, the clearing had to be continuous, because once more than six inches had accumulated, it was too difficult to move.

During one of these nights after a snowfall the clouds suddenly broke up and gave way to a sparkling sky. I looked up at the Piz Mezzaum, the

mountain over which the sun stood at noon and which now was glistening in the moonlight. Above the forest on the other side of Inn valley, a
naked shoulder rose up to a ravine from which the rock face of the mountain soared to the sky. The shoulder was steep, but not too steep. It would
have been a perfect slope to ski down. And because it was just under the
north face of the mountain, the sun barely touched it all through the winter and the snow on it had to be the most perfect dry powder.

That night, Robert, who was my classmate and the boy with whom I did
most of my Saturday and Sunday skiing, happened to be on the ice-clean-
ing shift after me. When he came, I said:

"Have you seen the slope under the Mezzaun?"

He looked up and saw exactly what I had seen.

"Jesus," he said, "that would be something, wouldn't it?"

That was how the idea started. Most of the other side of the Inn valley
was out of bounds for weekend skiing, most certainly the part under Piz
Mezzaun. But we had seen how bright it was in moonlight, and there
would be no one to stop us if we went up at night. The thought was irresistible. We needed a clear night and an almost full moon. And there was
another condition: no snow should have fallen for at least a week, because
new snow could at any time come down from the rocks above as a dust
avalanche. We had seen one that very winter and it was a sight we were
unlikely to forget. It came down the almost vertical rock face as a billow-
ing cloud. It seemed soft and slow. But that was an illusion. When it rolled
over the ravine, we suddenly heard the thundering roar of the air pressure it created and when it reached the first trees we saw them tossed into
the air like matchsticks. We had been told that people caught by a dust
avalanche frequently had their lungs burst. Having seen one, we could
believe it. It was not a risk we were prepared to take. So the weather had to
be right.

As it happened, we didn't have long to wait. Fine weather set in just
after the waxing half moon and we started our forecast of the moon's
timetable. We needed it to be fairly high in the sky from midnight to about
4 am and this had to be in the five days around full moon. The best fit
turned out to be the night just before it was going to be full and we kept
our fingers crossed that it would not suddenly decide to snow again. It
didn't, and on the evening of the fateful night we went to the locker room
where skis were being kept and prepared ours for the climb. This was not
unusual, because we often did something to our skis, in preparation for
the weekend. When we finished we did not put the skis back in their stalls
but carefully lowered them and our poles to the outside through a window that gave on the back of the building. No one ever went to that part
during winter, except where there was a path kept clear to the back door.

There were probably eight or ten feet of snow piled up against the back wall along its entire length and there was no way of getting to the window through which we had dropped our skis. We decided that we would have to creep out through the same window and put on skis there and then; and we would close the window when we came back.

A little after midnight we sneaked down the stairs on socks, made our way to the locker room, and put on ski boots, wind jackets, gloves, and woolen caps. When we came to the window we had chosen, we had a shock. It was still open from when we had dropped out our skis. We looked at each other and shook our heads. What an error to have left it open! Anyone might have noticed it, could have looked out, and seen our skis. But if anyone had, we thought, they would have closed the window. We stopped worrying and climbed out, which, wearing ski boots, was much more difficult than expected. Once out, we put on our skis and quietly slid round the building. We realized that we had to avoid the well-lit drive up to the school and kept our distance from it. We skirted the village and skied across the fields until we reached the bridge over the river Inn. By then we were far enough from the village and the school so that no one could see us. We crossed the bridge and started climbing.

The moon lit up the larger crystals on the surface of the untouched snow in a way we had never seen in sunlight. It left the big spruces we passed pitch black as silhouettes against the silvery landscape. The effect was totally enchanting and we climbed with more gusto than ever during the day. After about an hour we found the little bridge we had spotted during our reconnaissance as the only way of access to the slopes under Piz Mezzaun. From then on we had to find a way through thick forest, laying the track so that we could come down along it without too much difficulty. It took us half an hour to reach the tree line and the big slope that was our target. We took care to choose a way up that was unlikely to be seen from the village. We wanted our downhill tracks to look as though they had been made by creatures dropped from the sky.

The moon was getting close to the peak of Piz Mezzaun above us when we reached the top of the slope under the rocks. We had to hurry to have light on the way down. The run was a dream in well-settled powder that had never been touched by the sun. The part through the forest was awkward, pushing through branches at times, but it was manageable, and in less than half an hour we were at the bottom, crossing the bridge over the Inn on our way home. By four o'clock we were back in our beds, almost too excited to go to sleep.

The next morning we furtively looked to Piz Mezzaun and our tracks were plainly visible, a double pattern of linked Ss. The temptation to say that they were ours, was enormous. But we resisted. Yet things began to happen.

The mountain guides in the village of course look up at their mountains every morning and they at once spotted our tracks. They also knew that there had been no tracks up there the day before and that no tourist could have made them before eight o'clock in the morning. They did not approve of that kind of enterprise and it was probably they who reported it to the school administration. Anyway, when we came out from dinner that evening, the house master stopped me and took me aside. My heart started to beat and I was frantically searching for a way out. But I knew there wasn't any.

Without any preamble he asked me:

"Were you out skiing last night?"

There was no use denying it. So, as calmly as I could manage, I said:

"Yes — it was irresistible."

"We'll see about that," he said. "You'll be at the director's office at the ten o'clock break tomorrow."

I didn't sleep much that night and with the escapade the night before I must have looked somewhat haggard in the morning. I think that helped.

The housemaster was sitting beside the director behind the broad desk in the office. He looked at me and said:

"You know that breaking out at night is a serious offence? And skiing in forbidden areas is another, isn't it?"

He paused, expecting me to answer. I didn't.

"For each of them you could be expelled."

"I know," I said without looking at him.

The head master was about to go on, but the director spoke before him:

"Why did you do it?"

I wasn't sure what to say. But then it came out all by itself:

"I've been looking up at that slope every winter. There is no other anywhere near here where the powder doesn't get spoiled by the sun. And there's no danger of avalanches, except straight after a snowfall. The idea just came to me last month when we were clearing the ice and there was a full moon. It didn't seem such a terrible thing to do."

"I'm afraid it was, and I'll tell you why," The director said, and it didn't sound threatening. "It's not a question of rules in the first place, it's a question of consequences. What should we have told your parents if you had had an accident up there, broken a leg, something that can happen to the best skier? We would have to tell them that it happened in an area that is out of bounds for skiing and that you had gone there in moonlight. And what would they say? They would ask me what kind of a boarding school I was running; and they would have every right to blame me."

He looked at me, but I didn't know what to say. I was very close to tears and all I could stutter was:

"I am sorry."

"I hope you are," he said. "You happen to be the best skier and you know some things about mountains. Others will listen to you and try to do as you do. Whether you like it or not, they will see you as something of a model. So you have a responsibility. You are not a child any more and you cannot simply do what comes into your head. You have to think of the consequences, what it might do to others and also what it might do the school as a whole. In a community like ours we are all dependent on one another. The rules we make are for the beginning. You'll be fifteen in a few weeks. You have to see that our rules make sense. Do you understand that?"

"I think I do."

"You'd better! We'll trust you not to break them again. If you do, you'll be out."

That was the end of the session. I could hardly believe it. I was relieved but also shaken. I did not know it there and then, but it changed me. Later I realized that the short session had made me grow up a lot. I also learned later that the director, whose name suitably enough was Knabenhans ("Knaben" meaning "boys"), had a long-standing policy that is not at all common in boarding schools. Because our parents were not with us to defend us, he said, we needed someone to be on our side and he took that role upon himself, when we got into scrapes. I was immensely grateful to him and I understood that he was more interested in educating than in punishing.

Years after I had finished at Zuoz, I heard that he had been removed. He sometimes drank a little too much. We, of course, knew about it, but as far as we could see it never interfered with his being a competent and very fair director. The decision of the supervising board made me lose faith in such impersonal bodies of authority that clearly had no proper understanding of what mattered.

Gerda's Fracture 1931

Gerda was really a friend of my mother's. She was one of the best women skiers at the time. My mother and I had been skiing with her for several days in Kitzbühel during my holidays and I had developed a terrific crush on her. She was only about ten years older than I, but I was about fourteen at the time and she was of another generation. One day she said that she could ski only very early the next morning, because then she had to visit a relative.

"It'll be very icy," my mother said, "I don't think I'll do that."

When Gerda turned to me and said, "would you like to come?" I was in heaven.

We took the first gondola up to the Hahnenkamm and it was very cold, indeed. We put on our skis and Gerda took off like a bullet. The first slope was wide and long and not particularly steep. Halfway down there was a path crossing it, a step, about a foot high. Gerda came to it in the middle of a right-hand turn and, going at 40 or 50 miles an hour, she was in the air for quite a distance. When her skis hit the ground, it sounded like a shot. For a split second she lost her balance, but caught herself on her left leg and finished the turn until she came to a stop at the edge of the slope. When I reached her, she said:

"I've broken my leg."

"But you didn't fall?"

"I felt it snap. I can't put any weight on it."

She skied down to the village, on one leg most of the time, but still with a great deal of elegance. Walking to the doctor's office, she leant on my shoulder.

"It's much more difficult without skis," she said.

I waited with her while the X-ray photographs were being developed.

"I should have known better," she said. "Someone once told me that when you are very cold, your bones are like the mast of a sailing boat with all the tackling removed — it can snap at the first gust of wind."

When the doctor brought the X-rays, they showed it very clearly: there was a neat, transverse break in the fibula.

"So much for skiing this winter," she said.

When I left her, she gave me a peck on the cheek and smiled. "Thanks for being with me — I would probably have sat down and cried, had I been alone."

I never saw her again, but I remember her smile every time my legs get cold going up in a ski lift — and I take care to warm up.

Crossing the Rubicon 1932

It must have been during my first years at Zuoz, when I was thirteen or fourteen, that we read Caesar's *De bello gallico* as part of the Latin class. His famous expression "The die is cast" impressed me greatly. He apparently said it when he crossed the river Rubicon that separated Rome from enemies in the north. I saw him standing there, looking back over turbulent waters, proud of a decision that the river made irrevocable.

A few months later I was in the car with my parents, en route to a mid-summer holiday on the beaches of the Adriatic Sea. Rattling west on the dusty road from Modena to Bologna we crossed several stone bridges over the beds of brooks that came down from the Apennine Mountains and probably carried quite a lot of water in early spring, when the snow was melting in the higher regions. Now they were as dry as any African Wadi, just stones and gravel and whatever weeds had managed to take root. Insignificant though they seemed, they all had names and a sign at the beginning of the bridge told you what "river" you were about to cross. I was amused by the fact that these signs gave you the names of rivers that were hardly ever there.

One of these occasional rivers was the Rubicon and when I realized that Caesar probably walked across it in sandals it forever shook my faith in historical facts.

Marlene Dietrich 1933

At Zuoz, my boarding school, you got a single room when you were at least 15. Once that happened, you took pride in "decorating" your sanctuary. When I reached that important turning point, it was the fashion (and therefore considered a necessity) to have a deck chair. In those days it was a wooden structure that could be unfolded so one could lie back on a broad, colored strip of canvas that served as seat as well as back. It was a simple, prosaic item and most hotels had dozens of them on their terraces and balconies. To provide the illusion of luxury, the sophisticated schoolboy had to cover it with cushions and provide a romantic view to generate dreams while reclining. Most of us achieved this by sticking tourist posters of exotic places on the opposite wall. It was long before pin-up girls had been invented, but some of us had managed to garner photographs of favorite film stars, and if they bore an autograph they were among the most coveted possessions.

Given the quiet life my parents led, far from any metropolis where film stars congregated, I had never managed to conquer such a prize. The only thing I had was a picture of Marlene Dietrich cut out of a magazine. But I was able to make up for it with two autographed photographs that ranked as high on our scale of values. They were pictures of Hans Stuck and Louis Chiron, two of the most successful racing drivers of the day, whom we had met and skied with in past winters. As both my mother and I were more experienced and faster than they in the snow, I had no difficulty in obtaining a signed photograph from them. I pinned them on my wall and there they were, Stuck at the wheel of the Austro Daimler (one of the first vehicles designed by Ferdinand Porsche) with which he had become the champion of hill-climb races, Chiron leaning against his legendary Bugatti. I was enormously proud when a visitor to my room recognized them. But though I loved racing cars, I was not immune to other interests and the queen of my dreams was Marlene Dietrich. I had only seen her in one film and she had engendered feelings in me that were the very kind that the Knights of the Roundtable must have felt for Queen Guinevere. It was probably the purest longing I have ever had. If sex was the kind of thing we occasionally whispered about in terms that were unmentionable, it had nothing to do with my adoration for the mysterious Marlene, who seemed unreachable in every sense of the word.

When I was seventeen, I was for the first time allowed to spend a week during holidays away from home with Fery, the best friend I had in school. His family had a big house on the Mönchsberg above Salzburg and they invited me during the summer. Fery was a year older than I, he already had a driving license, and his widowed mother had given him a sports car. It was the time of the famous Salzburg Festival, and the old town was full of actors and famous people. The Festspiele in those days were something like the Cannes Film Festival after the war.

One morning, before driving to one of the lakes in the neighborhood, I went into a shop in the center of town to buy a pair of sunglasses. Fery was waiting outside in the car. I got the glasses and rushed out of the shop, with my head down and bumped into a passer-by. As I straightened myself, I was dumbfounded. I had rammed Marlene Dietrich. I stuttered a clumsy excuse. She smiled and walked on. I looked after her in shock, and as I climbed into the car, Fery said:

"Well, you certainly missed that opportunity."

Innumerable times, looking at her picture in my room at school during the following months, I relived the scene and thought of things I could have said to start a conversation … and perhaps? But, to be honest, I had no clear idea of how such a dream might have continued.

It may seem strange today, but at that time, as far as I knew, none of the boys of my age at Zuoz knew more about sex than what could be learned from Marguerite's *La Garçonne* or Lawrence's *Lady Chatterley's Lover*. Daphnis and Chloe had at least the sheep to give them an example. At Zuoz we didn't see sheep — or girls, for that matter. True, there was quite a bit of homosexual fumbling at school, but as far as I knew, no love affairs. Later, when I embarked on my first one, it became painfully obvious (not only to me) how much there was to learn.

Old Duke Clary 1933

There was another memorable event during my week's stay at Salzburg. The Café Bazar in the very heart of the town was a meeting-place for everyone. The famous people went there for a mid-morning coffee, afternoon tea, or a drink before dinner. If you managed to get a table with a good view and had nothing else to do, you were bound to see most of the notables the local paper, the *Salzburger Nachrichten,* focused on in its social column.

On my last afternoon I had an appointment there with Fery's brother and I arrived early. Walking between tables to find a free one, I heard someone say:

"Glasersfeld — sit down with me for a moment!"

I turned and saw a very old gentleman with a bushy moustache whom I had never seen before. He smiled and pointed to a chair beside him.

"I hope you don't mind being waylaid like this. I know who you are because Mrs. V told me you were staying with them. I am the Duke Clary and I am so old that no one wants to talk to me any more. So I sit here and every now and then I manage to snare someone. With you I have an excellent excuse: I knew your grandfather — as a very young man I served in his regiment, — let me see — almost eighty years ago!"

This was certainly a surprise for me. My father never talked about his family. All I knew about *his* father was that he had been a military man and had tried to force his son into a military career. He did not succeed, but seems to have lost his son's affection during the process. The only time I remember him being mentioned was when my father explained to a visitor that he had always been clean shaven because he had been terminally put off beards as a boy before he could grow one. The coterie of military men to which his father belonged changed the pattern of hair on their faces every few weeks so successfully that they were often quite difficult to recognize. Now I was curious to hear more, and as I squeezed into the chair beside old Clary, I said:

"What a wonderful coincidence! I know practically nothing about my grandfather."

"Well, I can tell you a little, but first I want to know about *your* father. What sort of a person is he? What does he do?"

I had to think for a moment. He did not press me; he just smiled and waited. After a while I said that my father was a very quiet man, that he liked the mountains and had hated the war. He had been cultural attaché at the Austrian embassy in Munich. He had joined the Camera Club there and since then had become a quite famous amateur who was invited to exhibit his photographs at salons all over the world.

"So he's become an artist. Not unusual for the sons of fathers who lack imagination. You grandfather had none. He was so straight that there was no room for any side glances. He was probably the most honest man who ever served the emperor. That's why he got the *von* rather than the stars of a general. His honesty would have severely upset the structure of the army."

Just then Fery's brother appeared and I had to make my excuses.

"I am so sorry," I said, "I wish I could sit with you a little tomorrow, but this is my last day in Salzburg. Maybe we can continue next year?"

"Maybe," the old duke said, "but I'm ninety-seven and I don't make plans, not even for tomorrow."

Final Exams 1935

Finishing high school at Zuoz, you had the privilege of going for two final exams called Matura. One was Swiss, the other German. With the two you had access to practically all European universities. The exams were administered, not by your teachers, but by "inspectors" from the Departments of Education of the two countries. This of course made everybody more nervous than if it had been an in-house event where what you had done through the years would have counted with the teachers. But as the subject matter was the same for the two exams, most of us felt that, having worked so hard, we might as well take both. There was a rule that candidates had to be eighteen years old. I was lucky. It was March 1935 and my eighteenth birthday was a few days before the exams began.

As it happened, it all went well and in his speech during our last dinner at the school, the director said that although we had been a most unruly bunch, our class had achieved the best results in several years. A Dutch class mate of mine and I got the highest number of sixes (the equivalent of A+) in the mathematical areas and after the dinner the Swiss inspector took the two of us aside. He told us that he was a professor at the Zürich Institute of Technology, the famous ETH, and if we wanted to study there, he would see to it that we could enter without another exam.

We took this to be a terrific compliment and were duly delighted. The next morning the Dutch boy said to me that he thought it was a wonderful opportunity but he really wanted to start his adult life in Holland. I said that I didn't mind the idea of living in Zürich, but that I would not go there until the fall semester because my parents had long ago mentioned that after finishing at Zuoz I should go to stay for a few months with a family they knew in Devonshire to polish my English.

Before I entered boarding school, my parents opened a bank account for me and put into it my monthly pocket money and some prizes whenever I brought home good marks. This had been going on for almost ten years and as there was practically no way of spending money at Zuoz, I never took much out of my account. I had my own way of providing a little pocket money. At the tennis club in Meran, I had spent a lot of time in the pro's shop while my mother was playing and I watched how they mended broken strings in rackets. All you needed was two straight awls to block strings in the holes of the frame, a pair of strong flat pliers to tighten them, and a supply of new gut. Tightening the string by hand was considered quite sufficient in those days. When I left for Zuoz, I bought a couple of awls and asked my mother for a spool of new gut string. With this modest equipment I was able to make enough money secretly mending tennis rackets to finance the obligatory Saturday visit to the confiserie, the pastry shop in the village (which, we always said, was better than the world-famous Hanselmann's at St. Moritz, eleven miles up the valley from Zuoz).

When I came home after leaving school, there was another exam that was far more important to me than the Matura. A driving license was, to me, the prerequisite of living; and if I was to go to England, I wanted to go by car. I had quite a respectable amount in my savings account and with my father's generous offer to make up the difference, I was able to buy the smallest car that was available at the time, an open Fiat two-seater that had a canvas top and removable celluloid windows for the doors. 105 kilometers an hour (65 m.p.h.) was the fastest it went, even after I had tried to trick up the engine. But to me it was a dream.

As my mother had occasionally let me drive her car round a track near the tennis club, I sailed through the driving test without difficulty. My mother remembered the advice she had received from our engineering friend Konrad when she had started to drive some fifteen years earlier.

"Driving to England will give you some experience," she said, "and I'll come with you to point out a few things that the test didn't bring up."

I noticed that my mother was treating me very differently now that I was out of school, almost as though she were no longer responsible for me. This quickly changed my attitude, too. I no longer resented advice from her and, in fact, learned a lot from her on that trip, and not only about driving a car. After a couple of weeks in Devonshire, I drove my mother to London and she went home by train.

The family I stayed with lived just outside Exeter and they suggested that, as the university there had open enrollment for single courses during the summer, I should take a course or two in English literature. This was a great idea. It brought me together with other young people and, above all, it not only forced me to speak English but also to write it, something I would not have done by myself. I liked the casual atmosphere at Exeter University, the fact that once you had registered for one course, you could sit in on others, and that it was always easy to find partners to play golf on week-ends. In fact, I liked it all so much that I stayed almost until Christmas.

Loch Ness 1935

At Exeter I met my first girl friend. She was called Eva — I thought this was a coincidence, but who knows? — and came from Canada. I think I was her second venture and we were still tentative and a little nervous. We both were going home for Christmas and knew that this would be a transient affair.

At the end of November I asked her if she would like to see Scotland. I wanted to drive there for a couple of weeks.

"Drive all the way?" she said.

"Why not? I've driven here from Italy, I don't mind driving all day and half the night. But we'll have to do it the cheapest way possible. 'Bed and Breakfasts' and sandwiches we can buy on the road."

"I don't mind that. I'd love to!"

The people I stayed with shook their heads when I told them. You'll be in fog and drizzle all the way, they said. November is not the time to go to Scotland.

They were quite wrong. We stayed a day in Wales on the way up, and had mostly sun and spectacular views when we went up Mt. Snowdon. It was a climb of more than three hours from where we left the car. It was Eva's first mountain, but there was a good path and we took it very gently.

It was worth the effort. Snowdon is over a thousand meters and there is nothing of half that height anywhere near. There was quite a wind and it brought a wisp of fog every now and then. In between it was clear and you could see almost the entire coast line of Wales and endless hills towards the east.

We spent a day at Edinburgh, visited the castle, and marveled at the charming intimacy of the old city. Then we went north to Inverness and turned south along the Loch Ness. It was again a sunny day and we stopped several times along the long, narrow Loch, looking for the monster. It did not appear, but by the time we got to Fort Arthur at the end of the Loch, it was dark.

Fort Arthur was a small place, a big hotel and little else. I looked at Eva. Let's try it, she said. Maybe they have a servant's room. We both went in. There was a big lounge and at the end the reception desk with no one behind it. But as we approached, a young woman came out and smiled at us.

"We're students, touring Scotland, and we wondered ..."

"I am afraid we are closing," she said, "our season is finished."

"We just wanted a bed for one night. Too bad. How much would it have cost?"

"Five guineas," she said. After a moment she asked: "How much did you pay for bed and breakfast on this trip?"

I laughed and said:

"Fourteen or fifteen shillings for both of us!"

"Well, we are closing, there are no guests here." She tilted her head and thought for a moment. "How would it be, if I gave you a room for one guinea?"

I turned to Eva — a guinea was twenty-one shillings — but she didn't hesitate.

"That would be wonderful! But can you do it?"

"Why not," the woman said. "We've had a very good summer. But the kitchen is closed. If you want something to eat, there's a tea room across the street; you may get a sandwich there. By the time you get back, the room will be ready."

We thanked her profusely and went across the street. They gave us a splendid sandwich with smoked trout and we had scones and jam for a sweet. When we came back to the hotel, we were led to a large room on the first floor. It was palatial, and they had lit a big fire in the fireplace. I don't remember the furniture, but there was a thick warm carpet. I have not forgotten it because we made love on it in front of the fire.

The next morning, the manager from the night before was not there. I paid our bill and asked for a sheet of paper. "Dear Manager," I wrote, "We shall never forget your generosity and we shall love Scotland forever." We both signed it, folded it in an envelope, and asked them to give it to the manager.

It changed my view of Scotland. From then on I have always spoken up when people said that the Scots were stingy.

Academic Disillusionment 1936

In the middle of December I packed my little car and set out on my long journey home. Before I reached Dover, for the Channel crossing, I got a taste of how cold it was going to be. The car had no heating and the celluloid windows left all sorts of cracks for icy air to blow in. Somewhere on the way I bought a pair of fleece-lined gloves, a woolen cap, and a military blanket. I quickly learned that putting the blanket over your knees was useless, because the cold blew in from underneath; so I put it flat on the seat, climbed in, and folded it over my legs from both sides. Wrapped up like that, with a large tin box of sandwiches and a thermos bottle beside me, I learned to drive in the snow. There was lots of it on the ground and it was falling thickly all the way through France and Switzerland. It was slow progress — I forget how many days it took — because rarely did I see enough to go faster than 25 m.p.h. But it made me form a lasting bond with my car and we arrived home all in one piece.

Shortly after New Year, I packed again and drove to Zürich to begin studying seriously (allowing a few week-ends to take part in ski races). Through a friend, I quickly found a room to live in and then went to the ETH to see the professor who had talked to us after the exam at Zuoz. All I remember of his name is that it began with K; I must have repressed it and for a very good reason. When I found him and mentioned what he had said about entering ETH without a further exam, he coldly said he did not remember anything about such a conversation and if I wanted to study at ETH I should have passed the exam in the preceding autumn. I was speechless. I simply could not believe that a university professor would do such a thing. I left in shock, went to my new room which I had rented for three months, wondered what I should do, and played with the idea to take more time off for ski races. Finally I called a friend, who had gone straight from Zuoz to Zürich University.

"Don't worry," he said, "with the Zuoz Matura you can enter here without any further ado."

So I ended up studying mathematics at Zürich University. People kept asking:

"If you wanted to study math, why didn't you go you the ETH?"

I told them the story about Prof. K, hoping that it would somehow get back to him and his superiors. The people were of course right. Math at ETH would have been more interesting. At the University, the main course I had to take was at eight in the morning, not an hour at which I was very alive. It was a course that a lot of students had to take and it was always crowded. To get a front seat you would have had to come a little after seven. I came at eight on good days and ten or fifteen minutes later on bad ones. So I had to sit in one of the last rows, far up in the auditorium. Even then I was usually not the last. The professor started at ten past eight and if there was any noise in the auditorium, he lowered his voice, so that a few rows up you heard nothing. By the time the noise died down and he spoke audibly, he had usually covered the black board with several yards of equations and you had not the slightest notion what they were about. When I tried afterwards to locate them in a textbook, I found that they mostly concerned things we had gone through during the last year at Zuoz and seemed just a more complicated way of doing them. My enthusiasm was severely dampened and I decided to study with books and fit in ski races, rather than kill myself by going to a lecture at eight a.m. When it got warm enough, I took a book and went to the swimming pool of the Dolder Hotel, where between vector analysis and infinite progressions one could see and sometimes get to know the prettiest girls of Zürich.

Before the end of the spring semester, my father wrote to me saying that, because of the international money situation, he could not promise to finance my studies in Switzerland; it would be much easier if I moved to Prague (which he advised me not to do) or to Vienna. I certainly did not want to go to Prague. I did not know Czech and I knew that I would have to do military service if I went there. So I opted for Vienna. But that was for the autumn and my friend Fery and I had long ago decided to drive to Berlin for the Olympic games that summer.

Olympic Games and the Cool, Blue Eyes of Lea 1936

Before the war, the International Ski Federation had the very reasonable rule that you had to be 18 years old to compete in international races. You also could not decide on your own to take part but had to be entered by an affiliated club. The winter of 1935/36, therefore, was the first in which I could start in big races. I was very pleased that a couple of times I finished among the first ten and realized that there were still things I had to learn.

The good skiers in those days were all from mountain villages, had learned to ski on their own, mostly on old skis a tourist had discarded, and sometimes on the curved boards of broken barrels. It was a crowd I had not met before. They were highly suspicious of what to them was a city person, but when the city person turned out to ski quite well, the ice was somewhat broken. I very much enjoyed their company. They were competitive, of course, but not as ruthless as they are today. Racing was still something you did for fun, not a lucrative profession. There was a lot of collegiality and for me this was a novel kind of education.

At several races I met a chap called Franz, who was the coach of some of the German skiers. He was not as good a skier as the Austrian coach, but I liked him better, because he was a worldly person with a wide range of interests. It was he who introduced a few of us to "autogenic training", a way of controlling your body that none of us had ever heard of. We became interested in it because of a mountaineering accident that happened that season. Four skiers had been caught in an avalanche and lay buried under the snow for several hours. When they were dug out, three of them had only minor damage from frostbite, the fourth was nearly dead and had to have toes amputated. The three lucky ones had apparently practiced what autogenic training had taught them about keeping your circulation going. We were duly impressed. Avalanches were very much part of our world, and to learn a way to survive them seemed eminently desirable. (I never had an opportunity to try out autogenic training under an avalanche; but some thirty years later, when I wanted to say something at the Wiener Memorial Conference in Genoa, I remembered the conscious relaxation and it immediately helped to overcome my nervousness.)

No one among the racing people talked about politics. But when Franz got to know me a little, he confided that he hated the Nazi movement. He had hopes that it would soon come to its end. Because he also coached some of the track and field teams he knew a lot of athletes and he said that many of them were planning a big show of opposition against Hitler at the 1936 Olympic games in Berlin. If I had friends, he suggested, we should come there and help, because foreigners would add weight to their demonstration.

I liked that idea and talked about it to my friend Fery. Though he was a year older than I, he too was naive enough to believe that such a thing was possible. It was a thrilling thing to think about, and so was the idea of a non-stop drive to Berlin. The summer before, we had driven in a thousand-mile rally together, and driving long distances had become a passion. We talked about the route we would take, and decided to go. A few months later I went to Salzburg, where Fery lived, and we set out for Berlin. Fery, his girl friend Lea, and I.

Lea had short blond hair and light blue eyes, so light that they made me think of something I had read, probably in the anthropological sketches by Frobenius. He recounted that, when for the first time they saw a person with blue eyes, some Africans thought it was the blue sky shining through them and that they were spirits from another world. It was an image that, I thought, fitted Lea; but naturally I did not say so.

When we arrived at a friend's house in Berlin, one of the first things he asked was:

"Did you see all the Storm Troopers in the streets? They are to keep order during the Olympic games."

We had noticed them.

"They always walk in twos," he said, "because one alone would be beaten up!"

We began to wonder how a counter demonstration could take place.

The next day, I tried to find Franz. He no longer lived at the address he had given me, and at the Olympic Village no one had heard of him.

Driving about in the Olympic Village, we came upon the theater that had been built for open-air performances. It had a huge stone entrance and men on a scaffolding seemed to be changing the inscription at the top of the arch with chisels and hammers. Later, we asked our friend what they might have been doing.

"Oh yes," he said, "that's the Dietrich Eckhart Theater. They had carved into the stone: *Ein Volk, ein Reich, ein Theater.* Only at the last moment someone realized how funny that was!" (In German, this is like saying "what a comedy".)

"Too true to be good," said Lea.

Going about Berlin and talking to the few young people we knew, we quickly realized that there was not going to be any demonstration. The streets and the traffic were strictly controlled by couples of Storm Troopers. They had obviously been ordered to be polite, especially to foreigners. The Olympic Games were to show the world how civilized the new Germany was. Fery's car had Austrian number plates, and when he inadvertently drove into a one-way street from the wrong end, we were stopped; but the uniformed man almost excused himself.

"You must have overlooked the sign," he said, "would you mind turning round?"

This would have sounded strange, coming from a German official in any age. Now, it seemed like a joke.

The house where we stayed with our friend was a large, old-fashioned building, from before the turn of the century, flanked as far as you could see by others of exactly the same style. It was a wide street and every morning Hitler's cortege passed through it on its way to the Olympic Stadium. We watched it on several mornings and it was an unforgettable sight. Not because of the many big Mercedes cars, the police on motorcycles, or Hitler raising his arm like an automaton to salute his people; but because of the hundreds of elderly and old women, who lined the windows and little balconies, screaming "Mein Führer! Mein Führer!" Our friend said that the street was inhabited mostly by the widows of officers who had died in the First World War.

When the Games began, all we could do was to stand up and applaud enthusiastically whenever a colored athlete beat the Aryans—and we were not the only ones doing this. We were happy that there were many opportunities. Among them Jesse Owens' three gold medals and the Japanese pole jumpers, who rose into the air as though they were weightless. We had no idea at that time that they would be Germany's allies. Hitler was present at one of these "alien" victories. He stood in his box, with his hands neatly folded over his crotch, not applauding. As our friend said, he was protecting his most faithful dependent.

When the Olympic games had ended, Lea wanted to go to Zürich. She had a house there and wanted to return home. This suited me very well, because I had to move from the University in Zürich to that of Vienna and I still had a number of things to do in Zürich. With all the restrictions on money transfers, my father had told me that there was no way he could send me Swiss franks.

We headed west and then followed the Rhine all the way until we came to the German frontier near Basel. It was the time when it was forbidden to take more money out of Germany than you had declared on entering the country. We knew about this and had made quite sure to comply. It was a serious matter because under the Nazis you could be hanged for a small breach of their rules. German customs officials, we had been told, were no longer interested in cigarettes or merchandise coming in, they now looked only for excess money going out.

The frontier station was crawling with men in different uniforms. We were told to get out of the car and were escorted into the building, as though we might try to run away. While we were being questioned — Where do you live? What were you doing in Germany? Where are you going? — we saw through a window that a team was starting to search our car. They seemed to be dismantling it. Lea was taken into a cubicle by a uniformed woman. Fery and I had to undress in another room and two SA-men looked at all the clothes we took off. They examined our wallets and everything else they found in our pockets. In Fery's jacket they came upon a sealed envelope.

"What is this?" the man asked.

"Good God," Fery said, "this is the birthday present my grandmother gave me when I was leaving home three weeks ago — she gives me twenty dollars every year!"

"Open it!"

Fery tore the envelope open and out came a fifty-dollar-bill.

"She's never done this before," he said, "it was twenty dollars as long as I can remember. She must be expecting to die."

The SA-man picked up the envelope. Written on it, instead of an address, was: To Fery, with best wishes for his 20th birthday, from Omama.

"The Third Reich will make good use of this," the man said. He gave Fery the torn envelope and slipped the dollar bill into the drawer of a big desk. He kept us in suspense for a long, long moment, studying our faces. But then he said:

" You may get dressed now — and for this time we'll let you go."

When we came out, they were putting back the carpets and seats of our car. The two Swiss frontier guards were leaning over the beam that lay across the road a few dozen yards away. When the Germans let us go, they opened the beam and as we rolled across, one of them said in his broad Swiss accent, loud enough for the Germans to hear:

"Ha, ha, those clowns have undressed you again!"

"I suppose they were suspicious," I said. "We have an Hungarian, a Swiss, and a Czech passport."

As the Swiss guard stamped our passports, he said, "They are doing it to everyone these days."

We drove off towards Zürich, shaken. There had been 19 men in four different kinds of uniform at the German post: Police, Custom Guards,

SA, and two SS-men. We were lucky, Lea said, and then we did not talk for a long time. I thought of what *could* have happened.

Lea seemed to have gone through the adventure unruffled. Nothing she did or said was ever troubled by hidden emotions. She was cool and seemed detached, no matter what happened. I never had any idea what she might be thinking, but to look at her was invariably a pleasure. Apparently she had been with Fery for quite some time. I was as envious as I allowed myself to be of something that belonged to my only true friend.

That evening we sat in the dark on the terrace of Lea's house, looking out over the lake, savoring the stillness of the night. It had been a long haul from Cologne along the endlessly curving road that follows the Rhine. There was no Autobahn then. Fery had been driving nearly all the way. We had been sitting side by side on the front seat of the open car and, whether I wanted to or not, time and time again I became aware of Lea's thigh along mine. Now, in the silence under the stars, I was shocked to realize that I was remembering the warmth of Lea's body. After a while Fery got up, stretched himself, and announced that his bedtime had come. Lea got up and embraced him. It was a long kiss, and when it ended she said,

"Good night — good night and good-bye ... You won't mind sleeping in the guest room?"

It was a question but did not sound like one. He remained motionless for a moment, and then he turned to me,

"I was afraid this would happen. I hope you two sleep well." And as he started towards the house, he added, "And so will I. I have to leave very early tomorrow."

I was speechless. Lea was sipping her drink, looking out over the lake again. The last steamer was creeping along, a pattern of lights on black glass. My mind was in turmoil, thoughts flashing up in bundles, not one coming to an end. Past, present, and future seemed inextricably entangled, a moving chamber of mirrors, I don't know for how long.

"How do these things happen ..." Lea said as she got up, and again she did not expect an answer. "Bring in the glasses, would you."

I followed her into the house. I was trembling and the glasses tinkled as I put them near the sink. Lea did not look at me. She took me by the hand and led me up the stairs to her bedroom.

By the time I woke up, Lea had made breakfast and Fery had gone. I stayed for five days with Lea. Then I, too, had to leave. I don't remember that we ever left the house. The morning after the last night, when I had packed my things and the cab was stopping in front of the door, Lea kissed me for the last time. Then she looked at me with her incredibly blue eyes and said:

"Good-bye." — And I knew that it was final.

Twenty years later, I was reading Aldous Huxley's *Time must have a stop*. At some point in the novel, a worldly woman says to the very young hero at the end of their affair: "Nature's lay idiot, I taught thee to love!" — I had remembered Lea all too often with shudders of nostalgia and regret. Now, for the first time, I could think of her with a deep, warm glow of gratitude.

Postscript

At that time — about 1936 — Fery and I and a couple of other young people we knew, who like us had been brought up in an ambience where the military and everything connected with it was viewed with ridicule and contempt, would have been ready to go to war against Hitler. What he represented seemed wholly unacceptable, and it was by no means only his attitude towards Jews. It was everything he said and did that seemed a throwback to barbarism. But then, when none of the other countries moved a finger to stop his march into Austria, we lost whatever fighting spirit we might have had.

Lesson from Hofmannsthal 1936

In Vienna, when I was nineteen, I read Hofmannsthal's *Andreas oder die vereinigten Fragmente*. I loved its romantic mysteriousness and, though I certainly could not have formulated it then, it taught me a bit of wisdom.

Andreas is a novel Hofmannsthal started and never finished. There is a draft of about half the story that seems almost finished, and then there are longer and shorter fragments but, as far as I remember, only a vague indication of an end. It is the story of a young man's first journey into the world. He is the son of Viennese patricians, civilized and well-read, and, like most of the children of the rich in those days before the First World War, utterly without living experience, let alone experience with women. The world he comes into after a horrible interlude on the journey is that of Venetian aristocrats, a world of glitter, sophistication, and even more like a stage than Shakespeare had in mind. He falls in love but the woman remains shrouded in mystery. At times there seem to be two of them, Maria and Mariquita, the spiritual and the sensual. On a walk, one day, he thinks he sees her from afar. Her clothes and everything about her seems somehow different, but he is sure it is she. He follows her and discovers that she is in fact a courtesan. Of course he could be mistaken. The woman he followed might be a sister or just another who looked strikingly like her, but his faith is profoundly shaken. More than ever he feels that he must know the "truth".

The fragments provide no solution and I have no idea how Hofmannsthal intended to end the novel. To me it seemed obvious: Andreas would begin to question Maria. At first she would give an evasive answer or two. He would not be satisfied and press on, but then she would simply say: If my love is not enough for you, yours is not enough for me. And that would be the end.

It is the experiences that matter, not the secondary interpretations we concoct. By assimilating what we experience to preconceived, generalized stories we run the risk of losing the very aspects that made the experience enchanting. Why should Andreas go and investigate the woman he has fallen in love with? Why does he have to know who she is and what she does when she is not with him? Why does he feel the need to turn her into a permanent object, into an entity that "exists" outside his own experience? — In doing all this, he ends up by destroying the perfection of his actual experience.

Like all profound wisdom, this must not to be used indiscriminately.

Loss of a Friend 1936

Helm was a young sports instructor from Berlin who had come to Zuoz in 1934 to teach us gymnastics. He was not a good skier and when he once saw me on a Saturday, he asked if I would mind teaching him on week-ends. I was duly flattered and we quickly became friends. It was through him that I first became interested in poetry. He knew a lot of Stefan George and Rilke by heart. After I finished at Zuoz, I saw him again during the Olympic Games. One evening I mentioned the excursions into the glaciers we made every spring, and he asked if I would take him along sometime. I said that I would let him know when the time came.

In the spring of 1937, before I embarked to Australia, we were going to spend a week at the "Hütte" of the Arlberg Ski Club. It was a private Alpine refuge hut from where there were several rewarding excursions into the Eastern Silvretta glaciers. I let Helm know about it and he joined us for the first three days. There was my mother, the photographer Lothar Rübelt, Martina, who had been on many mountains with me, and a young apprentice instructor from St. Anton. We had lovely weather and did some splendid runs that showed Helm that he still had a lot to learn.

The day he had to leave to get back to Berlin, we were standing in the late afternoon sun outside the hut. Martina gave him a peck on the cheek and said "See you next year!" As she went into the hut he put on his rucksack and turned to me:

"Isn't it time you got rid of her?"

I looked at him, not understanding.

" She's Jewish, isn't she?"

I was struck dumb. I just kept looking at him. Then I said the only thing that came to my mind:

"Don't ever come back!"

It was the first great shock in my eighteen years. I found it hard to believe that people could remain opaque for so long. I still had to learn to be wary before thinking of someone as a friend.

Chapter Two

1937–1938

Escape to Australia 1937

When I arrived in Vienna in September 1936 and went to inscribe myself at the university, I got a foretaste of what was to come. Every now and then there were two or three young men with crew cuts, nondescript breeches, and high boots marching along a corridor, trying hard to look like soldiers. While waiting at the office of admissions, I asked the chap beside me what was going on.

"They're our Nazi colleagues preparing for the glorious future," he said.

I thought he was being sarcastic, but I wasn't sure—and this uncertainty became the dominant feature of my stay in Vienna. More than once I noticed that acquaintances, who had always put on a cosmopolitan air, surreptitiously showed others the Swastika badge they were wearing under the lapel .

An older school companion from Zuoz, an Austrian American, who was studying chemistry at Vienna, had a largish apartment in a suburb and suggested that I share it for half the rent. A great solution, as it turned out, because we had very different timetables and hardly ever got in each other's way. I had brought a whole case of spaghetti from home and that saved us from starvation several times when we ran out of money.

The situation at the university was steadily deteriorating. The sporadic marching of booted individuals developed into more or less organized demonstrations and when that happened, some of the professors would decide to go home. They had my sympathy and I did the same and went less and less to lectures and seminars that were not certain to take place. Instead I devoted much time to reading. The friend with whom I shared the apartment had finished high school at Zuoz two years before me and had a wide circle of friends in Vienna. Among them was a couple of older students who had an interest in philosophy and often talked about the Vienna Circle. (Heinz von Foerster, who knew practically all the members of that group when he was a student, later told me that it was misleading to speak of the Vienna Circle as a school of philosophy, it was much more like a discussion group.) The only name my friend's friends mentioned was Wittgenstein and that was how I first heard of his *Tractatus*. As I have written in other places, I understood practically nothing of that book, but I was intrigued by the aphoristic style and it certainly did not put me off philosophy. At the time, however, I learned much more from Bertrand Russell's *Problems of Philosophy* and, wanting to start from the beginning, I bought a copy of Hermann Diels' *Fragments of the Pre-Socratics*. In between I kept returning to the *Tractatus* and one day it became clear to me that Wittgenstein suggested something that was quite impossible. In order to find out whether a picture was true or false, he wrote, we had to compare it with reality. But this is a comparison we cannot make because whatever we may consider reality is a picture we ourselves make of it. It was more than enough to nourish my interest in what knowledge was and how we came to have it.

At the same time, an evening's conversation made me curious about Freud. I bought a copy of his *Analysis of Dreams* and when someone told me that Freud was going to give a public lecture, I went to hear him speak. I was greatly impressed. What, in retrospect, had the greatest impact on me was an assertion that was soon forgotten by many psychoanalysts. Freud said that a valid analysis of a dream could be produced only by the dreamer; the associations that linked an underlying meaning to the manifest surface of the dream were the dreamer's and not anyone else's. It was the first suggestion of mental construction I had come across and it was a thought that I never let go.

As the end of the year came nearer, I thought a lot about what I should do. I had no intention of continuing at the University of Vienna, but there did not seem to be an alternative. I thought of returning to Exeter, but was pretty sure that financially it was not an option. There was also the problem of my passport. When I was born, my father was cultural attaché at the Austrian embassy in Munich. His property was in Prague, and when, after the First World War, Czechoslovakia was created, he automatically became a Czech citizen — and so did I. This meant that I would have to do military service in Czechoslovakia. It had already been postponed while I was studying in Zürich, but my passport was going to expire in about a year. Once that happened, I was afraid, there would be no escape.

Then I had a big stroke of luck. The Australian Ski Club—none of us had ever heard of people skiing in Australia—wrote to the European Ski Federation (FIS) that in order to advertise the ski-resort at Mount Kosciuszko they wanted to hold an international championship and were offering free passage to and from Sydney combined with a stay for three months to skiers who were ready to teach skiing for that period and enter the races at the end of it. The people at FIS were no doubt intrigued by the idea but they immediately saw a problem. The skiers who won races during the winter in those days did not ski all the year. They worked during the summer, mostly on farms, and could not afford to go to Australia just for skiing. So someone had the bright idea of writing to the few ski clubs that regularly sponsored racing, to find out whether there were any students who might be expected to do reasonably well in a race. That is how my name came up. I jumped at the opportunity. A Scandinavian Club nominated three young men, and Dick Durrance, who had spent most of his life in the Alps and was the only competitive skier in the United States, formed an American team with two of his colleagues from Dartmouth College.

None of the others accepted the teaching assignment, but their clubs made some arrangement with the Australians about financing the trip. I was thrilled with the idea and it was the first thing I told my mother when I returned from Vienna. I had written home about the Nazi demonstrations and the dismal situation at the university and I was sure that my parents would agree that there was no point in staying there. But my mother's reaction was still an unexpected one.

"Didn't you know", she said, "that the two sons of the Flexenhotel, where we have stayed in Zürs, have spent several summers teaching skiing in Australia and New Zealand? Anna Skardarasy, their mother, told me that she was planning to go out with them next summer. It's a great idea and now that you are going, I think I'll come along."

I was stunned. She used to leave my father alone at home quite frequently for a week or two—but to go to Australia for three months?

"Do you realize that this means going away for almost six months?"

"Oh, I wouldn't stay more than two or three weeks. I'd come back with Anna."

I remained a little uneasy. Not because of my father. I knew very well that he didn't mind being alone. He spent most of his time in his darkroom anyway. But I was still young enough to fear that traveling with a mother would be an impediment. Somewhere, of course, I knew that this was silly. After a few days on board I realized that, if anything, it was an advantage. My relation with the Skardarasy brothers, who were several years older than I, developed more easily because we had our mothers with us: it stopped them from patronizing me as a teenager.

The only thing I remember clearly from the seven-week journey is the stop at Colombo in Ceylon (now Sri Lanka). I was bowled over by the way people there moved. Even old men and women walked like dancers. The sidewalks were crowded, but there was no pushing and shoving, everybody seemed to be floating on invisible waves. We European tourists looked like cripples among them. In the shops, the first thing that happened was that you were offered coffee; and for seven shillings you could have silk shirts made to measure and delivered to the ship before it departed the next day. There was an air of gaiety about the city and on the way up to Kandy, the Buddhist sanctuary, we saw elephants rolling about and playing like children in a pond. On the surface it all felt like paradise, and for the first few days crossing the Indian Ocean I thought Ceylon was where I wanted to live. But then came Australia and when I returned, almost a year later, I was homesick for Europe and wanted to get back.

Skiing in the Antipodes 1937

We got off the boat at Melbourne because the Australian Ski Club had scheduled a brief stay for us at Mount Buffalo, a ski resort to be opened in the State of Victoria of which Melbourne is the capital. We were taken there by bus and all along I was looking out the window, expecting to see my first Australian mountains. There wasn't anything I would have called a mountain. The bus stopped at a big hotel and before we got out Ernst Skardarasy leant across and said to me:

"Don't worry, Mount Kosciuszko is not like this."

When we had our things settled in our rooms it was lunch time and we went to eat. It was pretty much like the English food on the ship, but there were some interesting exotic fruits afterwards. Kiwis and passion fruit had never been seen in Europe at that point.

Afterwards we were to go out to the "ski area". We followed the guide through what seemed the park of the hotel. There were oleanders and huge rhododendrons with patches of icy snow in between. And then there was a patch that was a bit inclined and that was the ski slope. At the bottom of it there were several dozen people waiting for our performance. Of course, there isn't much you can do on a patch of snow that is almost flat.

You can do a few jumps from a standing start and you can do what was then called a Reul turn. This is doing on skis what figure skaters do in between their more complicated feats; you push off into a turn and then you lift the outside ski like a clumsy ballet dancer. It's so unexpected that it usually brings the house down. And it certainly did at Mount Buffalo. We laughed a lot afterwards, because the Reul turn is not what beginners need to learn; it's of no practical use whatsoever.

The next morning we were asked to repeat our performance for another group of beginners and then, while Franz Skardarasy returned to Melbourne for his trip to New Zealand, we were sent off on a long train ride to Sydney. At the border between Virginia and New South Wales, the State we were heading for, we had to change trains because the width of the rail tracks in the two states was different and a train from one could not run on the rails in the other. It made you wonder how the European nations ever managed to agree on one type of rails.

There was little to see on the trip to Sydney except hour after hour of endless stretches of meager farm land and no houses or buildings of any sort in sight. The only startling feature was that every now and then a dog would be waiting along the railway tracks, A package of mail would be thrown to him from the train, he picked it up and set out on his way to an invisible distant farmstead. I was wondering how you could train a dog to go and meet a train that had not yet come at a place that was far out of sight. Months later, during the summer I stayed in Australia, I was taken to a sheep dog trial and realized that there was little they did not manage to train dogs to do. They could learn to perform different actions to ten or twelve different whistles, and they could be ordered to round up a bunch of sheep that were out of sight behind a hill. Yet, the people who trained these dogs had never heard of Professor Skinner, who created havoc among American psychologists by training pigeons to walk a figure of eight.

Mount Kosciuszko was indeed different from Mount Buffalo. The Chalet at Charlotte Pass, where we were to stay for the season, was quite a distance from where we were dropped after the train ride from Sydney. Our luggage was to be picked up by a tractor, but Ernst Skardarasy knew the way and we were to walk on skis. It was snowing thickly and the wind was against us. It wasn't much of a climb, Ernst said, but putting on skins would help against the wind. He was right. After half an hour it was a blizzard we were leaning into and without skins on our skis we would have been pushed backwards all the time. Even so, it was slow going. We had plowed on for well over two hours when Ernst said that we were about half way. After seven inactive weeks on board the ship I didn't look forward to another three hours of pushing against the wind. My mother, of course, did not complain. She merely remarked that it was rather like a snowstorm at four thousand meters in the Alps. I thought that if we turned around, the wind would blow us back effortlessly to where we had come from; but I had learned long ago that this was not the sort of thing you should say. So we put our heads down and pushed on. After about another hour, a noisy shadow appeared in the whiteness in front of us. It turned out to be a snow cat the people at the Chalet had sent to pick us up. We scraped off the ice that had formed on our fronts and gratefully climbed in to huddle together in relative warmth. This first experience convinced me that we were in for a winter just like in the mountains of Europe.

Waking up at the Chalet after the snowstorm, I thought I was still dreaming. The window framed what could have been a Japanese wood-cut: a couple of hills glistening in bright sunlight, here and there a clump of dwarfed trees each of whose leaves carried a little pad of sparkling snow. Later I was told that there were no native pines in Australia and that nearly all trees were Eucalyptus. The Eucalyptus trees obviously behaved as pines do in the Alps: the higher they climbed on the mountains, the shorter they got and the more contorted, until, near the tree line, they crept along the ground. But they were far more decorative than pines. Rather than shed leaves, they shed bark, and what was revealed under curled strips of bark was brightly colored, red, yellow, and bluish black.

After breakfast, we put on skis and climbed the hill facing the Chalet. The snow was fluffy powder and sparkled if you threw it into the air with the tip of a ski. It was like walking in crystalline feathers. As I reached the top of the hill, I could see that there were indeed mountains. Three or four of them, looking like the backs of giant hippos, flattish on top and getting steeper and steeper round the sides. Later, as we explored them, I realized that this was their danger: from the top you could never see how the slope ended. As you skied down, it got steadily steeper and, below you, it could turn into a rocky precipice that remained practically invisible from above. So you had to watch out. Fortunately, however, the hippo-mountains all had places where you could easily climb up and ski down.

Every two weeks a new bunch of eighty people eager to learn skiing arrived at the Chalet. Some had never seen snow, some had tried to learn to ski on their own. These were more difficult to teach than the absolute novices because they had acquired defensive habits, always leaning backwards and towards the slope. Those habits are difficult to get rid of. If you didn't keep your weight ahead of your skis you could not control them (This was long before the high, stiff skiing boot was introduced that allows people to sit back as far as they like). Anyway, most of our students learned something during their two weeks and left satisfied and even more enthusiastic than when they had come.

My mother was enchanted. She helped with the teaching and in between she went to all the slopes within about an hour from the Chalet, made an expert downhill track on them, and photographed it. After two weeks she left, having bestowed her skis, the equipment that goes with them, and most of her clothes to her favorite pupils. I accompanied her part of the way down to the train. Returning along the tracks we had made coming from the Chalet, I realized that this was good-bye for much longer than ever before. She had agreed that, having come out so far, it was reasonable for me to stay at least part of the summer in Australia. It gave me a strange feeling to think that it might be seven or eight months before I would see her again. I had never been on my own for so long, and I wondered. I kept wishing that I had told her how lucky I thought myself to have her as a mother. But then the teaching routine quickly took over and I rarely thought of Europe or home.

When the last ski class had left we had a couple of days to explore the further reaches of the Kosciuszko range. They were longish trips with several climbs and several descents, and it was then that from a distance we saw Mount Townsend. Ernst Skardarasy decided that it was the most likely site for a downhill race and that it would take place there. It took a little more than two hours to get to the bottom of Mount Townsend and then there was an hour's climb. Quite unimaginable today, when racers expect to be taken to the start by a hanging cabin or a ski lift.

When the competitors in the "championship" arrived, the atmosphere in the Chalet changed. Suddenly we were less than twenty people and for the first time there was space to move about without bumping into someone. When we went out skiing, I was, of course, curious to find out what the competition was like. I had seen Dick Durrance, the American champion, in a race in Austria the year before and knew that he was good. Now, when we were more or less playing on the slopes near the Chalet, I realized just how good he was. He was small and tough and very fit. His two colleagues, the Bradley brothers from Dartmouth College, called him the Rubber Ball because of his ability to bounce back into position after his very rare stumbles. He had his own style, keeping a low crouch on his skis and never letting them leave the ground for long. This made for speed. The Bradleys tried hard to imitate him, and I think this was a mistake. They were a head taller and probably weighed some twenty pounds more, which made it impossible for them to keep up the crouch when the terrain was uneven.

The races began with the slalom that Ernst Skardarasy had staked out on the steepest slope near the Chalet. It was a tight course and, as I expected, Durrance beat me by a couple of seconds in each run. The moment I had seen him on the first day, I realized that he would be quicker than I could ever be. So I was not really disappointed with my second place. I was looking forward to the downhill race and, as it happened, it went well for me and I won. There were two longish stretches in the run from Mount Townsend that could be taken straight, and there my greater weight was obviously an advantage.

After the race, on the way back to the Chalet, there was again an hour's climb and then a few beautiful slopes with perfect spring snow. This was long before skiing became a hopping game. When there was enough space, you made long drawn out turns during which you felt you were lying on air in a state of sublime balance. We used to say it was the second best feeling. And this is how I remember skiing in Australia.

Sharks and Other Perils 1937

When we left Mount Kosciuszko and returned to Sydney, we had a brief farewell celebration and later I said good-bye to the others when they were embarking for their home journey to Europe.

One of the people I had got to know a little better at the Chalet was a middle-aged man called Ken. He had a business renting out speedboats for people to scorch around the Sydney Harbor. He had been cross country skiing for many years and had no ambition to become a downhill skier. He merely wanted to learn a few tricks he could use when he found himself on steeper terrain. Ken was very pleased with what I showed him and we had a good many drinks together. When he heard that I was planning to stay in Sydney for part of the summer, he offered to help me find a flat. I was delighted, and we made arrangements for me to call him when I came down from Kosciuszko.

When I met him, after Skardarasy and the others had gone aboard their ship, he said that he had found a reasonable flat and he thought I would like it. When he took me there, I didn't; but I refrained from saying so. He had made provisional arrangements for me to stay there, and I was very grateful for that. I didn't want to have to stay at a hotel until I found a place to live. Now I could do it on my own.

But Ken also said something that interested me very much. He proposed to take me aquaplaning with one of his speedboats. Water skiing had not yet been invented. Aquaplaning meant that you stood on an oblong board that was being pulled by a rope from the boat, and you had a piece of rope from the front of the board with a cross bar as handle to hold on to. I had only seen it and was curious to feel what it was like. We made an arrangement for him to pick me up in a couple of days.

Sydney Harbor is a very large natural inlet that stretches some twenty miles inland. It is flanked by irregular hills and has innumerable little bays and peninsulas. The shipping harbor covers a small area a few miles in, the rest is a lovely place for boating.

The aquaplaning board floats behind the boat. You have to get hold of the wooden handle, I was told, and climb on the board, while the boat was gently accelerating. It sounded more difficult than it was. Ken obviously knew how to help by adjusting the speed of the boat, and in no time I was standing up and feeling my way, while Ken was going faster and faster. Making curves was the same as in parallel turns on skis, except that you had to put more weight on the inside leg and to control the inclination of the board with the outside one. If you could ski, there seemed to be no problem. But there was. The surface of the water had of course small ripples, which meant that the head of the board was constantly moving up and down. This vibration was easy to compensate with your thighs, but it was also communicated to the handle you were hanging on to, and after ten minutes your arms got tired. After twelve minutes they were burning. As there was no way to stop it, I let go and tumbled into the water.

The speedboat slowed down and started a wide turn to pick me up. It had been traveling at 30 or 40 miles an hour and turning back took quite some time. For a minute or so, I was happily swimming along, marveling how clean the water was. Then I remembered and was practically paralyzed. I remembered that someone had told me that if you looked down on Sydney Harbor from a plane, you could see sharks like in a gold fish bowl.

I did not know, should I stay still, or swim fast, or just splash? I did nothing and even stopped breathing. It seemed an eternity before the boat came and I could climb into safety.

"What's wrong with you?" Ken asked, because I just sat speechless.

"I remembered the sharks," I stuttered.

"We never think of them," he said.

That was very well for him to say. As an Australian he had been told from his birth on that there was a bigger chance to be killed by a car than to be attacked by a shark. Sure, I thought to myself, but with a little care I can stay out of the way of cars, whereas once I'm in the water, there is no escape from a shark. I could not get them out of my mind and I did not feel like aquaplaning again. The paper the day before had a front page story of a shark being caught and when it was cut open, they found a human arm in it that was still wearing a wristwatch. I remembered thinking what a good advertisement this would make for a waterproof watch. Now it had a different connotation.

* * *

The first two weeks in my flat were almost completely taken up with answering phone calls from people who had met me at Kosciuszko and who were now asking me to lunch, or dinner, or to do something with them. They were all incredibly hospitable and I didn't know how I could say no. I calculated that about eight times eighty people had come to the Chalet during the winter. It would mean at least five hundred invitations, and that was too many. At the end of the two weeks I had found a flat that I really liked. Another acquaintance from Kosciuszko had introduced me to an interior decorator who had lists of unoccupied flats. One of them was in a building near his own and it suited me perfectly. It gave me a way to escape. I was going to move without telling anyone. I paid my rent at the old flat and settled into the new one without leaving a forwarding address.

Ian, the interior decorator, made no bones about being homosexual. He didn't mind when I told him that I was not inclined that way and we became very good friends. One afternoon he phoned and asked me to come over to meet two friends of his who were curious to meet a skier. I assumed that they were male friends of his, but they were not. They were a startling pair of women: one a tall blonde who could have been one of Masaccio's angels, the other, at least a head shorter, a brunette who suggested Paris. As Ian led me into his living room, they were having a heated discussion. They spoke with a thick Australian accent, using language that was decidedly not "upper class". I listened in amazement. For a while they took no notice of me. Then the taller one turned my way, cocked her head, and asked:

"Looking for a tart?"

I just laughed and she shook her head and said to her friend:

"He doesn't believe us!"

Pointing to the blonde, Ian said:

"This is Irma, and this is Isabel—they like to find out how shockable people are."

"I'm sorry if I disappointed you," I said, and after this rather peculiar introduction we had some tea and got on very well together. So well, in fact, that they said they were going to ask me to their house. A few days later Ian took me there. It was a big, old house on Potts Point with grounds going down to a little bay in the harbor and a view right across to the

wooded hills on the other side. It was called Farnworth and Irma, her husband, and Isabel shared it. Cyril, Irma's husband was one of the top jour-
nalists of the main Sydney paper and mostly there were some of his
friends staying with him. On my first visit I was introduced to a game they
played every now and then. It was their form of skiing, they said. They
took kitchen trays up to the third floor, sat on them, and slithered down
the stairs, all of three floors. The art was to catch hold of the right rung in
the banister, so that you could swing yourself around at the landings and
head down the next flight of stairs. You had to learn not to lose contact
with the tray while you were making the turn. It was an outlandish sport
and rather astonishing that no one ever got hurt.

I took an instant liking to Isabel. She had a subtle wit and a thoroughly
British way of expressing it. Once we started talking to each other, I found
that far more interesting than scooting down the stairs on a tray.

New Prospects 1937

When I first visited Farnworth, Isabel seemed to like talking with me
about Europe and especially about Paris and then about other things. She
had studied painting in Paris for seven years, mostly with Picard Ledoux
who was famous for his figure drawings. Her mother, who had grown up
in England, had been married at the age of seventeen to an Australian
engineer with whom, it turned out, she had nothing in common. She
divorced him after a year, before Isabel was born. Because she was far
more literate than the average Australian she quickly found a job with a
publisher. When Isabel was in her early teens, her mother decided that
with the money she had put aside and the little she received from her
ex-husband they would have enough to realize an old dream and live in
Paris for a few years. That is how Isabel came to study there instead of finishing high school in Sydney. She and her mother looked a little alike and
the people they met usually thought they were sisters. It was, I gathered,
very much how they felt. Most of their friends were writers or artists and
through them Isabel received an exceptional education.

She loved to talk about their life in Paris. Her mother had become a
friend of Sylvia Beach, the owner of Shakespeare & Co., where Joyce's
Ulysses was published. (I had just read *Ulysses* and it became an immediate bond.) Her mother also met an English painter, whom she married
and with whom she had a son. This marriage did not last either, and

when, after seven years in Paris, their money was running out, she some-what regretfully took her children back to Australia. In Paris she had no chance of making money, but in Sydney both she and Isabel easily found jobs.

About two years before I met Isabel, her mother died after a short bout with cancer. It was then that Isabel escaped from loneliness by moving in with her friends at Farnworth. There was always something going on there, quite apart from the occasional downhill races on the stairs.

* * *

At that time, I realized that I would have to do something about my pass-port. It was going to expire during that summer and I was afraid that once it was invalid I might not have much control over what would happen to me. So I called up the Czech consulate and made an appointment.

When I was shown in to the consul, he took one look at me and said:

"Where did you get that tan?"

"I've just come down from Mount Kosciuszko. I spent three months there teaching skiing."

"Oh, skiing," he sighed and leant back with his hands folded behind his neck. "Tell me about it."

So I told him. About the arrangement with the Australian Ski Club, about the virgin snows on the mountains around the Chalet at Charlotte Pass, and about the races.

"Now I remember," he said. "I read about that in the papers. So you are the chap who won the downhill. They spelled your name in all sorts of funny ways! Where did you learn to ski? Did you race much in the Alps?"

I answered briefly and then he took over. He had been to many of the European ski resorts I knew and we had a great time talking about them, about the new fads, and about the basics of skiing. After well over an hour he looked at his watch and said:

"Good God, skiing makes me forget about time! — Why did you come to see me?"

I handed him my passport and explained that I needed an extension because, having traveled all that way, I wanted to stay in Australia a little longer. He skimmed through the pages that were covered with visas and other stamps. Then he shook his head.

"Do you know what I *should* do? I should give you an extension for three months — just enough for you to go to Prague and do military service — but this would be the end of your racing career, wouldn't it?"

He got up and went to another table where there was a whole battery of stamps. He chose one, pressed it into my passport, and added his signature. When he handed it back to me he said:

"You now have two more years. I wish you the best of luck!"

I was so relieved, I could have thrown my arms around him. But I didn't. I merely thanked him as warmly as I could and went on my way into what seemed a future of endless freedom.

* * *

I had spent a lot time at Farnworth and towards the end of the summer I mentioned to Isabel that, before leaving Australia, I wanted to spend a week or so driving into the interior.

"I've been to Melbourne several times," she said, "but I've never seen the Blue Mountains or any of the country west of Sydney. Would you take me along? — As a sister?"

I was delighted and went off to buy maps so that we could see where we might want to go. I had not really liked the idea of driving about all by myself, but I wouldn't have had the courage to ask Isabel. Now that she had suggested it, it seemed the perfect solution.

At the end of the first day we stopped at the only inn in a village some hundred miles inland. When I asked for two single rooms, the woman behind the counter hesitated and gave us the strangest look. She shoved the register across to us and we both wrote in our names and addresses.

She gave us two keys and said that breakfast was from seven to nine. As we walked towards the stairs with our little suitcases, she again shook her head in wonder.

At breakfast the next morning Isabel said she thought it was silly to pay for two rather awful rooms. We could save at least a pound each if we managed to sleep in one as brother and sister — what did I think about that?

I told her that in the refuge huts of the Alpine Clubs in the Alps women and men were always mixed up in dormitories and I was quite used to it.

"Let's try," she said, "but we'll have to sign in as a married couple. They never check, but hotels won't let you share a room unless you sign with the same name."

I suggested that, as Ian had introduced us to one another, we sign as Mr. & Mrs. Ian Long. She thought a little irony was appropriate and that's what we did.

The next day we came to the place where Canberra, the new capital of Australia was being built. It was a flat area between barely noticeable hills. A network of streets had been provisionally asphalted at right angles through pampas grass that let one see nothing but the sky. There was no building going on at the moment, but three or four large edifices seemed quite finished. They were far apart and looked like a giant's toys in the vast expanse of high grass. We stopped near one that stood at least four stories high. Above the entrance, carved in stone, it said something like Australian National Library. It was a totally empty shell without doors or windows. We thought it was a remarkable fact that the library was among the first three buildings of the new capital.

Towards evening, before we reached the village we were making for, it started to rain. A godsend after the day's heat of well over a hundred degrees. By the time we found the inn, it was not just raining any more, it was a tropical downpour. As we signed the register as Mr. & Mrs. Long, the inn keeper told us how pleased they were because it hadn't rained there for more than a year.

Looking out the window in the morning, it was still raining and there was nothing but water as far as we could see, no road, no anything. Fortunately the few houses of the village and the inn were on a little rise, but there was no other island in sight. While we were having breakfast, the innkeeper told us that after the long drought it might take a day or two before the water seeped away. We couldn't possibly drive on, he said; we'd get stuck in the mud or worse, and no one would come to pull us out. Given the view from our window, we were easily persuaded to stay.

There was absolutely nothing to do. We had brought nothing to read and the inn had no facilities like a ping-pong table or billiards. The only thing the innkeeper offered us was a pack of cards, but after a few listless hands of twenty-one and of poker, we decided we didn't feel like playing cards.

"Let's try another game," Isabel said. "I'll tell you a word, and you make up a story from it or around it; and then you give me a word, and I'll make up a story."

The word she gave me was "butterfly" and I couldn't think of any reasonable beginning. The only thing that came to my mind was that English, French, Italian, and German had completely unrelated words for it: butterfly, papillon, farfalla, Schmetterling. As I said the German word, I was reminded of my father's collection and I went on recounting how he told me the names of butterflies and beetles when we hiked in the mountains, and that I learned about mushrooms from him, and I ended in his darkroom where he taught me the basics of photography.

I have no idea where it came from, but I gave her the word "omelet".

"Funny that you should choose the one thing that I can cook quite well!" she said, "and as you are Austrian I might as well tell you that in

France they say that Austrians would rather make an omelet without eggs than without flour."

Then she went on to tell me how, when people came unexpectedly to visit them in their flat in Paris and there was no food in the house except eggs and a few left-overs, she would make omelets with whatever there was, and some of them were considered ingenious inventions. She talked about the people who ate the omelets and that some of them were connected to the theater, and this led to plays she had seen and a host of other associations. She had an enchanting way of recounting these things. For most people telling stories turns into a monologue and they seem unaware of the listener. Rather like a radio talk, where the speaker has no idea to whom he might be talking. When Isabel recounted something, I felt she was telling *me*, and what she said was always tailored to my reactions. It generated intimacy and the wonderfully reassuring mood of perfect understanding.

Before we knew it the day had gone and it was time to go to bed. Isabel went to the room first and I was to come when she was settled in bed, turned to the wall, so that I could get undressed and brush my teeth unobserved. When I climbed into my side of the bed, she didn't turn out the bedside lamp but said, "Shall we play one more?"

"By all means. I think it's my turn."

"All right," she said and looked at me with a smile that was in her eyes more than on her lips. "Go ahead!"

I hesitated for a moment and said, "The word is 'love'."

"Why?"

"I have fallen in love with you."

She slid across the space that divided us and put her arms around me and kissed me. It was the end of our platonic experiment. After a week, when we returned to Sydney, I knew that I had never been in love before. A few days later I had to go aboard the ship that was to take me back to Europe. I would have liked Isabel to come with me there and then, but that was impossible for all sorts of reasons. Besides, Isabel said she needed some time to think.

Leaving Australia 1938

The ship moved slowly and inexorably past Potts Point and Farnworth and for the first time in my life I was thoroughly depressed. Leaving

Isabel, uncertain whether I would ever see her again, was an unbelievable shock. John Fowles, I think in the novel *The Magus*, very accurately describes the state of mind of a young man, who has just ended a love affair. It is a to-and-fro, he says, between the regret of what was lost and the excitement about what might lie ahead. It fitted perfectly what I had experienced until then, but sailing away from Isabel was different. There had been no effort in our being together, no worrying about misunderstandings, no planning what to say and what not to say. It had been an immediate and unconditional fit. I now realized that in whatever relationships I had had before I had remained essentially alone. With Isabel there was no partition, no need for reserve, no feeling of separateness. As the ship moved out of the long inlet that forms a natural extension of Sydney harbor it began to rock in a gentle swell. For a few minutes, I thought I was going to be seasick. It had never happened to me before. I was sure it was not the sea but my state of mind that threatened a physical reaction.

Seven weeks on board ship are a very long time. In the dining room, I had been put at a table that was presided over by a clergyman who insisted on saying grace before meals. Even worse was a middle-aged businessman, who seemed to take it for granted that others would be interested in his exploits. The first evening he was merely boring; but on the second he got in his stride and explained that he was one of the main representatives of Vickers, the British armaments manufacturer. He was on his way home from China, he said, and business there had been wonderful. He only hoped that hostilities there would not cease too soon. I was horrified. The thought of having to listen to this kind of talk for the whole journey was unbearable. I got up before the "pudding" was served and went to the head steward at the end of the dining room. The night before I had noticed a table where there was lively conversation in Italian and I asked to be switched to that table. The steward looked at me and said:

"But they're all farm workers, you know?"

I told him that I didn't mind that at all and that I loved speaking Italian.

The table with the six or eight Italians was the chief amusement I had on the trip. Most of them had been in Australia for some thirty years and were returning to their homes in Italy for the first time. They had lots of stories about the Australian landowners and they told them with gusto. Sometimes I had difficulties with their dialect, but they loved explaining and did it in graphic terms. In between they wanted to hear from me what Italy was like now, whether Mussolini was as bad as he was painted in the Australian papers, whether Tosca was still a fashionable opera, and whether Italian women had taken to wearing short skirts. I told them that I was not very familiar with the south of Italy (which was where they were from). I did my best to prepare them for the shock they would suffer, having nothing but memories from before the First World War. We got on very well and I had a good time with them.

I wrote long letters to Isabel and posted them at every port of call. But as she had said she would let a few weeks go by before writing to me, I received no answers. Her first letter reached me at Port Said, almost at the end of the journey. It was a lovely letter and I was in heaven. Yes, she wrote, she had decided to come and live with me in Europe — but it would be June before she could leave Sydney, because her brother had to finish school.

I had left Sydney in the middle of January and when I finally landed at Genoa, it was March. For more than seven weeks I had not seen a newspaper and had no idea of what had been going on. I took a train and arrived home and found my parents in a somber mood.

"Hitler is going to march into Austria," my mother said.

My father shook his head. "The Allies have formally declared that he can't."

"Hitler no longer worries about the Allies. He'll take Vienna just as he took the Saarland," she insisted.

Unfortunately she was right. The Allies did not lift a finger. A concerted move would probably have prevented World War 2, but it did not happen.

A few days later, my old skiing friend, Martina, called from Vienna.

"I'm getting out," she said, "I've no intention of being caught here. I'm going to Paris and might even go as far as returning to my ex-husband in Argentina. But on the way I want to do a little skiing — it may be the last I get for a long time. Would you consider picking me up in Zürich and going to Davos for a few days? Remember the little inn we stayed at? I really need a holiday."

Recalling that phone call, I know that I hesitated for a moment, but not for long. My mother had told me that Martina's father had committed suicide a few weeks before. He was from an old Viennese family and just could not bear what was happening to Austria. I had not heard about that either, while I was on the boat. I felt I could not let her down.

"Send me a wire with the time your train gets to Zürich, and I'll be there."

I was a little preoccupied about Davos. Martina and I had shared a bed whenever we went skiing together. There were no complications. We liked each other and it was part of winter sports. So I knew what would happen. But it was a long time until June, I thought, and I did not feel I was being disloyal to Isabel. I considered writing to her, but then decided that such things were better told face to face.

Martina called me and I met her train just before midnight in Zürich. It happened to be one of the last before the German troops reached Vienna. There was not even standing room on it. The Swiss police was collecting the people who got off the train. I had no difficulty spotting Martina, she was the only one who had a suitcase and skis. With her Argentine passport she was quickly let go.

"Am I glad to see you!" she said. "I gave the men in my compartment all the Swiss francs I had. They were socialists, who had tried to put up a resistance against the Nazis in Vienna. They jumped on the train without passport, without money and with just the things they happened to have in their pockets. — Now I am penniless until I get to Paris. Do you mind?"

I easily convinced her that I was happy to see her, packed her and her skis into my car, and we drove off. It normally took about three hours to get to Davos (to average 40 miles an hour in those days you had to drive like a fiend). In the middle of the night, however, there was no traffic and you could go faster and we got to Davos at half past two. It took some time to wake up someone at the inn. I had told them that we would be arriving late and they had said we should just ring the bell. Eventually we climbed to our room and unpacked what we needed. On top of my suitcase I had a dressing gown I had bought on the ship's stop in Colombo. It was dark green silk with a few white herons flying across. When Martina saw it, she gasped: "Storks! Do you want to get me pregnant?"

We had a few days of happy spring skiing and, although we had only a vague idea of what was happening in Austria, a bad conscience. But what could we have done, if England and France did nothing?

Then Martina left for Paris. Some weeks later she sent me a note: Skiing was fun, but I'm leaving this sinking ship. Do the same. I liked you a lot, so please don't come to Argentina.

I never saw her again.

On the Road to Paris 1938

When I got to Genoa to meet the boat Isabel was coming on, I was told that there was a delay. It had been held up at Port Said and would arrive two days late. I did not want to sit about waiting in Genoa. My friend Fery had written that he would be in Monte Carlo for a week checking up on a hotel his family owned and that I should come to visit him for a day or two. So I got into my car and drove along the Riviera. Today it is a continuous built-up area from Genoa to Toulon, but in the 1930s it was still a lovely, winding drive through small tourist resorts separated by stretches of untouched beach and rocky coastline.

I had not seen Fery since our trip to the Olympic games in Berlin and felt a little uneasy about Lea. Did he know that I had stayed with her in Zürich? It was better to talk about it, I thought, but didn't quite know how to bring it up. I asked him if he had seen her. No, he said, but they were still writing to each other.

"Don't worry," he added with a malicious smile, "she told me about your adventure."

"Well, it wasn't me who ..."

"I said, don't worry! She made it quite clear that you hadn't planned it. In fact she didn't either. It just happened, she said. She is not someone who waits to be seduced. She gets what she wants, because she never has doubts about what it is. Anyway, I knew already in Berlin that we were close to the end." He laughed, and then he said: "But it never occurred to me that she had picked you!"

He told me a little about how depressing it was in Austria, how people whom he had considered quite civilized had become Nazis and that there was hardly anyone left with whom you could talk. I told him about Australia. I mentioned my passport and that I had made up my mind to get out of Europe before it expired.

"Why don't we go to Mexico or to South America—we could drive trucks together?"

"I can't. My mother is alone now, my brother is totally unreliable; I can't leave her."

There was nothing I could say. I thought of my parents. My mother was reliable and I trusted her: she would always know what to do.

* * *

It was midday when Isabel came ashore in Genoa and we spent the afternoon organizing her luggage to be sent to a friend of hers who had a big house near Venice. Then we put her brother on a train to Paris where Isabel had arranged for him to stay for some time with friends of her mother's. It was evening before we had finished with all that and we had literally had no time to talk to each other. We decided to get out of Genoa and stay the night somewhere along the Riviera. By the time we stopped at a little hotel in San Remo we had found each other again and were unspeakably happy. It felt like coming home.

On the drive, I told Isabel about Martina. I had nothing to gauge her reaction, but I felt I had to risk it. I could barely see her face in the dim light of the dashboard, but she had tilted her head and seemed to smile. There was a long pause before she said:

"I'm glad you told me. I, too, had a little business to finish before I left Sydney."

* * *

At breakfast the next morning Isabel asked whether we could go to Sanary on the way to Paris. Sanary was a small fishing village between Saint Tropez and Toulon, as yet untouched by tourists but a favorite summer hideout of painters from Paris. I thought that was why she wanted to go there, but I was wrong. A few months ago, she explained, an architect who had been an occasional visitor at Farnworth had eloped with the wife of a shoe polish magnate for whom he was building a house. They had left Australia and were living in a farm house they had rented in Sanary. Adrian, the architect, knew that Isabel, too, was planning to come to Europe, had asked her to visit them. Isabel, of course, was curious to find out how that ménage was going and as we were in no particular hurry to get to Paris, we drove to Sanary.

We had to ask for directions more than once, but eventually we found the farm. The front door was wide open, so we called, and as we got no answer, we went in. It was clear that they lived there, but they were not home. So we waited and looked around. After a while they came, not in a car but on bicycles. Adrian had a thin moustache and looked a little like Clark Gable but had all the signs of ready laughter. He was sun burnt and had an outdoor-look, quite unlike his female companion. She had flaming red hair, the figure of a fashion model, and the glitter of a make-up artist's masterpiece.

They were obviously delighted to see us, so much so that I wondered whether the simple life had begun to weigh on them.

The whole house had been whitewashed, inside and out, for the benefit of the foreign tenants, but after three weeks of occupancy, the inside walls were full of bloody spots where successful mosquitoes had been swatted. There was a mosquito net for the big bed, but Adrian and his redheaded concubine clearly did not spend all day under it. Also there was no sanitation in the house beyond a washbasin in the kitchen and a couple of chamber pots. Adrian had dug a ditch in the field behind the house and a spade stuck in the ground marked the latest entry; a reminder for the next user to cover up his.

The ex-millionairess still acted as though it was fun to rough it, but we wondered just how sincere it was. When she saw Isabel's brown corduroy slacks, she exclaimed (she didn't just say it):

"What a heavenly color! Onions, the color of onions. I'm going to have Schiaparelli make me a pair when we go to Paris next month."

I looked at Isabel and she slightly raised an eyebrow, but didn't say a word.

We were pretty sure that Adrian, who was hoping to make it as a free-lance artist, could not carry on this affair for very long.

We had dinner that night in a small restaurant in Sanary and for Isabel and me it was a true celebration. The next morning, scratching countless mosquito bites, we said good-bye and that we would see one another in Paris in a few weeks. We had no addresses to exchange because we had no idea where we were going to stay; we thought we would surely run into each other at the Café du Dôme if not at some other of the haunts in Montparnasse. As it happened, we didn't and we never heard how the unlikely love affair ended.

* * *

Sanary was not the only stop on our way to Paris. A few weeks earlier I had to have the car's valves adjusted. It was a new one and I had just finished running it in. It was a Fiat 1100 with a somewhat tricked up engine and a two-seater convertible body that I had had some hand in designing. It was a good deal faster than my first one and a real joy to drive. The mechanic who adjusted the valves did a great job, except that he left one of the steel caps, that should have been on a valve shaft, in the space where the oil circulates above the cylinder head. From there the oil drips back into the sump through four holes and, through a fifth one, on to the timing chain that drives the camshaft. The little steel cap had floated about in there for at least a thousand miles, and on the evening that we were approaching Paris at considerable speed in the Seine valley it decided to fall down through the only hole where it could do damage, the fifth hole that led to the timing chain. The effect was sudden and dramatic. The timing chain broke and instantly locked the main shaft of the engine and, with it, of course, the rear wheels. Luckily I was quick enough to disengage the clutch before we got into a real skid. I kept my foot on the clutch, shifted to neutral, and began thinking: a broken valve? A connecting rod? A split piston? All of that would have meant a new engine. I was horrified. The only redeeming feature was that it happened on top of a hill and the car kept coasting down very nicely taking us almost to the beginning of a little village.

The village was called Aisey-sur-Seine and when we had pushed the car a little further in, I was greatly relieved to find that there was a garage with a mechanic's workshop right next to a little inn. The garage was closed for the night, but the innkeeper received us with obvious delight. He had five rooms, he said, but they were usually empty, except during the fishing season, when groups of fishermen would come from Paris. When I told him why we had stopped there, he said he was very sorry and he would do his best to make us comfortable and the mechanic, he added, was a very reliable one.

He was right on both counts. The next morning, when I told the mechanic what had happened, he mentioned the same possibilities I had thought of but thought that they were all unlikely. We started dismantling the engine from the bottom and it took us to lunch time to find the jammed timing gear.

"I'll telephone to Paris for the parts we need," he said. "It'll be four or five days before you can drive again. There's nothing much to do at Aisey, but you'll enjoy the Chabrons' cooking. The fishermen who come here are very demanding gentlemen!"

Mme. Chabron cooked lunch, never less than four courses, and her husband cooked dinner, never less than five. It was the best food I had ever eaten and Isabel, who had known some of the best restaurants in Paris, confirmed that there was no better. She called it "one-flavor-cooking" because everything had the taste that seemed its natural one. We went for walks along the Seine, climbed over fences, and picked corn flowers at the edge of corn fields that were almost ripe. It was unhurried and peaceful and yet another opportunity for us to find that when we were together we never got bored.

One evening, when we came in to dinner, there was another party sitting round a table: one man and five good-looking women, each with a sumptuous head of hair in a different color. They were talking animatedly, and we were distracted from our delicious food, trying to get a clue as to who they were. They left before we had finished. But through the window behind our backs we saw them get into a large van that had painted on its side: Immédia, Teinture pour Cheveux.

Isabelle looked at me:

"Should I have asked them to dye my hair?"

"No," I said, "don't ever change anything, just stay as you are."

For me she remained the way she was for thirty-two years, and I was happy. But then, one day, she was suddenly dead.

Deciding on Dublin 1938

When Isabel and I came to Paris in the summer of 1938, I had the vague hope that I might be able to continue doing mathematics at the Sorbonne. I managed to get a visa for six months, but this was not enough to enroll at the Sorbonne. I would have needed an indefinite permit of residence, and with my Czech passport such a thing was out of the question at that time. Czechoslovakia was about to be taken over by Hitler.

It was then that we started to think of leaving Europe. We didn't really know where to go. Having won the first Australian downhill championship in 1937, I would have had no difficulty finding work there as ski instructor. It would have been reasonable to go to Australia, but neither Isabel nor I had much desire to return there—and in the meantime Paris was thoroughly enchanting.

Isabel visited friends from the years she had lived there with her mother, studying painting. We did not often frequent the Right Bank, except for visits to the Louvre and the Musée de l'Homme. Everything cost more there and we were having a wonderful time on practically nothing in the Latin Quarter on our side of the Seine. We stayed in the ramshackle Hotel de l'Observatoire on the Boulevard Saint Michel and almost every evening we had dinner for seven francs fifty a block away at Rosalie's "Prix Fixe" restaurant. Once Rosalie got to know you, she became your mother. I remember, I once mentioned that we couldn't go to a play she told us to see, because we were rather short of money, she immediately said, don't worry, you can pay me next month. The theatre and buying a book now and then were our only luxuries in those days.

On one of our rare excursions to the Right Bank we had a coffee at the Café Weber and watched the tourists. Suddenly a man stopped in front of our table and looked at me questioningly. It took me a moment to recognize him. He was a friend of my parents, who had lived in Meran while I was growing up there.

"Mr. Briscoe! I'm amazed that you recognized me, it must be more than ten years …"

"Twelve, I think. I didn't recognize you, but I had a suspicion."

I turned to Isabel:

"Mr. Briscoe started me off playing golf when I was seven or eight years old." And then I said, "This is Isabel Yves — we've been living together for quite some time."

"It's a pleasure to meet you," he said, but as I pulled out a chair for him to sit down he shook his head, "I'm so sorry I have to rush off now, but would you two be free tomorrow to have dinner with us?"

I looked at Isabel and she nodded.

"We would love to," she said.

He took out a business card, crossed it out, and wrote his home address on the back.

"Eight o'clock, tomorrow? — Splendid! À demain!" And he was gone.

I turned the card round and saw that it was an electrical firm he was running now.

"Mr. Briscoe is Irish," I explained to Isabel, "and had come to Meran at much the same time as my parents, about 1920. He was not yet 40 then, but he had made a lot of money with some business venture and had decided to retire. Like my parents he was building a house. So they got to know each other and he and my mother became founding members of the Meran Tennis and Golf Club. His wife was Viennese and they had a daughter about my age. Mitzi, too, was a single child and when I was seven or eight they invited me to play with her. They had a ping-pong table and playing ping-pong was what we did on the afternoons when I visited. But one day we decided to fold half of it down and pretended it was our house. We furnished it with cushions and played some board game with dice. The next time Mitzi brought in a big doll and said that now we were a family. Then she asked me whether I knew where babies came from. I said that they came out of their mothers, which was all I knew about the subject. She must have asked her mother to confirm what I had said. It was the last time I was invited. But Mr. Briscoe fortunately continued to play golf with me."

The next day we punctually arrived at his house for dinner, looking forward to a change from the "prix fixe" menus we had been having at Rosalie's. Not that they were not good — indeed we longingly thought of them in later years! — but I had told Isabel of the Austrian maid the Briscoes had in Meran, who got up at five o'clock every morning and baked a bunch of the small, crisp Viennese rolls for breakfast.

It was the same maid who opened the door for us that evening and her cooking had been honed by the years in Paris. Briscoe explained that both his wife and daughter had gone to London for a few days, something they did quite frequently. He told us that retirement in Meran became a little tedious after a few years and they had moved to Paris to start a new business.

"Now," he said, "with the political situation getting worse every day, we are thinking of returning to Dublin — we have not been back to Ireland since before Meran — but now I am curious to hear what you have been doing all this time and why you are here in Paris."

I gave him a quick run-down of what had happened since I left boarding school and explained that with my Czech passport I couldn't take up residence in France and that the passport was valid for just one more year and could not be renewed unless I went to Czechoslovakia to do military service. I had no intention of doing this because I had never set foot in Czechoslovakia and did not know a word of Czech. So the political situation was worrying us, too, and we had been thinking of going to Mexico.

"I wouldn't do that, if I were you. You've been to Australia and you know how ghastly it is to be so far away from Europe. If Hitler marches into Czechoslovakia — which he is sure to do — you can't get your passport renewed in Mexico and you may be stuck there for several years. Why don't you go to Ireland? If there's a war, Ireland is going to remain neutral and a war now is not going to last more than a few weeks. Then, if you don't like living in Ireland, it'll be much easier for you to go back to Italy or wherever you want to."

The mention of Ireland electrified us. Thanks to Isabel's connection to Sylvia Beach, the editor of Joyce's *Ulysses*, that book had become a sort of bible for us. The thought of going to Dublin, to see the Martello Tower and all the other places that played a part in Stephen Dedalus' day, was irresistible and we decided there and then that it was what we were going to do.

"We'll probably follow you," Briscoe said. "Anyway, I'll give you my brother's address. He's a member of the Parliament, the Dail as it's called, and you can go to him if you should need any help."

Although no one said it in so many words, the dinner became a sort of celebration of our decision. Briscoe had not read *Ulysses* and asked us to tell him about it. I didn't know where to begin and looked at Isabel. She leant back in her chair and thought for a moment.

"You know the pointillist painters? Seurat and Signac are the best known. They don't paint in strokes. They make little dabs of unmixed paint. The shape of the dabs is not significant, but they are placed in such a way that when you look at the canvas from a little distance you see not only figures and trees but you get a complete picture of the painter's experience. In a way this is like what Joyce did in *Ulysses* and he gives you one day in the lives of several Dublin people."

I was about to add something, but stopped myself in time. There was nothing worth adding to that description. As though I didn't love her before, I fell in love with her anew.

After dinner Briscoe switched on the radio to listen to the news. As usual it was bad. The Nazi propaganda in the Sudetenland, the German-speaking part of Czechoslovakia, had reached such a pitch that it was clear Hitler would occupy it very soon. It confirmed our decision.

"We'll see you in Dublin," we said to Briscoe as we left his house that night.

Chapter Three

1939–1946

Dublin Winter 1939

We left Paris just after New Year, managed to catch an early Calais-Dover ferry, and got to Holyhead just in time to drive the car on to the night-ferry to Dublin. I didn't know that the fare for the car included a cabin where you could sleep, with proper beds and a washbasin. We quickly pulled pajamas and a toothbrush out of a suitcase and climbed up from the hold to have a sandwich before going to bed. We found sandwiches in the bar and were surprised that it was a real bar with beer and bottles. So instead of having tea we had our first Irish whiskey.

When the car was unloaded the next morning, the customs people looked at our passports and asked how long we intended to stay.

"How long does it take," Isabel asked, "to get to know Ireland?"

The two men looked at each other and then one of them laughed and said:

"At least five years."

The other one picked up Isabel's British passport and said:

"That would be all right for you, but he has a Czech passport and he'll need a special permit. And if you want to stay longer than three months, you'll have to get customs clearance to register the car."

I received a temporary permit for two weeks and was told where I should apply for a longer one. After my experiences with customs officials in Central Europe, it all seemed incredibly smooth and easy. It left us wondering whether I would get an extended permit, but we didn't feel like worrying about that just now during our first hours in Dublin. Mr. Briscoe's brother will help, we said and left it at that.

After we found a hotel that was going to give us bed and breakfast at a reasonable price, we spent the rest of the day exploring what we expected to see in Dublin. We found the Martello Tower and Sandymount Beach and the street where a big clock prompted Stephen Dedalus' thoughts about aesthetics and reality. Though it had been drizzling rain nearly all the time, we were happy when we went to bed.

The next day I went to see about my permit of residence. Again everything was much friendlier and easier than I was used to from Central Europe. I ended up with a permit for three months on condition that I report to the passport office once a week. I was also told that, even if the three months were eventually extended, I could not get a work permit. I could do any kind of free-lance work or work on a farm, but that was it. The condition did not frighten me. I don't think I had ever considered having a regular job. Teaching skiing for three or four months, doing translations, or writing an article every now and then was fine, but nine-to-five employment was not. Anyway, three months seemed an eternity and I was sure that something would turn up.

* * *

There was one other person I had been told to look up in Dublin. It was a niece my father mentioned for the first time when he heard that we were going to Ireland. She was the daughter of his sister Rosalie, with whom he had never been on very good terms. The bulk of the inheritance their parents had left the two of them was a piece of land with three large buildings in the very center of Prague. Rosalie immediately made difficulties about how the inheritance should be divided. My father had no inclination to fight about money and the matter was settled in the simplest way. One of the houses was sold. Rosalie got the proceeds, and my father managed to add enough to make it half the inheritance. He did not want to talk about all that. It was my mother who told me about Rosalie. She had been married to a Baron Campe and left him after less than a year, before giving birth to a daughter. She had no intention of being a mother. She put the infant into a convent, made a token visit once a year, and devoted herself to Paris fashions, a succession of miniature French Griffons, and litigation about money. When the daughter, who was called Ellen, came of age at eighteen, she left the convent and within a few weeks had met a young Irishman, whom she followed to Dublin, where they got married. She made the mistake of telling her mother. According to Czech law at the time, a single daughter had to receive a sizeable portion—I think it was a third — of the parent's possessions as dowry. Rosalie, who had quite a history of suing people and was well acquainted with financial matters, immediately shifted her money to Switzerland, where it was out of Ellen's reach.

It was a great example of the wicked being rewarded and it always reminds me of the beginning of Sacha Guitry's novel, *Le roman d'un tricheur*. There the youngest of a large family, as punishment for some prank, is sent to bed without supper. He does not partake of the mushrooms they eat and in the morning he is the only one alive. My father never thought of shifting his money out of Czechoslovakia and therefore he lost most of it when first the Nazis and then the communists confiscated his property. Kurt Tucholski's quip "Money alone does not make you happy, you have to have it in Switzerland" was published only in the nineteen-thirties and by then it was too late to do anything about it. There were fierce restrictions on moving money from one country to another.

When I telephoned Ellen Campe, she was very surprised. She clearly had not expected ever to hear from relatives. But she sounded quite pleased and asked us to come to dinner one night.

We met her husband, who was some kind of financial adviser, and there were two boys who had not reached their teens. It was a friendly but uneventful evening and went by very fast with me answering her questions about my father and how I had grown up. Before we left, she told us that there was a dinner at the Academy of Art and if we liked she could take us with her. We might meet some of the older artists there. It sounded great and we said we would be delighted.

As the evening approached, Isabel and I became a little apprehensive. It was the older painters that worried us. We would be expected to know their work. But we could not remember ever hearing of an Irish painter in Paris. What would we talk about? We needn't have worried. There were about fifteen or sixteen people and nearly all, like Ellen Campe's husband, had something to do with the administration of the Academy and its gallery. They were only mildly interested in two young people who had just arrived from the continent. We sat at different ends of the long table and seemed to get through the dinner all right, as far as we could tell. But when we were leaving the building, Ellen Campe took us both by the arm and said that if we intended to stay and find work in Dublin, it would be better if we got married. It was, after all, a very catholic country.

Afterwards we wondered what had made her say this. We got the answer a few weeks later.

Meeting Erskine 1939

We were sitting in one of the pubs just off Grafton Street. I was brooding over my half pint of Guinness and Isabel over a sloe gin. We were depressed. It was the end of February. It was drizzling and we hadn't seen the sun since we arrived early in January. All the afternoon we had been showing our folder of sketches to shop owners and business people, telling them that we would be happy to take orders for show cards, posters, or any kind of advertisements. They were friendly and looked at what we had to show, but in the end they all said that they really had no need for show cards or posters and that their advertising was in the hands of an agency. It was not the first afternoon we had spent like this and we were coming to the point of realizing that there was no hope of earning a living that way.

There were not many people in the pub, and I was too absorbed in my gloomy thoughts to notice that two men had come in and now sat at the bar quite close beside us. Isabelle tapped me on the arm and drew my attention to them with a tilt of her head. It took me a moment to realize what she meant, but then I suddenly understood: they were speaking French. Naturally we began to listen.

We could only see the back of the head of the younger one who was talking about his last trip to Paris. He had a trace of an English accent but his French was quite perfect. He and Ruth, he was saying, had done some shopping on their last day and they ended up with so many parcels that they decided to take a taxi to return to the hotel. Getting in, Ruth dropped one on the floor of the cab, and as she already had too many on her lap, she dropped it on the front seat beside the driver. But then it was of course that very one that she wanted to have a look at during the drive. She had only begun to learn French and was eager to use what she knew while they were still in Paris. She leant forward and said to the driver:

"S'il vous plait, donnez moi la petite chose que vous avez en avant" (Please give me the little thing you have in front).

Both the men laughed, and so did we. This, of course, surprised them. The one whose back had been towards us turned round and asked:

"How come you understand French?"

We explained, and then he asked us what we were doing in Dublin. We gave him a very abbreviated version. When the two of them left, he asked where we were staying. We told him. My name is Erskine Childers, he said, I will call you next week.

We returned to our hotel in Harcourt Street and had sardines and crackers for supper, which we always did when we had been at the pub. We were excited. Apart from Ellen it was the first human contact since we had come to Dublin. We had no idea who Erskine Childers was and we were, of course, wondering whether he would actually call. But we were hoping. We really needed a change.

The week-end went by slowly. We didn't go out much. It was drizzling and cold all the time. It was still drizzling Monday and we didn't feel like doing anything because we didn't want to miss the call from Mr. Childers. It didn't come and we were pretty depressed. We were thinking about Mexico again, but without enthusiasm. We wanted to stay in Ireland, but though the permit I had been given allowed me to stay indefinitely, it still was not a work permit. Things looked pretty bleak and we spent two miserable days. But then Mr. Childers did call and everything changed. We went to have a drink with him at the pub where we had met and within a week he had taken us behind the stage at the Gate Theatre and, on Sunday, to the "open house" of Lord and Lady Glenavy. Their house was not really open to everyone and it was not common knowledge that people met there on Sunday evenings. You had to be introduced and the person who introduced you was somehow told if you were welcome to come again. In the years that followed we returned innumerable times to those Sunday evenings and never ceased to enjoy them.

Erskine Childers was the son of the Irish hero of the same name who had been imprisoned and shot by the British as a traitor because he fought for Irish independence. Before entering into that struggle, Erskine *père* had written *The Riddle of the Sands,* a documentary report of a sailing trip along the Dutch and German coast, warning the British before 1914 of the possibility of a German invasion. It was a book reread by many when Hitler came to power. Erskine *fils* was secretary to a ministry when we met him. He advanced to become minister of posts and telegraphs shortly after we left Ireland at the end of 1945 and was then made deputy prime minister. Some twenty–five years later he was president of the Irish Free State. He was the most unlikely person to be a successful politician in Ireland. He had a beautiful speaking voice with a British upper class accent. He was a literary, thoroughly civilized and cosmopolitan man without prejudices or bigotry of any kind.

We became very close friends and met all of his family. His grandmother was from an old Bostonian family and was widely known as Nonna Osgood. At the age of ninety, when we met her, she had crossed the Atlantic 84 times. When we were introduced to her, Isabel and I were placed on either side of her and she put one hand on Isabel's knee and one on mine and said:

"Imagine—these two young people are man and wife."

Later we were told that she had had a love affair with Franz Liszt and we wondered what might have been going through her head while she was sitting between us.

As it happens, we *were* married by then. A number of things had made clear to us that Ellen's advice was good advice. So we drove to Belfast in the North, where one could get a special license in a couple of hours and have a civil wedding the same day. We didn't even have to show our passports and wondered what would happen if we got married in someone else's name; there were people we knew who would have been greatly surprised to receive a marriage certificate in the mail. The only memorable thing about the ceremony was that one of the two witnesses who were called in from some other office was called Nelly Diamond, which sounded like a gangster's moll. It seemed a good omen to us, who didn't take the ceremony very seriously. But afterwards there wasn't ever a moment when we regretted making our togetherness official.

Very soon after war broke out there was no petrol for private cars. Erskine, as a member of the government, received a monthly allowance and was, for some time, allowed to drive his own car. We were living on our farm at Kilternan then, some thirteen miles from Dublin, and every now and then Erskine would come by and pick us up for a drive in the country or, if it was Sunday, take us to the Glenavys. Unless it was hay making time, work on the fields stopped at 6 pm and as in the summer months there was light until 10 or 11, such evening drives were a great pleasure for us. Except that Erskine drove like a maniac. I never had an objection to driving fast myself, but Erskine's style made us nervous. Fortunately we discovered that he loved singing. He had a small but very sweet voice that was perfect for some of the lilting Irish songs—and the moment he began to sing he slowed to about twenty miles an hour. So whenever he started to race, we'd say: "Oh Erskine, what was that lovely song about her going into the foggy dew?" He instantly slowed down and we had a wonderful drive in the Wicklow hills.

The Glenavys 1939

The year we arrived in Dublin, the Glenavys still lived in a large suburban house in Rathgar. Sunday nights they had "open house". This was a standing invitation to their friends to have supper there and to spend the evening in their company. It had been Erskine, who took us with him one Sunday evening. Gordon, Lord Glenavy, he had told us, was not only a director of the Bank of Ireland but also a philosopher and one of the most cultivated men in Dublin. The discussions on Sunday nights were always fun, he said, and Lady Glenavy was a successful painter and might enjoy talking about Paris with Isabel.

When we were introduced, Beaty, the lady of the house, took one look at us and said:

"Oh, I know you—you are living in sin!" and then she turned to the company.

"These two," she said, "succeeded in shocking the Irish Academy. It was hilarious. Someone had brought them to one of those stuffy Academy dinners where no one can ever get a conversation going. They were the youngest people ever. In one of the silences that are not infrequent at those functions, Isabel's (that is your name, isn't it?) Isabel's neighbor asked her how long they had been married. Two years, she said—and at that precise moment, at the other end of the table, this innocent young man was asked the same question and he answered: Oh about five years. The academicians froze with their forks in mid air. But President O'Brien, who's really a kind old thing under all his pompousness, broke the ice and asked Isabel who it was with whom she had studied painting in Paris."

Beaty could not have given us a better introduction. Everybody laughed, and we had a wonderful evening.

At some point Gordon said to me:

"Erskine told me that you're interested in philosophy—do you also play golf?"

I told him that I had played quite a lot, but it was some years ago and I no longer had any clubs.

"If you come with me next Saturday, you can share my clubs and see whether you want to take it up again."

It was the beginning of a friendship that had a profound influence on me. Gordon had read a great deal and was a wonderfully clear and above all totally dispassionate thinker. He was friends with Arnold Ussher, the doyen of Irish philosophy, and agreed with him in what they called "Philosophy of the changing point of view". It was a common sense way of thinking, sceptical of all metaphysics and, as I realized only very much later, not altogether different from Pragmatism.

That Saturday we had a leisurely game, and after the first few holes I now and then managed to hit the ball quite well. I decided to play more often—if only to continue the conversations with Gordon.

During those Saturday games and the many Sunday evenings at his house I learned an enormous amount from Gordon. The most important thing was that he introduced me to Berkeley and made me understand that, if you disregarded the Bishop's theological ontology, what he said about human knowledge made eminently good sense.

After a year or so, the Glenavys moved to a larger house. It was a beautiful eighteenth-century Manor, half way up the hill to the ruins of the Hellfire Club that stood out as landmark against the sky. Instead of playing golf on Saturdays, Gordon was now shaping and planting the grounds around the house to give it the proper stylish setting. He wore rubber boots and an old threadbare tweed jacket. One of those afternoons, a gentleman drove up, stepped out of the car, and asked:

"Is this Lord Glenavy's house?"

"It is," said Gordon.

"Is his lordship at home?"

"Yes, sir, but you'll have to ring the bell at the front door."

As the man walked up the gravel path to the front, Gordon dashed into the house from the back to meet the visitor formally as Lord Glenavy.

I took up playing golf with Gordon's son Paddy Campbell who was about my age. He was several inches taller than six feet and a scratch golfer. He liked me as a partner in Saturday foursomes at some of the clubs where one played for money. My game had improved, but I was always an irregular player and could never turn in scores like his. Yet I was mostly able to do two or three holes under par. That was all he needed for us to make quite a bit of money, because we played "best ball". This meant that each hole was competed for separately and the side that lost paid the other something like ten shillings or a pound, and for a birdie you got a shilling each from the opponents, and half a crown for an eagle.

Paddy had a very bad stammer from earliest childhood. No treatment had had any effect. When he was in his teens, his father sent him to a famous specialist in Berlin. Paddy stayed for several months with a family there and learned quite a bit of German—and when he spoke German, he didn't stammer; but nothing that was tried had any effect on Paddy's English. Finally, the specialist wrote to Gordon that he was helpless because Paddy had no intention of giving up his stammer. Indeed, Paddy had made a game of it. Whenever he got stuck on a consonant, say b-b-b ..., and someone—as people so often do to help the stammerer—would suggest a word that would fit the context, say, "book", he would come up with a far more complicated word such as "belletristic". It was an effective trick and gave him a lot of satisfaction.

One Sunday, Gordon had invited a visiting banker by the name of Gregory to dinner. No one except Gordon knew the man, and the conversation round the table was halting. In one of the pauses Paddy turned to the guest and started: "Mr. G-G-G ..." and someone made the mistake of suggesting "Gregory". As usual Paddy disregarded this and went on "Mr. G-G-G-Guggenheim!" There was an awkward moment, but Mr. Gregory didn't blink an eyelid. "Yes," he said, "I changed my name a few years ago because I had become a British citizen and it helped me to smuggle some of my family's money out of Germany." He then recounted the complicated machinations that had enabled him to do this, not only for himself, but also for a few others.

I don't know how Paddy had found out about Mr. G's change of name. But by then I had begun to suspect that Paddy often went to a certain amount of trouble to prepare his word tricks. They were not only amusing, he later made them the foundation of a career.

He had no sympathy for the military, but when war broke out, he felt he had to do something, if only because of his father's position. He joined the Irish Navy. None of us had ever heard of it, because of course it had never ruled the seas. It had no battle ships or destroyers, but a number of gun boats that operated much like the British Coast Guard. Paddy joined as an "able-bodied seaman" and I remember he appeared at a party in a white sailor's uniform which, he explained, had to be specially made for him because he was so tall. "I have chosen the right c-c-c..." he said, getting stuck on the c. Someone suggested "course". He gave them a scathing look and went on flying:

" ... the right career! Because there are only four chaps between me and the Admiral."

After the war, he somehow met one of the directors of the first independent television network that was started in Britain. The man was charmed by Paddy and hired him to run a talk show. As he had shrewdly foreseen, Paddy's stammer was an asset and the show became quite a success. This was, of course, after we had left Ireland and we never saw the show. But there was an instance we were told about. There was a discussion on agriculture, and at a certain point Paddy said:

"Cows, too, are very important because they make m-m-m-..."

And one of the discussants added "make milk". As usual, Paddy disregarded the suggestion and finished his sentence with "they m-m-make moo and much manure." After this, we were told, he was given the star role in an advertisement for milk.

From Joyce to Vico and Berkeley 1939

In the autumn of 1939 James Joyce's *Finnegans Wake* came out and the literary Dubliners—which probably made up half the population—were electrified. For seventeen years Joyce had published only bits of "Work in Progress" and he had lived in self-imposed exile in Paris for almost three decades. But Dublin had not lost interest in him. He was a constant presence in conversations. A year earlier Sam Beckett's novel *Murphy* had appeared and reminded everyone what Joyce had done for English literature.

One evening at the Glenavys, Michael MacLiammoir read the beginning and a few small sections of *Finnegans Wake*. He had an enchanting speaking voice and put on a slight Dublin accent; and everyone realized that this was the way the book should be read. The accent helped to make some of the puns comprehensible. But as there were many that involved other languages, a lot remained obscure.

Afterwards Michael, who was fluent in French and knew some Spanish, said it would be fun to get some polyglot people together to unravel a few pages. He looked at me and said:

"You speak German and Italian, why don't you try?"

"I've just come to Dublin, I only know a dozen people. You need someone who is at home here."

I looked at Will, who ran a big wholesale business. "You know hundreds of people and you know some Polish, too, don't you? Could you do it?"

He did, and so it came about that for a couple of evenings some fifteen people met, who could cover about twenty languages between them. We did not get beyond the first pages. Analyzing the puns was difficult, and the amusement to be got from them often did not seem worth the trouble of excavating it. Even so, one of them turned out to be of consequence for me. The first two lines of the book read:

"riverrun past Eve and Adam's, from swerve of shore to bend of bay, brings us by a commodius vicus of recirculation ..."

Vicus is Latin for village or hamlet. What could that have to do with recirculation? The only possibility, someone said, is that it refers to the Italian philosopher Giambattista Vico, who was the first to suggest a circular theory of history in which the sequence of birth, maturation, and decay is recurrent; a forerunner of Spengler and Toynbee.

In fact, allusions to Vico occur several times in *Finnegans Wake* and as I had read Spengler's *Decline of the West*, I was intrigued and went to the Dublin library. To my great surprise I there found an old Italian edition of Vico's *New Science*. Skimming through it, I became more interested in Vico's theory of knowledge than in his views about history and I was eventually led to the epistemological treatise which he published in 1710, some thirty years before his major work. 1710 was also the year of Berkeley's first publication.

When I later read most of Berkeley's works, this coincidence intrigued me. In the years after 1710, Berkeley had been in Naples for several months, where Vico was teaching at the university. He had met Prince Doria, to whom Vico had dedicated his thesis. Is it conceivable that the two philosophers did not meet one another? I corresponded with David Berman, the Berkeley expert at Trinity College, Dublin, and he told me that there was, indeed, a notation in Berkeley's diaries saying: "Tomorrow signor Giambattista", but nothing else. There must have been quite a lot of Giambattistas in Naples at hat time and the entry could hardly be considered a proof that they met. Later, when I was teaching at the University of Georgia, I submitted a research proposal to an appropriate agency in Washington. I wanted to go to Naples during the summer to look at the archives of the Institute for Vico Studies. If any evidence of a meeting existed, it most likely would be there. But the proposal was not accepted on the grounds that Vico was an obscure philosopher and I was not member of a department of philosophy. So much for the "uni" in university.

Returning to *Finnegans Wake*, after the brief concerted effort to trace puns I kept the book on my bedside table. I had discovered that when you opened it when your reading was becoming unfocused because sleep was intruding in conceptual sequences, some of it suddenly seemed to make sense. But of course it was not the kind of sense you could recall later. But there was some deeper satisfaction. I don't believe anyone has the stamina to actually *read* much more than a page of it. We normally recognize words as a whole when we read, but here you have to read letter for letter, which is too strenuous in the long run. And who would want to merge this strange fantasy with one's dreams every night? — Joyce died two years later, profoundly disappointed in the reaction to the book he had worked on for seventeen years.

* * *

I owe it to Gordon Glenavy that I came to understand Berkeley in a way that later enabled me to connect some of his explanations with the ideas of Silvio Ceccato and Jean Piaget. At the very beginning of his treatise on *The Principles of Human Understanding,* Berkeley writes that he finds all that has been said about "being" and "existence" wholly incomprehensible. We have tables, houses, trees, and a myriad other things in our perception, but where these things should reside when we are not perceiving them is quite unfathomable to him. This led many of his readers to the question whether or not a tree falling in the forest made a sound. The answer to this question is another question: What is sound? Surely sound is primarily a perception. What we perceive is what we see, hear, feel, taste, and smell. That it should exist, so as we perceive it, outside our perception, is an assumption that cannot be confirmed in any way. Physicists tell us that it is waves in a medium—but waves by themselves make no sound.

As I told Isabel what I had learned from Gordon, she said that she had long been waiting for such an explanation.

"I never told you, that my mother had me take religion lessons in Sydney before we moved to Paris. An old woman friend, whom she trusted a lot, advised her to do it. When your daughter grows up, she said, and doesn't need it, she'll have no difficulty getting rid of it; and if she finds it helpful, she'll have a basis to build on. My mother found this reasonable and so I learned a bit of religious history. One of the very few details I remember, is that Martin Luther somewhere crashed his fist on the table and shouted 'est, est, est!' when the question arose, whether the wine drunk at communion is or is not actually the blood of Christ. I found this both cannibalistic and incomprehensible. What could 'being' mean in that context? The wine in the bottle was the wine in the bottle. Perhaps one could pretend it were blood, but this was a fantasy and surely could not be covered by the mystical concept of being."

I put my arms round her and told her that she was simply wonderful.

Fortunate Accidents 1939

In the spring of 1939, at a party after an opening night at the Gate Theatre, we met William Heron. We ran into him several times during the following weeks. He was interested in poetry and at one point asked me about Rilke. The translations he had seen, he said, were not at all appealing. Did I think he was a real poet? I assured him that he was and that he was my model for whatever poetry I had written. I gave William the few Rilke poems I had translated into English, and it was they, I think, that made him consider me a reliable person. The next time we met he said:

"Rilke is certainly good— unless it's all in your translation."

It was the beginning of a real friendship. After a while, changing the subject, he asked a startling question in the staccato way that turned out to be one of his characteristics.

"I know that as a foreigner you can't get a proper job here. Would you be interested in farming?"

I was so surprised that I didn't answer at once, and he went on:

"I spent the last three years in Scotland as apprentice to a farmer. They are the best in the world. I have a little money, but not enough to buy a farm. I suspect that you have a little money, too. Would you consider buying a farm with me?"

"But I know absolutely nothing about farming!"

"That wouldn't matter. With all the mountaineering and skiing you have done you are physically fit and I can teach you all you have to know to do the field work."

I looked at Isabel. "It certainly would be better than the mangy hotel we're living in now," she said.

We went home and thought about it. The idea grew on us. At first it was living in the country that appealed to us. We were sure that a war was coming, and on a farm there was the possibility of becoming more or less self-sufficient. And doing fieldwork was certainly more attractive to me than ending up at a desk in some office. Of course, no money had been mentioned so far in our talk with William and he may have expected more than we were able to afford. We decided to risk two thousand pounds, which was about half of what we had.

When we saw William again, he said that such an amount would be more than sufficient because his brother, who had just been sacked from his job in some sales department, wanted to participate in the venture. He expected that the kind of farm he had in mind would not cost more than five thousand pounds. So we had several rounds of drinks and celebrated our rustic future.

The next day we picked up William and drove out into the country to look at places that were for sale. The first one on his list was just south of County Dublin, a charming eighteenth-century villa, relatively small, but with the most elegant divided staircase that led to several bedrooms upstairs. Each of them had a dressing room and built-in wardrobes with curved and exquisitely carved wooden doors. We were ready to fall in love with it. But William pointed to where the roof was leaking and when we went to look at the land, we discovered that it was less than four acres of arable land. William explained that we needed at least thirty acres to have a viable farm. Regretfully we went on to the next. We saw a dilapidated castle with no land at all, and several places with sufficient land but no house that could have accommodated as many people as we were going to be (William's brother Barney had a wife who was about to have a baby).

I don't remember how many days we spent driving around in the countryside and looking at farms, but I remember getting despondent. There was plenty of land that William considered worth buying, but even he agreed that the houses we saw would not do for us. When William came to the end of his list of possibilities, the idea began to look like a pipe dream and we felt thoroughly depressed. We did not see him for a few days, but then, one morning, he called. His aunt, who lived in the country south of Dublin, told him that a farm in a nice location not far from her was going to be for sale.

We got into the car, picked up William, and drove to the place as fast as we could. It was called Grovedale and was, indeed, in a lovely location. The land was on the southern slope of a hill, running down to a lively little stream, and there was a rocky outcrop with a few pine trees just behind the house. And the house—we could hardly believe it—had a large kitchen in the middle where you entered, two large and two small rooms on the right, and a much larger, two-storied wing on the left. It was as though it had been built to house a small and a larger family.

"It's just as well the owner isn't here," William said. "If he heard you enthuse about his shack, he'd double what he intended to ask for it." As we walked out to look at the stables and what else there was, he said to me: "You'll have a lot to learn, before I'll take you with me to the cattle market." I took this to indicate that he, too, approved of the house. In the cowshed, however, he made it quite clear that he wasn't going to admit it. "All this has to be rebuilt inside if we want to sell milk," he said. Then we went into the stable and he at once pointed to the structure holding the roof and said that it was rotting and would have to be replaced within the year. But I noticed that he liked the wooden partitions for four horses and the fact that the stable was large enough to hold a few implements as well; but he didn't say so. The only positive comment he made came after we walked round all the fields. "It'll take us a long time to cut these hedges down to size," he muttered more to himself than to us, "but the land would be worth it."

On the way back to Dublin, he kept telling us that we shouldn't get excited, because the man would probably ask far more than we could afford. He was going to contact him the next day, but a sale — if it could be concluded at all — might take weeks. On no account were we to meet the seller, because he would see us as rich foreigners. So we were left in limbo and tried quite unsuccessfully to stop thinking about it.

In fact, the bargaining took less than a week and William managed to buy Grovedale for a very good price. This was lucky, because a cart, a plow, and other implements had to be bought, as well as a pair of horses to pull them. William was looking after all that and we drove out to the farm every day, fixing up and painting our rooms and transforming one of the small ones into a bathroom. There was running water in the house, but like anywhere outside Dublin and other bigger places, there was no electricity. Yet, although at first we sometimes found ourselves groping for a light switch when entering a dark room, we got quickly used to candles and kerosene lamps.

* * *

Just then — it was a couple of weeks before the European war began — my parents decided to come to visit us in Ireland. I had not told them anything about the farm, and now that they had started on the long drive, it was too late to write. I was wondering how they would take the surprise.

My father looked at everything with some interest. We took him to the top of the hill behind the house, from where you could see just a tiny triangle of the Irish Sea, and he liked the view. Going back to the house over the fields, he said:

"You'll get a lot of exercise, but it will be much better than living in the city."

My mother did not quite manage to hide her shock. She didn't say so, but I was sure that she saw this as the end of her hope to have a son who was a physicist or an astronomer. But, as always, she was a good sport and didn't want to make us feel bad.

Then war broke out and there was no way my parents could drive back to Italy. It was very fortunate. With all the things they were known to have said about Hitler and his consorts while they were living in Meran, and with the fact that it had only been my father's father who converted from Judaism, the Nazis would have picked them up the moment they occupied Italy. We found accommodation for my parents at a small country club, a few miles from the farm, where Isabel and I could visit them every now and then on our bicycles. My father pottered around on the golf course and my mother found a place where she could ride horses, which consoled her a little for the lack of snow.

As soon as the war ended they wanted to go back, but to Switzerland rather than to Meran. At that time there was no possibility of going by car. This gave me an idea. Isabel was pregnant and I suggested to my mother that I sell my little sports car and give her whatever I received for it for hers. It was also a Fiat, but a four-seater and much more suitable for a family of three. My mother was glad to agree because the £300 she got out of that deal were a great help towards their tickets to Switzerland.

Reflection on Theories 1939

It seems that all my life I have had a weakness for theories. I think it began in my late teens when I met a young woman called Eva who had read much more than I had. She was able to talk about it intelligently and I was flattered that she was willing to talk about it with me. I had read little beyond some Hermann Hesse, Goethe's Werther, and other romantics, and, as counterpoint, all of Upton Sinclair's socialist novels that I could get hold of.

One day Eva mentioned psychology and I said that the only thing I knew that might count in that field was Hesse's *Narziss und Goldmund*. She laughed and said: "You'll have to try some of the hard stuff!" and if I was interested in psychological types, I should have a look at Otto Weininger's *Geschlecht und Charakter*. She lent it to me, and as I began to read it I realized that she had given it to me as some kind of a test.

I was instantly hooked by Weininger's idea that each human being was part male, part female, and that personality was a question of the percentages. Attraction between individuals was due to the desire to bring both the male and the female component up to one hundred percent. It was a beautifully neat theory, but it soon became clear to me that it depended on how one defined the characteristics of the two genders. I was unwilling to accept Weininger's notion of "woman as mother and whore".

"Good for you," Eva said when I returned the book to her. She went on to tell me that Weininger had developed that theory to account for his homosexual leanings. In his mid-twenties, however, he fell in love with a woman whom he simply could not fit to his own percentages. He killed himself — but I cannot remember whether it was because of the failure of his theory or because the woman did not return his love.

For me it was the end of Weininger but not of my appetite for theories. Early on I saw that they were useful because they made it possible to organize experience. Only much later I learned that they could never depict Reality. They could never be claimed to be "true" as pictures of an independent world; they applied to the world of experience from which they had been culled. If they were good theories, they were useful in ordering and systematizing the world we live in—and sometimes they could even serve to adjust it.

Theories are built by linking abstractions from experiential "facts" with the help of conceptual relations. Whether a theory is useful or not can be decided only by people who use it in the practice of living or thinking. It does not depend on the beauty or the elegance of its conceptual structure. But elegant theories have an attraction, even if they are of no use to you. One theory I came across will be of no use to most people; but its construction is so neat that I have never forgotten it.

It was the work of a landed baron in Southern Bavaria, sometime before the First World War. He was an expert water diviner and he compiled a map of all the subterranean waterways under his large property. During the summers there were frequent thunderstorms and as time went by, the baron noticed that lightening seemed to prefer to strike in places where two waterways crossed at different depths. One such crossing was under a corner of his rambling manor house, and when that corner was struck for the third time he formulated the conjecture that subterranean waterways emit or attract some form of radiation, which would of course be stronger wherever two waterways crossed.

In time he expanded his theory to explain all sorts of other things. If your bed stood over a waterway crossing, the risk of your getting cancer was greatly increased. Baron Pohl tested this extension of his theory with the help of the town council of a small town in his neighborhood. He made a map of the waterways under their town and checked it with the records of cancer deaths. As he expected, the study confirmed that nearly all the people who had died of cancer had lived above points that he had marked as crossings.

He recounted all this in his book on *Erdstrahlen* (earth rays), which, if I remember correctly, was published around 1930. It went unnoticed and although he pleaded with other towns to carry out the same test, it seems that nothing more was done.

The radiation, which the baron claimed to sense through his divining rod, was, he believed, noxious not only to humans but also to trees and shrubs and vegetation in general, except for a small number of poisonous plants that included some of the traditional medicinal herbs. Those, he said, are strengthened by the rays.

With the help of this addition a quite remarkable historical explanation could be formulated. If the rays impeded vegetation, it was obvious that the deer that lived in the dense forest that covered Bavaria before humans began to settle there, would follow paths of least resistance, which is to say, where trees and undergrowth were less dense. This, of course, were paths above underground waterways. When the humans appeared, they naturally found it easier to move along the paths made by the deer, and so it came about that the first country roads that crisscrossed the forests of Southern Bavaria all followed underground waterways.

The crown jewel of the theory, however, is this: according to Baron Pohl, the moon has an effect on the earth rays and they tend to be strongest when the moon is full. Since the earliest times, witches and herbal healers maintained that certain secret plants were most powerful if the were picked at a crossroads during the full moon. Thanks to Baron Pohl's theory we now know why this should be so: the stronger the earth rays, the more powerful must be the herbs. To me the combination of simple empirical observations and fantasy in this theory is enchanting. It's such a clear example of how theories are made.

David Robinson 1940

When Isabel and I came to Dublin we were still young enough to learn from people, not facts or information, but ways to deal with life. David Robinson was the son of a clergyman. As a young man he joined the Irish rebels, but this did not stop him from maintaining ties with personal friends in England. Every now and then he managed to skip across the Irish Channel and stay with them for weekends. But one day, in a roundup in County Dublin he was arrested and sent to prison in England. Many of the Irish rebels went on hunger strike when they were captured. De Valera, who later became president of the Free State, refused food for more than fifty days and wrote in his recollections that only the first week was difficult. Then, he found that his mind became exceptionally clear and he devoted himself to studying the theory of relativity. David Robinson had no love of physics or mathematics. His interest was in people and their strange exploits. While he was starving in prison, one of his British friends supplied him, one after the other, with the twelve volumes of Burton's translation of the Arabian Nights.

When David was finally released, Lady Astor picked him up at the prison gate. As he was led out, he was so weak that he fainted into her Rolls Royce.

We got to know him when he was in his late sixties — a wonderfully cultivated and worldly person. He was a senator in the Irish parliament, next to Erskine Childers probably the best-educated of the lot. He took a liking to us and invited us to listen in the Senate whenever there was something controversial going on. Some of the hottest battles in those days were about censorship. When Marie Stopes published her book on contraception in England, there was a fierce discussion in the Irish Senate. The Senator from West Cork, in one of those superb flights of Gaelic rhetoric, called the book "the fornicator's vademecum", and another speaker said that if this book were allowed into Ireland, Dublin would become a brothel city like Port Said. When we met David after the debate, he said:

"I am so glad to hear that Port Said is still as I remember it!"

A few months later he became ill with colon cancer. It was the virulent kind and he had to be hospitalized immediately. We visited him in hospital and were amazed. There he was sitting up in bed, beaming, his face framed by the collar of a lightly embroidered night shirt.

"Don't look so sad!" he said and began entertaining us with reminiscences. As we left, we said we hoped he was not suffering too much pain. "Oh, it's not bad, except when I have to shit," he said in a matter of fact way and added with a smile, "fortunately the food here does not tempt me to excesses."

Two days later he died.

Briscoe's Brother 1940

Mr. Briscoe, who had given us the idea of going to Ireland when we had dinner at his house in Paris, made the move to Dublin when we were just getting settled at Grovedale. He was amazed that we had chosen this solution to our problem. Farming was not among the things he would have considered. I told him that we had not gone to see his brother, the Member of Parliament, because there had been no difficulty about my permit to stay in Ireland and then things just happened by themselves. In fact, during our first three miserable months in Dublin I had thought several times about it, but I was very reluctant to ask for help, especially as the thought of a regular job filled me with terror.

Mr. Briscoe said we should meet him anyway and he would ask us to dinner the next time his brother came. He did, and inevitably we had to recount that meeting Erskine Childers had opened the way for us. I was afraid he might be irritated that we didn't call on him for help, but I was wrong. The story about hearing Erskine's French conversation in a bar amused him greatly and he told us a funny story about himself.

"When I was first elected," he said, "and made my first tour of the district, I had the idea that not everyone there knew that I was Jewish. I thought it might be just as well to leave it like that. So the first morning, when I was having breakfast with a group of notables, I made a point of ordering bacon. It would show them, I thought, that I certainly was not orthodox. Unfortunately I had quite forgotten that it was Friday."

The Fall of Paris 1940

It was drizzling when I went out after lunch to harrow the field where William had sown grass in the morning. Sowing was one thing I hadn't yet learned to do properly. William had shown me: you wore a canvas bag full of seed on your left side; it hung from a loop round your neck; you took a handful of seed with your right hand, swung it in a wide arc until your arm was stretched to the right, while you were taking a step, and during the next step you brought the arm back to the bag, letting the seed trickle out through your fingers all the time. It would have taken me a long time to learn to spread the seed evenly enough to satisfy William. So he decided to do it himself.

While the horses pulled the harrow up and down the field and I followed over the rough furrows of the freshly plowed field, the drizzle turned into rain and by the time Isabel was to bring me a cup of tea, it was pouring. It clearly was time to go home. I unhitched the horses from the harrow and led them, dragging their chains. At the stable, I took their harness off and gave them their quota of oats. It was earlier than usual, and they seemed to appreciate it. I was sodden and had a quick shower before I joined Isabel and William in the kitchen.

We had a battery-radio and they were listening to an English staging of a play by Sartre. It was close to six o'clock, and when the play ended, the BBC news came on. For more than a week we had been listening with growing apprehension about the German's advance in France. The Maginot line had been built with the assumption that there were rules that governed the conduct of war. Neutral countries, for instance, were not to be invaded. But Hitler marked the return to barbarism. For him there were no rules. That evening the final blow came: Paris had been taken.

Although it had been foreseeable, Isabel and I were stunned. After a moment she turned to me and could not speak — tears were running down her cheeks. I took her in my arms, too moved to say anything.

William switched off the radio, He was shaking his head and after a while he said:

" I suppose it was home to you both."

And he was right. Isabel had some factual justification having lived there for a number of years. I had not grown roots to any place while growing up, but Paris had become the city of cities for me because of the impressionists, its writers and its poets. As Lawrence Durrell wrote twenty-five years later in his novel *Clea*: "… the fall of France, an event which symbolised all too clearly the psychic collapse of Europe itself."

It was only in February 1943, when the German army at Stalingrad was finally defeated, that the shadow of doom over our lives began to lift.

Café Society 1941

The fact that during the war there was hardly any movement into or out of Dublin made social life a little like Sartre's play *Huis Clos*. The number of people who had a coffee at Mitchel's or a drink before dinner at The Buttery was limited. Everybody got to know everybody, and that was it. You had to put up with who there was because there were no newcomers. You came to know more and more about everyone and gossip tended to become incestuous.

Parties during those years had a way of extending into the next day. Whiskey and wine were scarce and expensive and after midnight the host's supply tended to run out. On a Saturday it sometimes happened that someone said: "I have a bottle at home, let's go to my house." A few hardy guests would take him up on the invitation. When the dawn showed in the windows but, in spite of the empty bottle, the conversation wasn't flagging, the new host might disappear for a while and return with fried eggs and bacon and toast and a big pot of tea. It could be eight or nine on the Sunday morning before everyone went home. Remembering the Dublin parties after forty years in the United States, it strikes me that there was never any music. What kept the party going was talk, never about the war or politics, but talk about books, plays, sometimes largely invented experiences, and always with an undercurrent of hilarious, amiable rather than spiteful, subtly malicious gossip.

More than once it happened to us that people would tell us about the marvelous things that occurred at a recent party they had heard of, and it took quite some time before we realized they were describing a party we had been to. Inventing stories, sometimes grotesque, sometimes funny, was of course a national talent and the reason why quite an inordinate amount of English literature was written by Irish authors.

* * *

Among the regular patrons of The Buttery was a couple that was difficult to overlook: a startlingly good-looking woman and a slender middle-aged man, well over six feet tall, with a crown of white hair around a domed, totally bald pate. Mister H had joined British foreign service and was sent as an attaché to the Berlin embassy in the late 1920s. He inherited a vast amount of money from his Irish father, began to lead a busy social life in Berlin, and met and married a German countess. It was not known whether he had been aware of the fact that marrying a German citizen would end his diplomatic career. It did, and he and his beautiful wife came to Dublin just before the war began. He joined one of the golf clubs where Paddy Campbell hunted for victims, and that was how I came to know Mr. H. He liked playing with us because Paddy was the son of Lord Glenavy and he did not mind that he lost some money every time. He was a tremendous snob. He had given a Bentley to his wife as a wedding present, but no one had ever seen her at its wheel. He drove it, but as it was legally hers, he had her crest discreetly put on the driver's door.

At some party Mr. H had drunk a little too much. He began to reminisce about his days in Berlin, the sparkling social life during the early thirties, and how it came to an end when the Nazis took over everything a couple of years later. Except for Göring, he said. Göring continued to give splendid parties, especially shooting week-ends in the country. Few people had been listening, I think, but at this point someone piped up:

"What did you shoot? Pheasants and ducks, or Jews?"

It was never forgotten. Towards the end of the war some bombs fell into the sea near Dublin harbor. A mistake, Erskine told us, and probably not even from a German bomber. But someone remarked that it was strange that the Hs had left town for that day. Promptly the joke spread that Göring had probably warned them.

* * *

The Irish Free State's neutrality during the war was a political affair and did not reflect the attitude of the average citizen. The vast majority was not at all indifferent as to whom they wanted to win the war. Only the IRA sympathized with Hitler, and Erskine estimated that it had no more than 180 or 200 members at that time. His government also estimated that more Irish citizens were volunteering in the British army than would have been conscripted if the Free State had still belonged to Britain. All of these volunteers would have laid down their arms if Churchill had actually occupied the Irish ports, as he threatened more than once (because these ports would have been helpful in the battle against the U-boats).

There was also another characteristic statistic. The German propaganda machine had an inaccurate picture of the Free State. From their radio broadcast to Ireland it appeared that they knew where Dublin's Jewish quarter was, but had no inkling that practically no one among the population was hoping that England would lose the war. During the war years dozens of German agents were dropped into the Irish landscape by parachute in order to organize a "fifth column". All of them were convinced that they would be warmly welcomed, but in fact all of them were delivered to the police within days of their landing. According to the rules of neutrality, they were interned until the end of the war. At times there were also quite a few British and American airmen, whose bombers had to make emergency landings because of some failure or battle damage; but at the end of the war not one of them was still in the internment camp. They had all been smuggled across the border to Northern Ireland.

One day a flying boat of the British Coastguard landed and slid into the Dublin Harbor. The pilot told the harbor master that they had a small electrical failure and that they could easily fix it if only they had a soldering iron. If they could repair it within twenty-four hours, the harbor master said, Irish neutrality would allow them to fly away. The pilot phoned a friend in Dublin, who came to pick the whole crew up and had already organized a party. The Coast Guard people had not had a party for quite some time and proved indefatigable, so the party was extended several times. The morning after the second night they came back to the harbor with a borrowed soldering iron, found their rubber dinghy, and rowed unnoticed to their plane. Several people heard the engines when they started and saw the flying boat glide out of the harbor and take off into the eastern sky. It was not long before the responsible minister heard of the escape. He was furious. Neutrality was a delicate matter.

"How could you permit such a thing?" he shouted at the harbor master, "You know perfectly well that we are neutral …"

"Of course I know that — but no one ever explained to me against whom we should be neutral."

Paddy Perrot 1941

When the weather was too bad to work in the fields and William had some business in Dublin and went in with the horse and trap, I would sometimes go with him, spend a few hours at the library and return on the Enniskerry bus. One of these times, Paddy Perrot was on the bus when I got in.

"What takes you out of the city?" I asked.

"Once a year," he said, "the Powerscourts give a party for the Arts — this time they thought of the Gate Theatre."

Lord Powerscourt had a large estate between Enniskerry and the old Lead Mines Tower that was on the hill south of our farm. Paddy was the dress designer at the Gate and one of the original friends of Michael MacLiammoir. He was tall and lanky, a little like a daddy longlegs, but he moved with the languid elegance of a cat and gave you the impression of a thoroughly disillusioned Mephistopheles. "It's so unfair," he once said to Shelah Richards when she was trying on the spectacular dress he had designed for her leading role, "It is so unfair that you women are allowed to put these things on and yet have no idea how to wear them!"

During the long damp winters he went out as little as he could. But when he did, he wore a long camel hair coat that softly hugged his contours like a sumptuous dressing gown.

Although the bus was fairly full of farmers returning from some market, he had spread himself, reclining over two seats and bemoaning in his ultra-cultivated voice the sad state of the theatre, the lack of interest and support shown by the plebeian population and the frustration this meant for him, because he was never given the means to realize his designs to the full.

"Have you never thought of going to New York?" I asked him after a while.

"New York?" He said incredulously, throwing back his head, "my dear, I'd rather till the soil!"

And then, remembering perhaps that this was exactly what I and most of the other passengers were doing, he added, looking at his beautiful long-fingered hands,

"Not that there's anything wrong with tilling the soil — it's probably the second oldest profession."

One of the farmers sitting behind me leant forward and said: " 'tis a great thing that God tempers the wind to the shorn lamb."

Just then the bus was stopping at the Golden Ball, which was as far as I was going.

"Enjoy the party!" I said and jumped off. Walking home along the Ballicorus Road, through fading light and a soft drizzle, I thought what a wonderful little world Dublin was, that Paddy could indulge his aesthetics and a farmer could quote Sterne. (I had erroneously attributed the quotation to Yeats, but my editor fortunately spotted the mistake.)

The Chisler 1942

Shortly after the war came closer (the declaration of war was followed by a few months of non-action in Central Europe), the Irish government made a decision that turned out to be a boon for some small farmers like us. With unusual foresight, they calculated that food was likely to get short and that it would be helpful if farmers, rather than producing only oats for horses and barley for the brewers of stout, would start growing wheat. They knew that wheat was chancy, given the Irish climate, and they also knew that it was not easy to change farmers' habits. So they decided to offer quite a substantial subsidy to those who were sufficiently adventurous to cultivate a new crop.

Our farm was on the southern slope of a hill not far from the border of County Wicklow and we were told that the position was favorable for wheat. So we tried, and though as beginners we had no great expectations, it turned out to be a success.

During the second year, favored by an unusually sunny summer and a few dry days during harvesting time — a rare stroke of luck in that part of the world — we had what you might call a bumper crop. Our wheat was considered top quality, and given the subsidized price, we suddenly had some unexpected cash. There were many things we thought of doing with it. After long and sometimes heated discussion we eliminated all but two possibilities. We could have bought a third draft horse to fall back on, in case something happened to one of the pair we had. This would be a wise investment, because if we were left with only one horse, we could neither plow nor cut hay. On the other hand, we could buy two more cows and venture into regular milk production. This would give us something we did not have but badly needed: a steady source of cash.

Money, they say, attracts more money; and since we had some in hand, we gave up the idea of a spare horse and decided to go into the dairy business. I was a little apprehensive about this. Until then, William and I had both milked the cows we had—something that has to be done regularly every twelve hours, and as there was no electricity, it had to be done by hand. What worried me was that there were fairly frequent occasions when it was necessary for William to attend to other urgent jobs and I had to do the milking alone. I did not cherish the thought of being left to milk six or seven cows by myself.

"If we buy two more cows," I said, "it will shorten the time I have to work in the fields, and it's often too short even now. But if we actually get a dairy contract, money will be coming in every month, and I suggest that we use some of it to hire help for the milking."

William was very shocked.

"Just because you don't like getting up in the morning," he said.

"Of course—but think what would happen if I cut one of my milking fingers and you would have to do it all for a week? That seems a far greater risk to me than one of the horses breaking a leg."

This argument prevailed, largely because of an immutable condition of the dairy business. If the daily milk pail was not ready and did not contain the required number of gallons when the dairy-van comes to pick up, there was a hefty fine to pay.

John, the man we occasionally hired to help at threshing time and harvesting, soon found what Irish farmers call a "chisler"—a young lad to do milking and other odd jobs. His name was Terry and he turned out to be not only a competent milker (which John had promised) but also good company (which I had not expected). Far from being reluctant to speak to foreigners like myself, he obviously enjoyed it and he had that remarkable endemic talent which, in my view, explains the inordinate Irish share of English literature. It is the art of spinning a tale, not to impart information, but simply to amuse.

He was somewhere between 16 and 20 years old and lived with two much older brothers who had a farm a few miles from ours. He came on his bicycle at six o'clock in the morning, milked the cows, fed the pigs, and did whatever other little jobs William assigned to him. Then he had lunch with us and cycled back home. Sometimes he stayed for the afternoon and did the evening's milking, too.

In the twilight of the early morning, the tea kettle that William, who invariably was already up and out, left simmering for me on the stove, and the piece of toast I made for myself, rarely made the rest of the day seem a desirable proposition. The cold drizzle when you crossed the yard and the dank darkness of the cowshed were not given to improve your mood. But in time you came to think that the wholesome animal warmth that radiated from the cow into your body as you sat on the milking stool and leant against her furry side was a decidedly positive feature. I would not normally have felt much like communicating under these circumstances; but for Terry the early morning was not depressing. He was bright, alert, and ready to talk.

He was also remarkably tactful and did not push me too hard at the beginning. But after a while we had some great conversations, across the cows, you might say. He gently coaxed me to tell him about continental Europe, about where I came from, and how I had come to Ireland. He was fascinated by the Alps, of which I told him that they were ten times higher than Mount Sugarloaf, which you could see from the top of our hill. This was lucky for me, because of the mountains I had a good many stories. And I learned a lot from him about how real farmers go on and, after we had got used to each other, about the peculiarity of everyday life with his two brothers. They were both unmarried and had inherited the farm from their father. They had worked together quite happily, but about a year ago they had a disagreement and a quarrel. They cut it short and went to the pub to get a little drunk. When they came home, the quarrel started again, fiercer than before. Terry was in bed upstairs and heard them shout at each other but could not make out how it ended. When he came down in the morning, they were both standing in the kitchen. Their expression told him that it wasn't the moment to say Good Morning. As he poured himself a cup of tea, Tim, the older, said:

"Tell him that I'm going to plow the long field," and with a jerk of his head he indicated that he meant his brother as he opened the door to the yard.

That was how it started. At first, Terry did not understand what was going on, but it became clear to him when they continued not to speak to each other directly but only through him. He realized that they had made a kind of pact not to address each other. He thought it was because they were afraid the quarrel would start up again and something terrible would happen. It frightened him and he continued to act as the intermediary – there was not much they had to tell each other, because their lives were governed by the needs of the farm, and they both knew those very well. Somehow it worked, but there obviously was not much conversation round the kitchen table. Sometimes Terry would try to talk to them both, but they always reacted as though the other were not there. I concluded that it was probably the reason why Terry was so voluble when he came to milk our cows and I wondered whether the brothers' Trappist pact would last forever.

Then, one morning, when I stumbled still half asleep into the cow shed, Terry was not there. Usually he was already milking when I arrived. I wondered what could have happened to him. He had never missed a day. Then I heard his bicycle outside and he came bursting in.

"They're talking!" he shouted from the door. He was beside himself with joy and could not wait to tell me about it.

When he had come home after lunch the day before, Tim was harnessing one of their horses for the two-wheeled farm cart.

"Tell him, I'm going to Dundrum to buy seed potatoes," he said.

Terry went into the house to deliver the message.

"Tell him to make sure he doesn't go without money — as he did last year," said the younger brother.

Terry caught Tim just as he was climbing into the cart. As casually as he could he asked: "Do you have the money?"

"Did he say that?" asked Tim about to fly into a rage — but automatically his hand went to his hip pocket. "Jesus! he's right, I've forgotten it again!"

For a long moment he stood in the cart, the reigns in his left hand, motionless. Then he jumped down and with slow, stately steps walked to the house. That evening the brothers were talking to each other again, tentatively, as though they had been separated for a long time.

Schrödinger 1942

I don't remember how it came about that my mother met Schrödinger. It was shortly before a physicists' get-together he organized at the Institute of Advanced Studies and he casually mentioned that he always wanted a social afternoon at these meetings with some younger people, so that the physicists did not have to talk about physics all the time. Their wives, he said, thought that, when talking to their husbands' colleagues they had to talk about their science, and this was obviously a disaster.

My mother said that her son and his wife had friends among the theatre people and painters and they might be able to create some diversion. Schrödinger loved the idea and that was how we were introduced to him. We had mobilized our actress friend Shelah Richards and a couple of other young people who, we thought, might entertain the physicists. Apart from Schrödinger, there were Paul Dirac, Max Born and a charming woman who, I think, may have been Lise Meitner. She talked about electrons as though they were love birds she kept as pets in a cage at home. And there were several other physicists of whom I remember only that their wives wore dresses they had clearly knitted themselves.

The party, Schrödinger said, was a great success and during the following years he invited my mother, Isabel, and myself several times to tea at his house. The door to his study was usually closed and above it there was a red light; it meant that he was not to be disturbed. Once, however, the door was open and he was just putting some books back on a shelf. I took the opportunity to walk in and say hallo. On his desk I saw a reprint with the unforgettable title: "The proper vibrations of the expanding universe." Had I needed a hint, this would have stopped me from bothering him with naïve questions about philosophy. But having heard a couple of his public lectures at the Institute of Advanced Studies, I realized that I didn't know nearly enough to reach from my level of understanding to his.

My mother rightly had no qualms. She had come across a logical puzzle that had kept her busy for several days and she was curious how he would react to it. She did a good job of clearly laying it out and wrote it on a postcard to him.

> A tyrant has three prisoners. They are all supposed to be intelligent and he really doesn't like executing intellectuals. He presents them with a test. He shows them five patches, two black and three white. Each of the prisoners gets one of the patches stuck on his forehead and they are led into a room where they can see one another. The one who first finds out what color patch he is wearing will go free.

A week or so later, my mother received the following letter.

Dublin Institute for Advanced Studies, 28 February, 1942

Dear Mrs. Von Glasersfeld,

Many thanks for your postcard. You are a rare case. There are very few people—and among these only a minute fraction are women—to whom such questions leave no peace until they have solved them. You certainly have never had serious difficulties with mathematics and could probably achieve original results in that field.

Concerning the five-hats-problem (or five-patches-problem) which, for me, belongs to a more interesting category than all others, the following came to my mind. Two quite separate remarks.

1) The clever competitor who finds out that he has a white patch could actually be blind, provided that the other two are sighted. Because he (A) must say to himself: if I (A) had a black patch, B would see it and conclude from C's silence that he (B) has a white patch and would therefore speak up. Because both are silent, I (A) have not a black but a white patch.

2) But the problem is more interesting the way it is put—namely so that one says at once: B and C see white patches; A sees this and concludes from the fact that B and C remain silent, that he himself (A) must have a white patch.

The interesting point is, I think, this. A uses for his conclusion the following two premises

    1) B and C see white patches;

    2) both are silent.

He interprets 2): my own (A's) patch must have such a color that neither B nor C has sufficient premises to infer the color of their own (B's respectively C's) patch. Consequently, A further concludes, my patch (A's) cannot be black, because otherwise B would conclude from C's silence that his (B's) is white—and C would do the same. Hence—A further concludes—my (A's) patch must be white.

The result of this conclusion, however, is in conflict with the premises. For according to the result—derived from premises 1) and 2)—both these premises are available to B and C, too. A's supposition (underlined in red above) is therefore not justified.

If you think about this for any length of time, you go mad. I have come to the following provisional result.

A's method of concluding (from 1) and 2) → "my patch is white") is of such a peculiar kind that, logically speaking, one can call it neither correct nor false.

a) For if it were correct, it would ensue that B and C have in any case (whether A's patch is white or black) sufficient premises to come to a conclusion. But then A cannot infer the colour of his own patch from their silence.

b) But if it is false, any criticism of A's method becomes void, because in fact a white patch and only a white patch on his own forehead can explain B's and C's silence. In which case his way of concluding is not false.

If A is blind, it seems to me, the paradox disappears. But then the problem, looked at closely, is very complicated.

With respectful greetings,

E. Schrödinger[1]

---

[1]   My mother was rightly pleased to receive this letter. She fully deserved the compliments, she was an exceptionally straight thinker. She never went into mathematics, but she understood everything about Newton's universe. I know this, because she explained it to me long before I entered school.

    Translating the letter, I used the address and the salutation that Schrödinger might have used had he written in English. The ones he chose in German—*Hochverehrte gnädige Frau* and *Mit den ergebensten Grüssen und Handküssen*—have no equivalent in present-day English.

Mushrooms 1942

The field above the drive that led from the Ballicorus Road to our farm had not been plowed for several years and we used it as pasture because it grew excellent grass. We called it the Westfield and hardly ever walked into it. The horses that were left there over night were well trained like good dogs and came trotting when I rattled a bucket at the gate. They knew that they were getting some oats and I don't think they minded being harnessed and doing some work. In fact they seemed to get bored and were always glad of any diversion. When they were pulling the plow or the harrow up and down a field, it was always they who saw Isabel first when she came from the farm house to bring me elevenses halfway through the morning or at tea time in the afternoon.

"I made a discovery," Isabel said at one of these occasions, "there are mushrooms in the Westfield. I happened to look after the postman as he was leaving today, and was surprised to see him enter the field. I wondered why he didn't walk on the drive. So I walked up to the gate and watched. He was picking mushrooms. When he left, I went into the field, more or less to the places where he had been, and found these."

She showed me a handful of small white mushrooms.

"He probably left them quite deliberately for tomorrow, because they would grow bigger. Are we going to do something about this?"

"He's a nice man," I said, "we'll have to think about it."

We talked about it at supper that evening.

"He's probably been doing it for years," William said, "and by now he thinks it's like a right of way."

"And his wife expects them and will be raging if he doesn't bring them home!" Isabel added. "But I'd like to cook them for us, just the same."

We laughed at ourselves for making things so complicated. Legally there was no problem at all. The land was ours, so the mushrooms belonged to us. But we all agreed that the postman was a nice old codger

---

[continued from previous page]
Concerning the 5-patches problem it is, I think, important to remember that logic pertains to a static universe from which time is excluded. The tyrant, unlike Schrödinger, was more interested in practical considerations than in pure logic. Who of the three prisoners reached a conclusion first was, to him, the most intelligent.

and probably didn't have much else to celebrate with his wife. So from then on, Isabel went out to the Westfield every morning, picked some of the mushrooms, and left some for the postman.

We had no doubt that he noticed that we took some, but also that we left some. Though he quite liked talking whenever there was someone to talk to when he came to the house, he never mentioned mushrooms and we left it at that. William threatened several times that given the necessary rotation of crops, the Westfield would soon have to be plowed for something else to grow in it. But he, too, liked mushrooms, and so it was postponed.

The discovery of the postman led to another adventure. There was a bowl of mushrooms Isabel had brought from the Westfield in front of us on the lunch table.

"I think I was told that one can grow mushrooms in a dark room if one has sufficient dung," Isabel said. "We certainly have a lot of dung; and don't we have an empty shed near the stable that has no windows? Couldn't we try?"

I looked at William, but he was speechless. The Scottish farmer, who had trained him, clearly had not been into mushrooms.

"I'll prepare the soil," I said, "if you can provide the seeds or whatever you call it."

William had recovered. "Mycelium, I believe it's called. I think I've seen a man who sells things like that at the market. I'll look the next time I go."

"Make sure you get instructions what to do with it."

"I'm sure that's in the big book I have," he said, and that evening he brought it out.

We all studied it, and when I had a moment during the next week or so, I started to prepare soil for the bed. We had plenty of horse manure, which was supposed to be the best. Eventually William brought a small cardboard box from the market. That was it, and Isabel and I started to load the little dark shed. We religiously followed the instructions, and when it was all set we closed the door and put a padlock on it, so that no one would accidentally let light in. It was supposed to take a month and a half or two. After six weeks we gingerly opened the door a crack and looked in. Nothing. Everything was exactly as we had left it. We looked two or three more times, but when no mushroom had appeared after two and a half months, we gave up. A dismal failure, we thought.

It was well over three months when, passing in the dim light of early morning, I thought I saw something white under the shack's door. But the chisler had already arrived and I had to go and milk the cows. When I brought the full milk pails to the kitchen, I told Isabel, I thought the mushrooms had moved. We walked out and saw that there were small mushrooms squeezing through the crack all round the door. We picked some of them off and carefully opened the door. It was an incredible sight, just like a fairy tale. There were mushrooms everywhere, not only on the bed, but crawling up the walls and especially the door posts, as though they were desperately trying to escape.

It took us more than an hour to pick them all and when we finished, we had had four or five big buckets full. What could we do with them? We thought of taking horse and cart to hawk them round town, but that would take a whole day at least, and we had the hay to bring in and then the wheat. In the evening Isabel walked down to the Kilternan shop, where there was a phone, and tried to ring all our friends, to tell them that we had as many mushrooms as they wanted, but they would have to come and get them. No one had a car, but two said they might cycle out to us. They never did. We were left to eat mushrooms until they came out of our ears. We dried some and gave some to our neighboring farmers, but they had probably never eaten them and were very suspicious. It confirmed their idea that we were at least partially mad.

We made plans how we might organize the distribution in the future, but we never got round to it, and for the rest of our farming life we just shared the mushrooms from Westfield with our postman.

Molly O'Rourke 1940

The Galway Blazers was the decidedly upper class hunt club of County Galway. None except landed gentry had ever been accepted as members. But times were changing and the Galway Blazers did there best to adapt. They had broken an old rule when they unanimously elected Molly O'Rourke as their Master of Foxhounds. No one ever regretted her election. She rode like a man and drank like a man and had far more wits and authority than was needed for the job. When a businessman who had made an enormous amount of money wanted to join the club there was of course some consternation. But this man could no doubt be of advantage in mobilizing much needed funds. After a lengthy discussion it was decided to risk making yet another exception.

At the first hunt that he rode with, he showed a great deal of enthusiasm. Afterwards Molly O'Rourke took him aside.

"You will have to remember," she said, "our hunting cry is 'Tally Ho!'… not 'Git after the fucker!'"

Doubles Player 1945

When the war in Europe ended in 1945, my mother wanted to reconnect with some of the people she had known and she wrote to addresses she happened to have. From some of them she got answers. Her tennis friend in the Toscana reported about the sad fate of all those, who because of their international attitude were persecuted by the Nazis. Among them was also Count Salm, whose partner my mother had occasionally been in mixed doubles. He was an exceptional doubles player and my mother was always delighted when he asked her to play with him. He was also an international playboy, but tennis was, as far as I know, the only thing my mother played with him. As a boy I was enormously impressed with him, not only because of his tennis but also because he treated me almost like an adult and always had amusing stories to tell.

In the mid-twenties a scandal exploded around Ludwig Salm. An ex-girlfriend of his had emigrated from Vienna to Chicago. There she opened a fashion boutique which was immediately successful. One day she mentioned in one of her letters to him, that among her clients were a few of the richest heiresses in Chicago. That gave him an idea, because like many Austrian aristocrats he was quite often short of cash. He visited his friend, and got to know Milicent Rogers, the daughter of lots of oil and Dodge Automobiles. After a little while they eloped because her family adamantly opposed a marriage. When father Rogers was informed of their wedding, he was beside himself and did some drastic things to make Milicent change her mind. He flooded her with threats and evidence — some of it fake — of Ludwig's earlier indiscretions. In time this worked. She returned to Chicago and Salm was given a settlement for the divorce. As a final comment, my mother's sister, who happened to be working in Chicago at that time, sent her an article from the *Chicago Tribune* that was headed by something like *"How I caught my million dollar bride"* and was signed by Ludwig Salm. It was the last straw for my mother. Although it turned out later that Salm had had nothing to do with the article, my mother had condemned him.

The news she now received from her friend was shattering. When a military victory of the Germans had become less and less likely, the

Gestapo tried to keep people in order by acts of terror. In Austria hundreds of "suspects" were hauled in for cross examination and forced to denounce friends, who had made statements about the Nazi regime. Salm was arrested because he had often carelessly made disparaging statements against Hitler and his cronies. As he was standing in front of the Gestapo boss's desk and was urged to denounce names and addresses he foresaw that he probably could not withstand the methods the questioners would use on him. But he was still a good athlete and easily fast enough to surprise his captors. He dashed to the window and threw himself out. Wherever it was, it was high enough for the fall to kill him.

My mother was rarely moved to tears, but her friend's letter with the news about Salm's suicide did it. She pulled out her handkerchief and said after a while:

"This extinguishes whatever nasty things he did in his life."

And I, too, felt that it justified my affection for him.

Leaving Ireland 1946

In the summer of 1944 we were quite sure that the war would come to an end before the next year and we decided to have a child. As it happened, the war lasted a bit longer. Nevertheless we were somewhat gratified that our daughter Sandra came into the world two weeks after Hitler's suicide. Erskine's wife Ruth, who had raised their five children, still had a passion for babies and invited us to stay with them after Isabel came out of the nursing home. It was a great solution for us, because we had worried about bringing the newborn baby to the farm, miles from Dublin and with only a horse-drawn buggy and my bicycle as a connection.

By then we had already decided to sell the farm. William had fallen in love with a young Englishwoman whom Erskine had brought a couple of times on his visits, and he wanted to go to England with her. And we, we had visions of the Mediterranean, of sun-scorched hills and beaches, and a strong desire to escape dampness and drizzle. It wasn't that we didn't love Ireland. We did. But the lack of sun had taken its toll. We were riddled with rheumatism and felt that we would be stiffs before long if we could not dry ourselves out in real sun.

We moved into the Childers' house and stayed there much longer than expected. Ruth decided to take the opportunity to introduce Rory, her younger son, to her home in the United States. With Isabel in her house, she was confident that Erskine and the other children would be well looked after, and she stayed in the States for several months. Being about half way between the ages of the parents and the two oldest children, Isabel and I could be friends with both and serve as a buffer whenever there were conflicts. During the week, I usually cycled out to the farm to help William prepare everything for the sale. It was concluded very fast, because one of our neighbors had wanted to buy our farm for several years. Had we waited and sold the farm a year or two later, we would have got two or three times as much for it because Ireland was becoming a haven for all sorts of people from abroad. But we didn't know this, and it probably would not have changed our minds.

Living in the Childers' house brought with it a lot of diversions. We had fun with the children and as Erskine was the liaison person between the government and visitors from abroad he very often invited the foreigners to dinner. When they hailed from France, we learned to predict that they would politely decline the invitation, saying that unfortunately they were suffering from a slight indisposition — by this they clearly meant that they would get the indisposition if they had to put Irish food in their stomach.

One of those dinners remained vivid in my memory. The guest was the British biologist Julian Huxley, who was returning from Los Alamos where he had been invited to witness the first explosion of an atomic bomb. His description was a subjective confirmation of what we had seen on the newsreels, but he added something that had not been made public. He recounted that the physicist, who had chaperoned him during the visit, quite casually said that they were not absolutely sure that the explosion would not trigger a chain reaction. It was the sort of revelation that left you speechless.

That summer I was issued an Irish passport and for the first time in my life I felt I had a citizenship I could live with. We were sure we would not leave Ireland for good, but when Ruth returned in the autumn, our desire for a holiday in the sun took over. We put our furniture and other possessions in storage. What we wanted to take with us we packed in my mother's old car. An important item was a box that contained a small spirit stove, a can of oat flakes, and a few other things. We wanted to be able to make porridge for Sandra wherever we happened to be. This was a great help, because we could buy a bottle of milk and things to eat for ourselves on the way and didn't have to stop at restaurants. But it took quite a juggling act because the back seats of the car, which were piled high with luggage, had to be partially cleared to make space for the spirit stove. It was December, and for most of the second half of the journey it was snowing. It was not easy going. Like all reasonably priced cars before the war, the Fiat had no heating. (Porsche's design of the air-cooled Volkswagen provided heating for the cabin, but when it was built, this heating was difficult to switch on and sometimes impossible to switch off — which was no fun in the summer.)

When it came to making lunch, I had to open the back door, arrange the spirit stove on the seat, and stir the porridge for some fifteen minutes. Whatever warmth we had generated in the car evaporated. Isabel and Sandra were wrapped in a blanket like one big cocoon and were more or less all right, but my feet almost froze off. When the cooking was finished, I ran up and down on the road for a few minutes to get my feet ready for driving.

The last straw came in Lausanne. It was late evening when we got there and I had to take gas for the last stretch to Château d'Oex, the village where my parents had settled. But I had no Swiss francs. The gas station would not take British pounds or French francs. I offered my wristwatch as deposit, but in Switzerland, I suppose, that was a futile gesture. I saw a hotel a little way up the street and went there to ask if they would change some money. No, they said, they could only do this for guests of the hotel. I explained that I had to buy gas to bring a baby to its grandmother at Château d'Oex, but it cut no ice at all. They would change money for guests and for no one else. Clearly they thought they would make much more if we had to take a room for the night than if they gave us a bad exchange for the English money. It annoyed me — and when you are annoyed you are likely to take unreasonable risks. To hell with them, I thought, we probably have enough gas to get to Château d'Oex.

So we drove off. As we got higher into the mountains, it got much colder. Our breath froze on the inside of the windscreen and I had to take off a glove and melt the frosted layer with my hand. Soon there was just a little hole that I kept clear with my thumb. Fortunately it did not take long before through it I caught a glimpse of the village of Château d'Oex; and with what I was sure was the very last drop of gas we made it to the house where my parents lived. It was almost midnight and my mother opened the door in her dressing gown. She was very cross.

"This is not how I wanted my grandchild to see me for the first time," she said, and no explanation seemed to appease her.

But when Sandra was put to bed and we were having a cup of tea, things were smoothed out again and we could look forward to a long and unencumbered sleep. The next day I thought for a moment of what might have happened if there had been a little less gas in the tank. It's a thought that I quickly repressed. But it's the kind that tends to turn up when you are thinking of the past.

With eight years skiing in the Dolomites 1925

After climbing Piz Balü 1931

My father Leopold von Glasersfeld in the Dolomites

With my mother Helene von Glasersfeld in the Dolomites 1933

In Meran 1935

Mount Snowdon, Wales

My skiing friend Martina 1937

Racing in St Anton 1935

Ploughing at Grovedale in Ireland 1941

Grossvenediger, Austria

Isabel and Sandra 1946

Chapter Four

1947–1958

First Visit to Meran 1947

A week or so after we had arrived in Château d'Oex, my mother said she would like me to drive her to Meran. She wanted to see if anything was left in the house, and if there was, we could retrieve skiing clothes and my skis, too, so that I could start again. I said I'd love to do this, but I wondered how we could get there in mid winter when all the mountain passes were closed.

"No problem," she said, "we drive to Brig, put the car on a train through the Simplon tunnel and are in Italy."

She clearly had found out all about this before she made the suggestion to me.

It worked exactly as she said and we easily made it to Meran in one day. The next morning we went to see the lawyer who had been left in charge of the house when my parents left for Ireland in 1939. He explained that the house had not been empty for long because he had found a tenant, an Italian dentist with his family, who had lived in it all through the war and was, indeed, still there. They were extremely nice people, the lawyer said, and it was thanks to them that most of our things had survived. He made an appointment for us and we went to see them.

It was very strange coming back to the house after eight years. Trees and shrubs had grown so much that you couldn't see the house from the private lane which led to it. The dentist and his wife led us to what had been my father's study and I noticed that nothing much had changed. The big furniture was still where it had stood and some of the pictures were still hanging where they had been, but there was a new carpet that almost covered the entire floor.

"As you see, we've been using the large furniture you had," said the dentist while he was opening the door to the dining room and I could see that the big oval table was still there. "All the things that could be moved and carried we put in the attic and no one has touched them. When the Germans came to sequester things, we said we had rented the house empty and all the contents belonged to us. Later I learned that the uniformed man who had led the group that came to take things away was from the shop where Mr. Von Glasersfeld had bought all his cameras and photo supplies. I thanked heaven that he apparently had never visited the house before and could not recognize any of the furniture!"

"We would have lost everything if it hadn't been for you," my mother said, "I don't know how we can thank you."

"Well, the only thanks I would ask for is that you don't throw us out immediately ..."

"Rest assured," my mother said, "you can stay as long as you like!"

The dentist shook his head.

"No, we have already decided to find a place nearer the center of town, but at the moment it is practically impossible to find anything that could include my practice. So it may take time."

My mother told him not to worry because they had no plans to return to Meran for the time being. All we wanted was to see if there still were some winter things we could take to Switzerland.

We climbed up to the attic and were amazed. Everything was nicely stacked, what had been there originally had not been moved but left accessible, and there were our skis and rucksacks and everything that went with them. While picking a couple of pullovers out of the old moth-proof chest where woolen things used to be kept, I saw the big canvas bags that, as I remembered after a moment's wonder, contained the expedition tent my mother had bought in the early 1930s when she and some skiing friends were planning to explore spring skiing in the Caucasus. The expedition was never made, but we had used the tent one summer driving along the French Riviera. Camping as a form of holiday did not exist in those days. In Monte Carlo we met some people my mother knew from tennis tournaments and they asked in which hotel we were staying. They couldn't believe that we were sleeping in a tent. They probably thought that my mother said it because she would not admit that we stayed in one of the cheaper hotels.

The tent, I now thought, would make it possible for us to move around Italy without paying for hotels when we left Château d'Oex in the spring. By the time we finished, we had a lot of things in the car. It was a convertible four-seater with a canvas top that had a glass window set into the back, and the whole back could be folded down, so you could put up the roof as a sunshade in the summer. I never really appreciated this feature, but now it was the very thing that made it possible for us to bring along our skis, sticking out at the back, over the bag of the tent that I had strapped over the rear bumper. We once more thanked the family, wished them good luck in finding a new house, and told them that we would probably be back later in the spring.

* * *

The next two months I spent getting used to skis again, after almost ten years in Ireland. I also started to show Isabel how to use them. She had seen a few flakes of snow during the winters on the farm and in Paris as a teenager, but she had never been on a slope, let alone in the mountains. I knew that I had to proceed very slowly, and I did. For a couple of days we just slid about on flat ground and learned to turn, step by step, without treading on our own skis. Then we moved to the bottom of the village practice slope, which was just behind the house we lived in, and started sliding down almost imperceptible inclines. Then there came slightly steeper ones, where there was nothing to run into at the bottom. And I showed Isabel how to do a "snowplow" so that she could brake and stop whenever she wanted to. At that point she had never fallen, and I thought this was very important, because confidence is half the battle in learning to ski. Once you are sliding, you have to learn to control an automatic instinctive reaction: if the slope gets a little steeper, instinct makes you lean back — and the moment you do this, your skis run away from under you and you fall backwards. So whenever it gets steeper, you have to lean forward. Children learn this without thinking, but an adult has to repeat it to herself innumerable times.

Luggi, who had been my main teacher when I went for an instructor's diploma in the 1930s, had a golden rule: "The less you push a learner at the beginning, the faster he will get on later." It certainly worked with Isabel. I gave her plenty of time to find her balance on skis and when it came to switching from simple snowplow turns to starting turns on steeper slopes, she was quick to catch on. She made perfect turns, as long as she didn't look down the slope. Steepness frightened her long after she had mastered the technique to cope with it. The first time I took her up one of the mountains around Château'Oex, I made a seat with our skis when we were on top to sit down for our lunch.

"You expect me to eat on this precipice?" she said.

"Over the top it's windy and here we are warm in the sun," I said; "one season is not enough to feel comfortable on steep slopes. It'll get better, you'll see."

For a while we munched our sandwiches in silence. Suddenly she turned to me:

"Are you sorry that I'm not Martina?"

"Good God! All these years you remembered that name!"

She had that mischievous smile that was in her eyes rather than around her lips.

"That's why *I* never told you a name. But answer my question!"

No, I realized, was not a viable answer. I slowly faced her and looked straight into her smiling eyes.

"Well, it would be nice if you could ski like Martina, but how often will we go skiing? Maybe twelve or fifteen days a year—that leaves three hundred and fifty to get through."

Her smile spread over her face as she said:

"So let's get back to those Stemmbogens!"

It became very clear to me that the paralyzing effect of steepness was due to the idea rather than to lack of technique. If you don't see the steepness, it doesn't frighten you. At the end of the season, we climbed the Wildhorn. On the way down, the end of the glacier forms a long very steep slope. It had been a beautiful day, but by the time we came down, fog had come up from the valley and below the top of the steep slope you couldn't see anything. I wondered how Isabel would cope with this. I stayed close behind her and told her what to do, and she did it. She made perfect turns and never noticed just how steep it was. I would have liked to show her our tracks when we had reached the bottom, so she could see what she had mastered; but the fog hid them and there was nothing but unbroken whiteness when you looked up.

In the years to come, Isabel lost the fear of "precipices" and could make turns on any slope. But every now and then it would return. I never discovered something visual that might have triggered it and we couldn't find a psychological reason. Whatever it was, it remained buried in her subconscious.

Two Break-downs and a Horrible Shock 1947

When May came the skiing season ended, because the Alpine Club closed its refuge huts. By then, Isabel and I had been on top of all the mountains accessible on skis and within easy reach from Château d'Oex; including the glacier covered Wildhorn and Les Diablerets. Both of these I had climbed with my mother, because I wanted to see them before taking Isabel.

On the climb to the Diablerets, there was a very steep slope you have to stump up right after leaving the hut, where we stayed the night. It's uncomfortable because you have to carry your skis and to be careful not to slip, because you'd be sliding down a long way. I left this to the end of the season, hoping that by then Isabel would be quite used to steep slopes. When we came to it, I took both her skis and mine on my shoulder and made her use the track of deep steps that led like stairs straight up the slope. She went up without a murmur. Having reached the flat top, I asked her to turn round and look down. She couldn't believe it.

"I came up this?" she said, "I'm glad you didn't tell me beforehand."

"It was a fitting end to your slope adaptation," I told her, "I'll never lead you into anything worse."

* * *

We had planned to leave Château d'Oex towards the end of spring, but as we were getting ready I was struck with nausea and high fever.

"Ah, you have jaundice!" the doctor said, "a typical springtime disease."

He gave me a prescription, told me a few things I shouldn't eat and that I shouldn't smoke. The fever went down fairly quickly, but when he came to see me a few days later, I still felt awful.

"Sometimes it lasts quite a while," he said cheerfully, "you just have to be patient."

After six weeks nothing much had changed and he decided to send me to the hospital in Lausanne to be examined.

They took blood tests and when the specialist had finished examining me and I lay stark naked on the stretcher before him, he tapped me lightly on the tummy and said:

"You have infectious hepatitis. We can get rid of it, but your liver has been badly damaged and we can't repair that."

"But the doctor told me it was jaundice?"

The specialist smiled.

"It was," he said, "but that's just the first symptom."

"And what do I have to do now?"

"You'll have to take the pills I am prescribing and try to get used to a diet with little fat and spices, without coffee, wine, or alcohol of any sort."

"What about smoking?" I asked, because that had been the worst deprivation during the past weeks.

"Well, smoking isn't good for you, but it won't do much more harm to your liver."

I got dressed and left in a daze. I think it was the wholly detached attitude of the specialist that for some time stopped me grasping what it all meant. On the way to where I had parked I bought a packet of cigarettes. I got into the car, lit the first one, and just sat there until I'd finished it. Then I lit a second one and started on the way home. And began to think. Sure, I'd had colds and sprained ankles and things like that, but I had never been really ill. What the specialist had said seemed quite unbelievable and I was thoroughly shaken. How could I have picked up such a thing?

Driving up the steeper section of the road, just before Château d'Oex, a big truck was coming down and I stopped at the side to let it pass. When I started off again and accelerated in second gear, there was an ominous rattling from the engine. It lost some power but kept pulling and continued to rattle. It was a noise I thought I recognized: a cracked connecting-rod bearing. Driving on could severely damage the crankshaft. Having the car towed home would cost a fortune in Swiss Francs, but I thought of a compromise. If I took out the sparkplug of the affected cylinder, there would be no pressure on the particular bearing. But I had to find out which one it was. I took out the first one and started the engine, but the clanking was still sharp and metallic. I put back that plug and removed the next one. I was lucky. Now the noise was a much softer even rattle and I didn't have to try any further. I left the second sparkplug out so that there would be no explosion in that cylinder and nothing knocking the crankshaft. I slowly drove home on five cylinders instead of six.

When Isabel came out to greet me, I said:

"Both the car and I are cripples."

I explained the two disasters and she looked at me and said:

"Let's get out of here."

I agreed. But first something had to be done about the car.

At the service station where I had changed oil a couple of times I had met an Italian mechanic. Because I spoke Italian, he told me he had been there for three years, trying to save enough money to buy a place at home in Italy; so he was working for the service station and, in his spare time, on his own in the garage of the house where he lived. I explained to him what I wanted to do. I knew that you couldn't just take out a connecting rod, because without that bearing the oil pressure would drop so low that other parts were at risk. But if we took out the cracked shell of the bearing, the space between the connecting rod and the crankshaft could be filled with a piece of leather from a belt or something like it. It would get soaked with oil and there would be practically no friction and no pressure if we took the sparkplug out of that cylinder.

He laughed.

"I've never heard anything like it!" he said, but after a moment he added: "I don't see why it shouldn't work."

So that's what we did. It took a week-end to finish, but then we packed the car, strapped the tent to its back, and were ready to go. When you get to Meran, my father said, try to sell the house. He had no intention of returning there and if I managed the sale, I could have my share immediately. That was good to know, it seemed to extend our stay in Italy indefinitely.

The first night on the way was the first time we used the big tent. It took us more than an hour to put it up and to get everything settled for the night. Later, after some practice, we did it in fifteen minutes.

The tent was large, about nine by nine feet with a solid rubber floor that went up a few inches on the four sides. In the central part it was high enough to stand up. We worked out the best arrangement for the two rubber mattresses and the canvas cot I had made for Sandra, so that we could store all the other things we had to bring in from the car. I had made the cot large enough to serve as a playpen because Sandra was already an enthusiastic walker.

We slept very well that night and the sun was quite high when we got up and started to cook breakfast. Isabel was stirring the porridge for Sandra and I was in the tent, folding up mattresses and blankets. When I came out and looked around, there was no Sandra.

"Where is she?"

Isabel jumped up.

"Oh, God, she was here a moment ago!"

We were in the upper Rhine Valley and had put the tent near the bank of the river. There was a slight rise and then a slope of rough rocks down to the flowing water. Our hearts stopped for a moment, but when we looked over the rise, there was Sandra climbing up from wherever she had been. She must have slipped on the way down, but was stopped by one of the rocks that jutted out. She had a slight cut on her forehead and the moment she saw us she started crying. And so did we. She might have been swept all the way down to Holland. It was a lesson we never forgot. There were of course other shocks and crises, but nothing like that first one.

* * *

The next day we arrived at Meran and went straight up to the house. I told Mrs. Dentist that my parents had decided to sell the house, but there was no hurry and they had no intention of hoofing them out. They had started to look already, she said, but it was difficult because her husband wanted a place that could include his practice. I told her not to worry and that we were going to find some place to live and would probably come to take a bed and some other furniture from the attic.

"I'm not making a suggestion," she said, "but you may not remember that there is a large room, a kitchen, and a toilet in the basement here, where your maid and her husband used to live."

I had, indeed, forgotten about the basement and when Mrs. Dentist showed it to us it seemed far more desirable than some dingy two-room apartment that would cost a lot of money. The room was beside the garage and next door to the heating furnace. It was quite big and had two large windows towards the garden. I looked at Isabel.

"Why not," she said, "it's a garden flat."

By the time we had furnished it with things from the attic, including a big old-fashioned sitzbath, it was very livable and we stayed there for several weeks before we strapped the tent on the car again and headed south. But I could not get over the fact that my parents would have a servant live in their house without a proper bathroom.

Filming in Tuscany 1947

During the first days in Meran I ran into some acquaintances from before the war. Mario, whom I had known since elementary school, had also grown up with both German and Italian and was now earning his living as tourist guide and interpreter. We occasionally met in the Piccolo Bar, a tiny meeting place without tables in the main street, and he always had new stories about the "Piefkes", the German tourists, who on coming to the South Tyrol invariably bought a pair of leather shorts and then strutted about with snow-white legs. Our dearest guests, he said, because they'll eat whatever is put before them and no matter what wine is served, they love it.

One day Mario came with a proposition. Some months ago he had been hired as interpreter by a German film company that was going to make a film in Tuscany. The company then kept postponing the work in Italy and now he preferred to take a job that didn't require leaving Meran. Would I like to replace him with the film company? The idea of spending a few weeks in Tuscany was very tempting. When I told Isabel about it, she said that with the money I got for that work we could make a longer trip later in the summer and have some leisure to look at all the things in Florence, Perugia, and Siena. She thought that would be worth a few weeks without me.

I had no conception of what my work would be. Someone had explained to me that it would mainly be dealing with all sorts of local offices, finding suitable places for takes, and organizing extras. The location would be Greve, the capital of the Chianti region. Lodgings had already been arranged and Greve was waiting impatiently for the foreigners to arrive. The little town had never been touched by tourism and its inhabitants expected all sorts of advantages from the coming occupation by a film company.

What Mario had told me did not really frighten me, but on the drive down I did have some preoccupations, because I had never worked as an interpreter. But the thought that tomorrow I would wake up in the heart of Tuscany helped me to get over them.

It was afternoon when I arrived in Greve, just in time for the billeting. I was directed to room in a house on the central square (which in fact was a triangle) and was relieved to find that it had access to a bathroom. Then I was supposed to report to the producer of the film. He was of course much too busy to deal with an interpreter and one of his assistants merely told me to be ready at half past six in the morning. Breakfast, I was then told, began at six. For an inveterate night person this was quite a shock. But Tuscany, I said to myself, was worth a few sacrifices.

When I came to the breakfast buffet at a quarter past six I was pleasantly surprised. There was crisp fresh bread, jam, and hot black coffee. I was barely chewing my first slice, when a secretary came running and told me I had to rush to the general staff that was about to leave in order to look for a good Italian landscape. The general staff consisted of the producer, the director, the camera man, and the architect. The producer, the almighty boss, took the architect in his car; the other three and the interpreter followed in a second one. It went up the hill south of Greve and down the other side, past beautifully proportioned peasant houses, each with its own little tower, past renaissance villas with long cypress-lined drives, past vineyards and olive groves and enchanting views into distant chains of ochre, green, and purple hills.

"What a landscape," said the director.

"Incredible," said the camera man and added after a moment, "that's where I'd like sometime to make a documentary!" The deeper sense of this statement I came to understand later.

When we came to a stop, the producer had already taken his stance in the middle of a largish square of asphalt. Before him, some shabby houses formed an angle, that could be in the poorer section of any small town.

"Something like this, I thought, would be right for the osteria," he said, and tried to suggest some atmosphere by swinging his arm through the air.

"A bit stark," muttered the director while he was searching with a view finder for something that might be photogenic. "The script asks for trees and a pergola, doesn't it?"

He flips through the pages and reads:

"Rural osteria, garden, flowering shrubs, and a pergola with climbing roses."

"We can put it there. That's no problem at all. Just look at those miserable houses—that's Italy! And it's romantic, too; exactly what we need."

If it weren't for the blue sky and the chirping of the cicadas, I say to myself, this could be in Birmingham or in some impoverished suburb of Munich.

"Well, if it really has to be—but romantic?" He slowly shakes his head from side. Then an idea comes to him: "But what's the light situation here?"

The camera man has caught the short glance. The film is to be in color, and for color one needed sunlight in those days. With great carefulness he studies his compass and although the square is obviously open towards south, he says:

"Not too good, before noon we can't work here."

"Well, I can see, the gentlemen are against me," says the producer with an expression of profound boredom. "And where is the location that you would suggest?"

The car with the director quickly takes off, and I get in beside the driver in the producer's car. Sitting next to the producer in the back, the architect remained very quiet in the background. He leisurely lit a cigarette and spoke up:

"It would be no problem at all, in no time we'll have an osteria better than anything you could find in Tuscany."

The producer just shrugged his shoulders. After a while he leant forward and looked at the odometer.

"Twelve more kilometers! How long it takes to get there, once again does not seem to bother our professionals. But every minute in Italy costs us a fortune."

The location we eventually came to was partly encircled by stone oaks and flowering oleander bushes, but there was also a view of attractive houses, vineyards and cypress trees.

The producer climbed out of the car, stuck his hands in his pockets, and looked disparagingly round the whole circle.

"No," he finally said, "this doesn't convince me. This is not the real Italy. It's what you might see on a tourist poster."

"But here we can shoot in every direction and always have a decent background," the camera man tried a technical argument; but the wily architect was ready with an answer.

"When there are actors in the picture, no one ever looks at the background anyway!"

It was becoming clear to me why the camera man would have preferred to make a documentary. His name was Paul and he was Austrian. He had made some mountain films and spoke with awe of Arnold Fanck, whom my father often cited as a master photographer and about whom I knew quite a lot because Luggi had been his camera man on several occasions. So I could tell Paul some stories about Fanck and we quickly became friends. He had never heard of the problems Fanck had in Greenland when he was making a film called *SOS Iceberg*. No one had warned them about mosquitoes before they were on location and after two days the faces of Leni Riefenstahl and the male lead were so swollen with bites that they could only be photographed from a distance.

"That's interesting," said Paul, "it's probably the reason why that picture has even more beautiful landscapes than his others."

What the German company was going to make here was, he said, what is called a "Schnulze". I was not familiar with that word, but I had seen the main actors, a rather slight Italian radio tenor and a remarkably well-stocked young woman, who could present what was needed without much acting.

My work was much more varied than I had expected. Almost every day I was given a new task. Once I was told at six in the morning that by noon a steam roller was needed at that and that location. Although I believed that my Italian was fairly good, I had no idea what I should say for steam roller. I went to the friendly woman at the tobacconist's, who had already helped me once. She spoke the most perfect Tuscan dialect which, apart from two phonemes, is the purest Italian you can find and therefore, unlike the other Italian dialects, easy to understand for foreigners. When I tried to explain to her what I needed a word for, she gave me a slip of paper and a pencil. I had barely made an outline and she said:

"Ah, un compressore!"

How logical, I thought: a steamroller compresses the gravel.

With the highway people I already had an acquaintance. At the very beginning of shooting I had realized that I needed a couple of portable barriers so that I could divert traffic when work was to be done on a road. The road police told me that I could get them from the local highway administration. From then on I carried them on the roof of my little Fiat as a permanent part of my equipment.

The man at the highway office laughed when I explained that we needed a *compressore*. The barriers, he said, he could give me for nothing, but a *compressore* cost money. Did I need it for one day, for two or three? Evidently nothing struck him as unusual when you were dealing with film people. He even let me use his telephone, and so a price could be bargained, I showed him on his map where the steam roller was needed. It would be there at two o'clock, but only if I first brought him a check. I liked that idea because it added at least another thirty kilometers to my daily travel account and the fact that I was paid for the use of my car was a welcome increase of earnings.

Another task I had was to maintain relations with the parish priest of San Leonino. I had managed to get his permission for the company to shoot a scene in front of his charming little church. However, he had picked up the (no doubt false) information that another film company had presented a priest with a baby Fiat for the same permission and I seemed to be unable to convince him that this company was not going to do this. The producer apparently did not want to cloud relations with the church and I was therefore sent innumerable times to San Leonino in order to placate the priest. Finally I told him that this German film would probably inspire an American company to make a similar one and the Americans, of course, had much more money. It seemed to persuade him and we parted on amicable terms.

When they were actually shooting, I had little to do. Paul, the camera man, knew a little Italian and was able to communicate when he needed. There was also the uncouth Bavarian whose job it was to direct the extras. He had picked up a few words of Italian and despised me because I tried to be relatively polite with people. Whenever a scene was ready, he would shout innumerable times: "silenzia!" It made the extras laugh, because the word is really "silenzio". He also had orders to stop the shooting if he discovered some serious disturbance within the framed scene. This led to the biggest fiasco of the whole enterprise. When the scene in the garden of the false osteria was being shot, the buxom heroine sat under an artfully arranged branch of a rose bush and waited for the love song the tenor was about to start. It was a sunny day, but every now and then a cloud cast its shadow over the scene.

"Stop!" the camera man would shout, and the scene had to be started again. The third or fourth time, when everything seemed to be running perfectly, a butterfly fluttered in and landed without hesitation on the heroine's shoulder. What could have been more romantic? But the supervisor of extras shouted "Stop! Stop!" and the take had to be ended.

"You bloody idiot!" shouted the camera man and the director, too, was in a rage. There was nothing to be done, however, but to repeat the scene without the butterfly.

I was busy every day from six in the morning until after supper at night and lost a few pounds during the six weeks. But as most of it was really entertaining, I felt very well. I wrote long letters to Isabel about the things that happened, some of which I later used in sketches for the paper I started working for. Besides, the constant driving around the region of Greve gave me an acquaintance with Tuscany that was more intimate than the usually hurried passing through on vacation.

Val di Sogno 1947

A few kilometers south of the little ancient town of Malcesine, on the eastern shore of Lake Garda, there is a semicircular bay that has the romantic name Val di Sogno, Valley of Dreams. Next to it is a smaller bay that had for at least four centuries belonged to the family that owned the villa on its southern point. The villa had its own chapel, on a rock looking out over the lake. It was called San Vigilio and has, though few people know this, been immortalized by the romantic German painter Böcklin as the "Toteninsel", that is, the Island of the Dead. Reproductions of the painting, a rare example of somber kitsch, were very popular in boarding houses, much like the stag that, as "Monarch of the Glen", graced the walls in the dreary Victorian bed-and-breakfast establishments of Britain. It can only have been the unfortunate association of cypress trees and cemeteries that made the painter choose that lugubrious title.

The bay of Val di Sogno had an intimate sweetness that had no match anywhere on the northern Italian lakes. There is a tiny island facing it; a minute pebble beach, a bit of shrubbery, and two graceful trees, not large enough to block the view of the spectacular rock face on the western shore two kilometers across the lake.

As a teenager I had fallen in love with the place (partly no doubt because it seemed a real adventure to swim across to the island). When we returned to Meran after the war, it was the one place I wanted to see again. It was not far, but getting there was not as easy as it had been. The Germans, retreating out of Italy during the last days of the war, had dynamited some of the tunnels of the road that led to Malcesine along the lake from its northern end. Why, one might ask, as the war was ending anyway. The reason was no doubt the same that made them blow up the 14th century bridge to the Scaliger Castle in Verona. The bridge was an architectural treasure much too narrow for military vehicles, and it led nowhere except to the castle. It was destroyed out of spite.

When we drove down to the lake it was a decade since I had last seen it in 1937. I jotted down a few lines, which somehow survived in the back of a notebook. They better express what I felt than I could say it now:

> This little piece of my world may well be the only one that has not changed during the past ten years, ten years that are among the worst in history. The lake is as alive as ever and the rock face of the opposite shore as high and vertical as it was. The color of these rocks changes from red to golden and to black according to weather and hour of the day. High up above the rock face there is the village of Tremosine: houses, paths, and fields, far enough for people and their fates to disappear, yet not so far as to hide the centuries of their work. After the years of war it is profoundly moving to see that man's interference with nature is here not manifest in wounds but is merged with the landscape as though humans and their doings had grown out of it.

The little town of Malcesine had not changed much either. The one café spread a few more tables and chairs on the pavement around the little harbor, and there was a sign in the window that read "Deutscher Kaffee". A strange message, given the fact that people in Germany sometimes advertised "Bohnenkaffe" (coffee made from coffee beans) to differentiate it from concoctions made from other black vegetable substances. But Germans were the first tourists to swarm around the lake and the poor villagers desperately needed business, never mind where it came from.

Signora Martini, the owner of the grocery store, who had known me as a boy when I had come to the lake with my parents, greeted me as though I were part of her family and when I introduced Isabel and Sandra, she hugged them and made them part of it, too. She sat us down on chairs behind the counter, brought out glasses, a bottle of wine, and a *biscotto* for Sandra and she wanted to hear where we had been and what we had done during the war. While she was serving an odd customer, I told her a little about the farm we had in Ireland and listened to some of her experiences with the Germans.

"And now they come here," she said, "and behave as though they owned the place!"

She paused and I took the opportunity to get in the question I wanted to ask.

"Who owns the olive grove that slopes down to Val di Sogno? We thought we might camp there for a few days."

"Camp?"

"We have a big tent to sleep in and most of the day we'd spend in the water anyway."

"A tent? You mean like the military?"

"It's not a military tent, Signora Martini, it's the sort they use on expeditions. It's large and quite comfortable."

"But the child? What do you do with the child?"

"Oh, she has slept in it several times. She doesn't mind a bit—she likes it! She has a cot she can stand up in and there's enough room for her to play."

Signora Martini remained unconvinced but she did tell me that the olive grove was part of a fisherman's property, whose name was Luigi. The grove went up the hill in several terraces, but at the bottom there was a bit of flat space with an enormous fig tree and a high stone wall along the narrow sand road that separated it from the pebble beach. At the far corner of the property there was a weathered shack with a big door and a loft above it. The door was open as we arrived, and a tall, middle-aged man was inspecting fishing nets that lay spread out on the grass. He looked up as I got out of the car.

"You can't get out on the main road, that way," he said. "I'll open the gate here so you can turn."

"Thank you. But I've come to speak to signor Luigi."

He tilted his head and looked at me with some suspicion.

"That's me," he said, "what can I do for you?"

I tried to make my explanation short and to the point, but also wanted to make sure he didn't take us for German tourists. I told him that we came from Ireland, that I had been brought up north from here in Meran and had come to love Val di Sogno during many visits before the war. Finally I said that we were not rich and were trying to stretch a holiday by sleeping in a tent. Would he allow us to pitch it on his land?

He slowly took the few steps to the gate and unhitched the chain to open it.

"Come in and have a look."

There was quite a lot of space on the side away from the shack and I said I'd like to put the tent in the shade of the fig tree, so that it wouldn't get too hot during the day. He asked how high it was, and I said not quite as high as your wall. That's good, he said, because people passing by on the road won't see it. By then Isabel and Sandra had come out of the car and I introduced them

He shook his head.

"I never heard of such a thing — but if you want to, you can try. There are two things, though. Don't leave the car outside. Park it inside along the wall so people cannot see it; and don't forget to close the gate every time you leave."

I thanked him and told him how delighted I was that he would let us camp on his land. We shook hands and I said, we'd be there in a few days.

It worked out beautifully. We put up the tent and along the wall I built a shelter with a few big stones for our little cooking stove. The lake was just across the sand road outside. The beach of worn round pebbles was below a low dry wall, but there was also a little pier to sunbathe and to dive into the water.

We soon became friends with Luigi. The evening after our first night he came on a sort of formal visit. He brought a bowl of cherries and sat down on the big blanket where we had had our supper. I offered him a cup of wine and as he took it he laughed.

"You know," he said, "I've often drunk it out of the bottle, but never out of *plastica!*" He looked up into the fig tree. "The figs will soon be ripe," he said. "Take as many as you like. We have them near the house and never get round to picking them down here; they don't ripen all at once but go on all through the summer."

It was like the Garden of Eden. The tree had large round branches and you could walk out on them quite far. For figs that I could not reach with my hand I had tied a knife to a stick. With this I cut them off when Isabel was standing below to catch them before they splattered on the ground. Most of them were so ripe that the smooth green skin was beginning to split. All through the summer I climbed in to the fig tree to fetch fruit for our breakfast.

When the weather was right, Luigi would come down with his son at three in the morning, get nets from the shack, and go out fishing in the boat that was anchored near the pier. If we were awake when he came back, he showed us the catch. It wasn't very much.

"We couldn't live from this," he said, "if we didn't grow olives and peaches. The fishing is strictly regulated, but there are too many fishermen nowadays and not enough fish. We eat them ourselves — take what you like!" There were only two large ones, the famous Garda trout that have pink flesh like salmon; all the rest were small and I took a couple that would fit into our pan.

"Who regulates the fishing?" I asked.

"There is the *Codice della pesca* (fishery code) that was written by Lodovico il Moro. It is still in force and says who is allowed to fish and where. If you are interested, there's a copy in the Town Hall in Malcesine."

Il Moro was the nickname of Lodovico Sforza, the Duke of Milan in the 15th century. The next time I walked to Malcesine, I had a look at the Codice. It was a well-worn copy and the language was not exactly modern Italian. I did not spend much time on it, but realized that it was exhaustive. It covered everything in minute detail: the parts of the lake that belonged to each community; that beaches were public property and could not be closed by anyone; and many other points that I no longer remember. The fact that it was still in force and used to settle all disputes about fishing, certainly was an exceptional compliment to Lodovico il Moro.

On one of the holidays that came, we went up all the terraces to Luigi's house and brought a big cake we had bought at the pastry shop. We were introduced to the whole family and they brought out wine and the grandmother directed the cutting of the cake. She asked questions about the tent, but it was clear that she found our way of living incomprehensible and quite unsuitable. When the time came to leave, we had difficulty tearing Sandra away from the black cat she had been playing with. Francesca, one of Luigi's children, said the cat's mother was going to have kittens again and Sandra could have one of them. Sandra did not yet understand Italian but she guessed that it had something to do with her. So I translated it, hoping that it would be quickly forgotten; but that, of course, was not going to happen. Every day she asked when the kitten was coming.

A few weeks later, when the kittens had been weaned, Francesca came down one evening and brought one. It was black like its mother, but had a white triangle on its chest and two white paws. It was irresistible, so what could we do but keep it. Isabel was cooking some fish in milk for Sandra and put an extra bit in for the kitten. It loved it. It was restless during the first night in the tent and complained quite a bit; but it adapted quickly because Sandra was a very attentive companion. We called it Mehitabel, because Isabel had been reading the story of Archie and Mehitabel aloud to Sandra. Before a week had passed Mehitabel was established as a member of the family.

I had read that it was easy to train dogs to come when you called them. All you had to do was give them a tidbit to eat every time you called out their name. You just had to keep a few dog biscuits in your pocket and repeat the procedure for a week or so. I saw no reason why it should not work with a cat. It might take a bit longer because of their more independent character, but I didn't believe that they were immune to seduction. The problem was to find the right bait. The solution came when we were making a spaghetti sauce with dried anchovies. The kitten was instantly attracted by the smell and when I gave it a little shred, it wanted more and more and more. That's it, I thought, and began to carry a dried anchovy with me in a little box. Whenever the kitten was some distance away I would call "Mehitabel" and then give her a shred of the dried fish. After three weeks it worked infallibly: When I called her, she came running, and it did not cease to work even if sometimes she got no anchovy.

During the summer a thunderstorm would sometimes move up the lake from the open south and get stuck between the mountains on either side. The sound of thunderclaps was echoed to and fro and often still reverberated when the next flash of lightning came. If it happened at night and rain wet the canvas above us, it was as though a light bulb were being switched on and off. The first time it happened, Sandra, who was just about two then, sat up and we explained that the sky did this when it was feeling too hot. She flopped back on her pillow and went to sleep. At the next storm she barely stirred.

One day Signora Martini came by. She was so curious to see our encampment that she got her son to drive her out the few kilometers from Malcesine. As she looked into our tent she said to Sandra:

"But aren't you afraid to sleep there in the dark?"

I was glad that Sandra did not yet understand Italian. I translated: She asks if the cot isn't too small for you, and Sandra shook her head. Later I said to Isabel, that's how idiotic grown-ups get children to be afraid of the dark.

* * *

The most important event of that summer was meeting Silvio Ceccato. Working with him, off and on, for the next fifteen years laid down solid foundations to the way of thinking I had haltingly embarked on when I started reading Berkeley and Vico in Dublin.

Sitting on the low stone seat I had built against the little wall on the beach, I had my typewriter on my knees. I was doing translations for tourist offices and was also trying to write a thriller in the hope of making some real money. Although I finished a manuscript, it was a dismal failure. The agent I sent it to in New York eventually wrote back saying that it was quite a good story but there was too much philosophy in it.

So I was typing away there in bathing trunks, while Isabel was stretched out on the pier, reading or drawing; and Sandra was with her when she was not arranging and rearranging her collection of pebbles on the beach. Looking out over the lake, I always noticed whatever boats passed outside our enchanted bay. When the weather was fine—almost all the time—a wind punctually blew down the lake until noon, stopped for a couple of hours, and started up towards the north for the rest of the afternoon. Almost every day two or three of the big cutters that transported heavy goods would sail down in the morning and up again before the evening. Hardly anyone rowed past, but there was one boat I began to notice. It passed on our side of the little island and the lady who sat under the canopy seemed very interested in what she saw on the beach. One day she came on foot, accompanied by a servant, and stopped above the little wall behind me.

"Forgive my curiosity," she said, "I have seen you from our boat, sitting here with a typewriter, and I would love to know what you are writing."

I explained that I wrote small things like articles for tourist offices and occasional notes about books that I happened to read ... No, they were not novels. They dealt with science and philosophy.

"Philosophy!" she said, "My son is a philosopher! He is coming to visit me next weekend. He would be delighted to find someone to talk to here, because with me he gets bored very quickly... I am Irma Ceccato. We have the villa beyond the point, going to Malcesine. Would you come and have tea with us on Saturday?"

I was a bit stunned. I told her my name and to gain a little time, I said that there was also my wife Isabel and daughter Sandra, pointing to the pier where they lay stretched out with their heads raised like two seals. Signora Ceccato waved to them and assured me that of course she meant the three of us. "Saturday at four?"

When you are living in a tent, tea in a civilized villa is not unattractive; and though I was apprehensive of a philosopher interfering with our Arcadian summer I was also curious to meet him. So I said that we would be delighted to be there on Saturday.

That afternoon determined my future. Silvio Ceccato was three years older than I and had just written an introduction to the Italian translation of Wittgenstein's *Tractatus*. We couldn't have found more fertile common ground for a first conversation. I told him how much I liked Wittgenstein's way of writing and many of his aphorisms, but that I didn't agree with his notion that we could check the truth of the pictures we have of things with the things as they really are. I saw no way that could be done.

"You are right," he said, "but that isn't only Wittgenstein's delusion, it's the perennial delusion of Western philosophy."

That statement laid the foundation to a lasting friendship. We talked once more while he stayed with his mother and then he invited us to visit them at Vicenza, where the family had their home just below the castles of Romeo Montecchi and Giulia Capelletti. We went there for a few days and I met three of Silvio's six friends who formed the group around him that was attempting to rewrite the theory of knowledge and language. That time at Vicenza there were Enzo Morpurgo, a psychologist who practiced in Milan, Enrico Maretti, an engineer from Alfa Romeo, and Ferruccio Rossi Landi, a linguist who was about to get a Ph.D. at Cambridge. As I became a more or less regular member of the group, which met three or four times a year for a day or two, I met the other three: Vittorio Somenzi, a physicist from Rome, Giuseppe Vaccarino, a logician and philosopher from Messina, and Enrico Albani, one of the first computer specialists in Italy.

What made me useful to the group was that I spoke more than one language. There was no money involved and the collaboration was strictly voluntary. Only when Ceccato started the journal *Methodos,* I was paid a pittance by the editor for translating articles. More than ten years later, when Ceccato founded the Center for Cybernetics at Milan University, I got my first research job.

In retrospect I can say that what I learned by being part of Ceccato's group throughout the years was far more than a replacement of whatever academic education might have given me.

Breitmoos and the Royal Engineers 1948

If you drive from Kitzbühel, the famous ski resort, to Jochberg and beyond, the road climbs to the Passthurn, one of the passes that was kept plowed and drivable all winter even in those days. A mile or so down the other side of the Pass, there is a big old peasant inn called Breitmoos. It lies on a sunny slope and has a great view of the valley below and the glacier-capped peaks of the Tauern Mountains. This is where in the winter of '47/'48 Walter and I taught several hundred Royal Engineers the beginnings of skiing. The Royal Engineers were a detachment of the British army responsible for building bridges and communications in general.

Almost immediately after the end of the war, Churchill suggested that the Allies might quite soon have to fight a war against the Soviet Union. When this idea seeped into the higher echelons of the Ministry of Defence, someone thought that, because Russia was a notoriously cold country, it would be useful if parts of the infantry were capable of moving in deep snow. It was not an easy problem for generals to solve, but as so often private connections opened a way. Walter, a member of an old Scottish family, had been a parachutist during the war and the commander of his unit was well acquainted with Walter's family and knew that he was an expert skier. It did not take long for Walter to be charged with organizing ski-instruction for the Engineers.

The way Walter and I met was, like so many things in my life, a fortunate accident. Early that winter of '46, when I was teaching Isabel skiing, I occasionally went by myself on one of the trails that were easily accessible from Château d'Oex. On one of these runs, I saw a young woman skiing extraordinarily well. She had a style that I recognized at once. I followed her, and when she stopped I pulled up beside her and said:

"You didn't learn this here, did you?"

"How did you know?"

"Well, I spent the more significant parts of my youth in St. Anton and you somehow look like home."

"I hoped I had developed a personal style!" she said, "Anyway, we probably have friends in common. But I have to run now. Let's have a drink later—about six at the Bar du Midi?"

"I'd love to!" I said, and she was off.

* * *

I found her in the Bar, sitting with a tall red-haired man who got up the moment I approached their table.

"Don't leave, Walter,", she said, catching his arm, "he is an Austrian skier!" Then she turned to me: "This is Walter Ogilvie and I'm Rhona MacCloud; we're both roving representatives of the Ski Club of Great Britain—and you?"

"I'm Ernst von Glasersfeld, representing nothing and not doing much roving these days."

"Glasersfeld," she repeated, "I've heard of you! You were in Australia and beat Dick Durrance!"

I don't blush easily, but at that occasion I'm sure I did. I had never met anyone who had heard of me and it was a shaking experience.

"Only in the downhill," I muttered, "he was too fast for me in the slalom".

"And what are you doing here, on these innocuous slopes?" Walter asked, and I told them that my parents had settled in Château d'Oex after the war and we had just come from Ireland to visit them.

Walter looked at me with a funny little smile. "You were in Ireland during the war?"

I knew exactly what he was getting at.

"Look," I said, "I came back from Australia a few weeks before the Germans marched into Austria. I would have been quite willing to fight Hitler then. But no one else was. That put me off politics for good and I became a farmer in County Dublin."

"You may have a point there," Walter said. "I was younger and joined up with one of those old Scottish regiments that still wear kilts; but as I became a parachutist—which I thought was another smart way to move downhill—I never had to wear a kilt. It would have blown over my head as I floated down dangling on my chute, and the army did not want me to expose my parts to the enemy. Actually I was lucky. I was never dropped into enemy territory because the war ended before I finished training. But I had my thrills just the same. You can't imagine what it feels like when you begin to twist as you are in the air and the ropes are screwing your helmet down on your head."

"Are you going back to Ireland?" Rhona asked.

"Not immediately. We sold the farm and we'll go to Italy for a year or so, just to dry out. 'We' includes my wife and child. I've also been charged to sell my father's house in Meran and that may take some time. I'll probably have to find some job there, though I don't know what. Next winter I may teach skiing. It's one thing I can do. When Hitler took Austria, it somewhat curtailed my options: it stopped me from getting a Ph.D. in mathematics and from taking the final exam as a ski instructor on the Arlberg."

Isabel and I met them for drinks a couple of times and one day I went skiing with them. Rhona was a pleasure to watch, Walter was good but obviously had not been schooled the way she had. When they left, Walter said he might come through Meran on his way to Venice where he had some business during the summer and I gave him the address of our house.

* * *

He did come, but it was after we had taken off with our tent. He left a message with the dentist family, which I found on one of my short day-trips to Meran from Lake Garda. He needed to talk to me, it said, and there was a phone number. I was duly intrigued and called him that evening from Malcesine on the way back to Val di Sogno.

He told me about his job with the Royal Engineers and asked if I would be willing to spend the winter in Austria teaching them to ski. We'd be staying at an inn on the Passthurn, the salary was small, but bed and board would be free for Isabel and Sandra as well.

"Hold on for a moment," I said, because Isabel was standing beside me. "Would you like to spend next winter skiing in Austria?" I asked her. "Why not?" she said and I told Walter that we would join him—enthusiastically.

He visited us on his way back from Venice and told us some of the details. It was a network of strange coincidences. First, that the commander of Walter's unit knew that Walter was a good skier; second that the commander found a retired senior officer who had lots of experience of the Alps and could supervise a training camp; third, that this senior officer happened to own a suitably isolated inn called Breitmoos in the mountains of Austria where a venture that was not to generate publicity could be located.

Walter suggested that Isabel and I should get settled at Breitmoos in mid-November. Charles Olgin, the senior officer, would be there already and Walter would come a couple of weeks later.

"What sort of a name is Olgin?" I asked Walter.

"Russian. He came to England as an émigré when he was in his early teens. He studied engineering, joined the army, and has been out-Britishing the British ever since. You won't believe it, he has no trace of an accent and Colonel Blimp is lax about conventions in comparison to Olgin. He was instantly impressed by your 'von' and didn't ask if you were an "all right" foreigner which, I know, he would normally have done. But he's a good chap fundamentally. About his name—there's a rumor that he is descended somewhat illegitimately from a grand duchess Olga, but I wouldn't vouch for it and I certainly wouldn't ask him!"

* * *

We punctually arrived at Breitmoos on a sunny day that was as warm on Passthurn as it had been in Meran, on the southern side of the Alps. There was no sign of snow anywhere, but Olgin received us with so much enthusiasm and charm that the absence of snow didn't seem to matter. We had a nice big room with a small adjacent one for Sandra, the food tasted great after a summer of cooking on a spirit burner, and the weather was subtropical, perfect for exploring the neighborhood of Passthurn for ski slopes and excursions.

Olgin's table in the *Gaststube*, the dining room of the inn, was by the big tiled stove and ours next to it. Olgin ate in silence and with a great deal of concentration, but when he had finished he turned to us, ready for conversation. Sometimes he ordered an *Achtel* (one eighth of a liter) of Schnaps, of which he regularly drank a quarter with his supper. He was a tall rather lanky man, but his movements, especially at table, had something of a studied elegance. It made me think of a play we had seen in Paris before the war. A socialite woman had met an attractive young man and, to see whether he had presentable manners, she invited him to tea and served him a very ripe peach. The part was played by Louis Jouvet and his conversation was so riveting that the lady quite forgot to watch how he was managing the peach.

On one of the first evenings, Olgin explained that he was an engineer and had become interested in the mechanics of skiing. Although he wasn't good enough to experience it regularly, he said, there was that strange feeling of complete balance all through a parallel turn. He asked if I had I ever thought about how that worked.

I hadn't, I said, but I'd be very interested, because we had often said that this feeling was the second best one could have. He disregarded my remark as though he had not heard it, but during the next few days we spent many hours working at an attempt to solve the problem. The only thing I remember contributing was the idea that, as you put your weight forward on your skis, which was crucial in a parallel turn, the skis acted like springs. This occurred to me because I remembered a physics problem we had been given at Zuoz, namely to specify what forces were involved when a person jumped up and down on a trampoline. The trampoline could be considered a spring and it seemed to me that skis functioned like that, too.

"You're right," Olgin said, "I hadn't thought of it." And he added with a funny smile: "Probably because I don't lean forward enough on my skis. But this, you know, makes the problem even more complicated than I thought it was. There are a lot of elements involved: gravity, speed, centrifugal force, the inclination of the slope, the friction of the snow determining your backward/forward balance point, and now also the flexibility of the skis that work like blades and God knows what else."

It turned out to be too difficult. We filled sheets with diagrams and Olgin composed formulas and used a sophisticated slide rule, but when snow began to fall and the first batch of Royal Engineers arrived, the problem was still unsolved; and then, in the rush of activities, it was soon forgotten.

* * *

Olgin had his quarters in a separate building that had originally been the stables of a farm. For his wife Louise he had turned the chicken coop into a two-room apartment and a bathroom. During our stay at Breitmoos Louise once came for a few days. She was a good-looking, elegant woman, who lived in Paris, and nothing was further from her intentions than to get herself stuck on skis. During her visit she asked Isabel and myself for a drink to her apartment, which she called "my henhouse". I have a little trouble with my heart she said and made a sweeping movement with her arm, indicating the walls of the room. Pinned up with thumb tacks, there was a continuous display of cardiograms. These are the only mountains I'm interested in, she said. That's why I visit Charles for not more than a few days at a time.

Olgin treated her with great respect and was unfailingly polite, even formal with her. No one would have guessed that they were married. When she arrived, he introduced her to us, but he never mentioned her in a conversation. It seemed an intriguing situation, but Walter, who usually knew all about people's background and quirks, had no explanation. Though he had known Olgin for many years, he had no idea who Louise had been and how they got married. It seemed utterly impossible to question Olgin about it and so their marriage remained a mystery.

* * *

The Royal Engineers came in lots of about thirty and stayed for two weeks. None of them had ever been on mountains, let alone on skis; but they were physically very fit, much more so than the beginners I had taught before. For the first week we had them walking on the flat, learning to climb up small rises and sliding down gentle slopes. During the second, we showed them how to do the "snowplow" and to shift their weight to the outside ski to make a turn. They quickly gained confidence and enjoyed it enormously. The last two days we took them to steeper slopes and showed them that what they had learned was working just as well in deep snow, provided they did it properly.

At supper time, the *Gaststube* was crammed and they had a great time. Herr Maxi, the establishment's sturdy grey tomcat sat on the shelf between Olgin and the stove and scanned the scene for leftovers he might be offered. One night when Schnitzel was being served, Olgin got up to get some pepper from a dresser near the kitchen door. Herr Maxi's eyes followed him until he was halfway across the room. Then, without any particular haste, Herr Maxi jumped down on the table and, without disturbing Schnapps or cutlery, picked up Olgin's Schnitzel and returned to his perch. As fast as the cat, Olgin was back at his table, snatched his

Schnitzel, and put it back on his plate. The entire room burst out laughing and Olgin, mustering the true British self-control he had acquired, swallowed his irritation, smiled, and said:

"Plucky little beggar, isn't he!"

Resterhöhe was the name of the mountain that rose up steeply behind Breitmoos. The slope was thickly forested and above it, near the summit, which was some two thousand feet higher than Breitmoos, was a building, almost like an Alpine Club refuge hut, where hikers could spend a night and get something to eat. It had been built for the summer, but now that skiers occasionally came across from Kitzbühel, there was a couple living there in the winter, too. There were nice open slopes down to the Passthurn and a cable lift up from there that served as supply line for the hut on top. It was a large, open wooden box and of course not licensed for the transport of people. But after Walter and I had climbed up and talked with the couple on top, they said they would let us use it every now and then if we were never more than two and if there was no one about to see us get in. It had been tested for more than a ton and was quite safe, and they themselves rode up in it when they went to buy supplies.

Walter and I didn't use it often, but if we happened to wake up early on the first clear morning after a snowfall, it was irresistible to go for a quick run before we started working with the soldiers. On one of these mornings, when we came up to the hut, there was Herr Maxi. He had been with us in the Gaststube the night before. Why on earth would he climb two thousand feet through some ten inches of new snow? The woman laughed when she saw our astonishment.

"He's a faithful gentleman," she said, "he comes up every time our cat is in heat."

* * *

The last batch of Royal Engineers came at the end of March and the second week of their stay was the most beautiful weather. Walter and I thought how nice it would be if we could provide a finale to the season and take our students up a real mountain. We mentioned it to Olgin as a sort of joke, but to our surprise he immediately caught on.

"Splendid idea," he said, "the chaps will never forget it! Of course, if you make it the Venediger you'll need to have at least two guides with you; but we can do that—the army can pay for it out of the reserve they allowed in case of an emergency."

Clearly there was a bit of Russian left under his British skin.

The Grossvenediger is one of the highest peaks in Austria, all glacier practically, and very easy skiing. To get to the Kürsinger Hütte, where you could stay the night before the climb to the top, was a long way from Breitmoos: by bus down into the Pinzgau valley and then a long climb to the Hütte. The Royal Engineers did not mind a bit. Carrying their skis, a spare pullover, and a toothbrush was far less than they had to carry on their military training marches. Six hours up an easy path was nothing to them and when, during the last half hour on the approach to the Hütte, they could see the glistening summit of the Grossvenediger, they started to sing.

Early the next morning we showed them how to put skins on their skis. Then, with the two guides leading the way, we started our climb. There were a couple of inches of powder on a hard surface — ideal conditions for climbing up as for skiing down. After an easy four hours we were on the summit. It was a cloudless day and even Walter and I, who had never been so high in that part of the Alps, were impressed. The view was spectacular and the Royal Engineers were duly overwhelmed. We shared a few apples and bits of chocolate and then we started on the run down. We told them that each should make the slow turns they had learned, not to let it run fast, and never to go out further to the sides than the tracks of the guides. Walter and I watched and were delighted. Not one of them fell or lost control. When they stopped for a rest quite some way down on the glacier, we let fly — wanting them to see what they might learn in the future. They didn't even look. They were so enchanted that they were able to manage and ski down without panic or stress that they couldn't care less about what we could do.

Back at the Hütte we ordered some wine and it turned into a pretty jolly evening. As long as there was any daylight at all, they kept going out to the front of the Hütte to admire the tracks they had made on the glacier.

The Cybernetics of Snow Drifts 1948

Surely you have at some time admired the smooth elegant edges the wind designs on snow drifts or sand. How does it do it, without blueprint or ruler? The wind does not *draw* them at all. Snow crystals or grains of sand are not fixed; each can move more or less freely — and the wind moves it as long as it gets sufficient purchase on it; but whenever a crystal or a grain comes to lie so that most of its wind-side is protected by others, the wind can no longer move it.

One could say the patterns on the sand are due to the grains moving out of the wind and, in doing this, they build up smooth, slightly rising surfaces until cohesion is broken because a collection of them offers sufficient resistance to the general pressure of the wind. This will generate ridges at a right angle relative to the direction of the wind. On the lee side of the ridges a vortex may develop, deepen the gap, and smooth the edge on top.

This can be seen as a cybernetic process. It is based on mobile elements *avoiding* the motion to which the wind pushes to impel them. In getting out of the wind, they generate a pattern that is not predictable from any one of the elements or from the force that generates it. It is a pattern that *emerges* from random interactions.

* * *

What is cybernetics? Norbert Wiener, who wrote the book with this title that inspired a new way of looking at things, circumscribed it as "communication and control in the animal and the machine". As a discipline cybernetics was launched by the 1946 Josiah Macy Conference in New York and immediately split into two branches: a technological one that produced thermostatic gadgets, automatic pilots, heat-seeking missiles, and played a leading role in the development of computers; and the philosophical branch that made the notions of purpose and goal-directedness respectable in the human sciences and opened a new path for the theory of knowledge. It was this second and for some time very unpopular area that interested me and helped me a great deal in clarifying my own ideas. For me, as I later came to say, cybernetics is the art of creating equilibrium in a world of possibilities and constraints. This is not just a romantic description, it portrays the new way of thinking quite accurately.

Cybernetics differs from the traditional scientific procedure, because it does not try to explain phenomena by searching for their causes, but rather by specifying the constraints that determine the direction of their development. The patterns of sand and snow are a good illustration. The characteristic patterns are not simply caused by the wind. They appear because the wind tends to push the grains or flakes along, but friction and their own weight allow them to pile up to a certain extent. Their individual positions that collectively generate the pattern, therefore, mark a labile equilibrium between the force that pushes them and the force that holds them down.

A First Steady Job 1949

When Otto Beer first suggested the job I was frightened. We had met Otto early on in Meran while we were still living in the basement. He was an editor of the *Standpunkt*, an intellectual weekly that had been started shortly after the war in an attempt to calm the politically still turbulent German-speaking region of the South Tyrol that was now under Italian rule. He was editing the Kulturteil of the paper, the part that dealt with literature, art, and science. It had acquired a quite disproportionate reputation for its book reviews and consequently received loads of review copies from German, Austrian, and Swiss publishers. Once Otto took me to his office and showed them to me. They were piled in high stacks beside his desk.

"Would you like to try and write some reviews?"

"I've never done it, but I regularly read them in *The New Yorker*."

"That's the very style we are aiming at. Of course we don't pay as much! In fact, we pay very little; but if I accept the review, you can keep the book."

"I'd love to try," I said, and he gave me two from two different stacks. One was a travel book, the other was a popular science text on modern physics. I did half a page on the first and four pages on the second and Isabel helped to make them more reader-friendly. I notice that he didn't give you a novel, she said and laughed. Both my reviews were accepted and it became a regular thing. During the summer, when we were camping, I always took a whole batch of books back to the lake with me when we made one of our regular visits to Meran. I liked writing the reviews and, though the *Standpunkt* did indeed not pay much, it was welcome pocket money.

During the second camping summer, the money from the sale of the farm was running low and the sale of the house was still not in sight. We were not sure what we should do. I began to think that I had better try to find a job as ski instructor.

Then, on one of my brief visits to Meran, when I gave Otto Beer the reviews I had finished, he provided a staggering surprise.

"I've been offered a nice job with the biggest daily in Vienna," he said, "and I'm going there at the end of the year." He leaned back in his chair and looked at me tilting his head. "Would you take my place here at the *Standpunkt*?"

"What did you say?" — I couldn't believe it.

He knew that I had heard perfectly well. He said:

"I see no reason why you couldn't edit the Kulturteil. You write good German and you know your grammar. That's very important for the *Standpunkt* because most of the contributions need some correcting in that area. It has to be done tactfully — which you might do even better than I! — and you have to keep in touch with our correspondents; and try to connect with new ones. And you'll have to write a little more yourself."

"But I've never done anything like that before!"

"Don't worry. You can come and sit with me for a couple of weeks while I'm still here, and I'll show you all there is to know. It isn't much, believe me. It's all a question of good judgment ultimately, and your reviews have shown that you have some."

It seemed like a miracle, but I was shaken. I had never had a nine-to-five job and it frightened me. On the other hand, it solved the financial problem and it didn't force me to do something that I hated. Beer had already discussed it with the two other editors (one for politics and one for economy), and they had agreed. So who was I to say no.

When I returned to Val di Sogno and told Isabel, she said it couldn't be better, and I realized that, though she hadn't shown it in any way, she must have been a little worried about our future. Her reaction helped to lay my fears about taking a regular job and we happily spent the last two months of camping at the lake.

When we returned to Meran, I went about a dozen times to Otto Beer's office. I realized that no one appeared there before ten in the morning, but sometimes you had to stay until eight or nine at night. This suited me much better than getting up an hour earlier. The secretary was a motherly, middle-aged woman, who knew how to make the editors' lives easier.

"Don't mind," Otto said, "if once a month or so she isn't here in the morning, she's worth it." She had a hangover every now and then, he explained.

Otto taught me how to mark manuscripts for the typesetters and to estimate their length in print. He showed me how to correct proofs and gave me his evaluation of the regular contributors and advice how to deal with them. A couple of times I went with him to the printer's at the near town of Bolzano and he showed me how to lay out the pages. The *Standpunkt* being a weekly, this happened once every week. It was being supervised by a retired Austrian journalist known as the "Corrector". He was extremely competent and very nice as well. Whenever I had a problem in the years that followed, I would call him and he invariably helped me solve it. Much of what I learned in those two weeks not only served me well while I was editor but turned out to be useful in things I undertook many years later.

* * *

Now that I was going to have a job, Isabel and I decided to look for a reasonable flat. As the dentist's wife had said, they were difficult to find. When we had almost given up hope, a gentleman we met at a friend's party said he lived in a village near Meran and there was an old tower near his property that had just been transformed into apartments. The village was called Partschins and it lay on a sunny slope a few miles west of the town. The tower was a large rectangular building that had been used for grain storage in the Middle Ages. But it clearly had been used in other ways, too, because it was called *Gaudententurm* (revelers' tower).

The second floor apartment was just what we needed. The owner had put in a bathroom and a small system of central heating. The living room was large, with a big tiled stove, old wooden floor, and huge beams carrying the ceiling. It cost a little more than we had expected, but we thought, what the hell, the name alone is worth it.

The flat, of course, was unfurnished. We found most of the essential things in my parents' attic, but we now developed a craving for the books, the pictures, and the silver we had stored in Dublin before we left. In view of the steady income we were going to have, we thought it a good moment to retrieve the things from Dublin. There was furniture we decided to give away and what we wanted to bring over had to be packed for transport. It wasn't the sort of thing a friend could do for you. So we decided that I should go to Dublin and do it myself.

It took more than a day to get there (by train, of course), but as one crossed the Irish Channel during the night and I had a compartment all to myself, I slept well and arrived in fairly good shape. I called Shelah Richards, with whom we had been staying the last two weeks before we left for Switzerland. I explained why I was in Dublin and she immediately said that if I could finish my packing in three days I could stay with her and then travel with her to Paris, where she was going for the first night of Orson Welles' *Dr. Faustus*. Three days, I thought, would be quite sufficient and spending a day in the train with Shelah and then staying overnight in Paris was too good to be missed.

"Lovely," I said, "I accept both invitations, provided that I can take you out to dinner every night."

"Thank you, but then I'll take you to dinner in Paris and to Orson's show as well."

And that was what happened. On the way, Shelah filled me in about the event in Paris. Orson Welles had written two small sketches and they were being shown for the first time. The first was a skit on Hollywood's beginning predilection for religious films; the second was a somewhat surrealist fantasy based on the Faustus story, presented partly as monologue, partly as song, and accompanied throughout by spectacular lighting effects. Its greatest attraction was the fabulous modulation of Orson Welles' voice, reciting bits of Marlowe, Milton, and Dante, and the ravishing appearance of Eartha Kitt, whom he had cast as Helen of Troy. The only thing I remember of the plot is that it ends with the suggestion that a ticking time bomb is the ultimate result of the human search for knowledge.

The late supper after the show lasted far into the small hours. I was constantly torn between listening to Orson's highly articulate stream of consciousness and studying the incomparable features of Ms. Kitt. Orson came late, but when at long last he bounced up to the gallery where our table had been arranged and everybody had started eating an hour ago, he looked just the way he had in *The Third Man:* an oversized panther ready to pounce on anyone who might dare to criticize him. But he turned out to be in a most affable mood and especially delighted to see Shelah, whom he had known at the Gate Theatre, where he started his acting career twenty years earlier at the age of sixteen. His laughter was contagious and his flights of fantasy uninhibited. He could switch from sophisticated intellectual to schoolboy or caveman and his expressions would follow to suit. Someone mentioned his film *The Magnificent Ambersons* and I asked him if it was there that he first used the focusing of the camera to draw the spectators' attention to a specific spot. He looked at me with big round eyes.

"How did you notice it? Hardly any of the critics did, and I thought it was a stupendous innovation!"

I explained that my father was a great photographer and I had learned a few bits from him. Photographically, Orson said, the best thing he had so far done was *Othello*, but they hadn't yet got round to cutting it. For some reason the script, the film, and he were never in the same place. As soon as it was done, he wanted to go to London to play *King Lear*. Why should Lear always be impersonated by wizened old men? After all, Lear was a knight, a hunter, and a man of nature, and Orson began to recite whole sections of the play to prove it. There was daylight outside when the party broke up and as Orson woke up his chauffeur he looked back at us as though to say, what a pity that you sleep away your lives.

When I returned to Meran I wrote my first article that was not a book review. It was about my evening with Orson Welles.

The Passion for Snow 1950

My mother had two sports. Both she and her sister had played tennis since their childhood and as adults both were successful in many tournaments; my mother, who loved playing the net, competed mostly in mixed doubles, her sister in singles. But tennis was my mother's second sport. Her first one, without question, was skiing. In the late 1920s, she changed from telemarks to the Arlberg style developed by Hannes Schneider at St. Anton. She did very well in a number of races, but what she liked best was excursions into the high mountains.

I have a photograph of myself, aged two and a half or three, sliding about on my mother's skis. The next winter I got my own and she taught me the telemark. From some of her expert friends I learned the various jump-turns. Telemarks and jump-turns were practically the only way of making turns in those days, because there was deep snow wherever you went. True, there was also the "Scherenkristiana". You had to have a certain speed to do it and it never felt quite safe. You put your weight on what was going to be the outside ski in the turn, and then you opened your skis a little in front and sort of steered with the unweighted inside ski. There was always the danger that the point of that weightless ski was pushed further away from the other and you fell flat on your face between them.

Ski lifts and cable cars did not yet exist and the snow was all yours. When you climbed a mountain, you were usually alone and you rarely saw other people's tracks.

After we had moved to Meran at the beginning of the twenties, my mother went skiing in the Dolomites. The Val Gardena, only a couple of hours by car from our house, was her favorite haunt. When I reached the age of six, she began to take me along. She took great care to take me only when the weather was fine, when it was not too cold, and when the snow conditions were the easiest. She did not want me to be put off by any discomfort. Of course, I did not like the climbing up, but my mother always managed to coax me along and I still remember the intense pleasure of reaching the top, with nothing ahead but the run down. Being much lighter than the adults was a disadvantage on flattish slopes, because you did not get up enough speed to keep up with them. My mother often foresaw this, and let me hold on to one of her poles, so that her weight would pull me along.

The next winter, my mother wanted to meet some of her friends, who were competitive ski jumpers, at Cortina d'Ampezzo, where there was a jumping championship. She and one of her regular tour companions, who lived close to us and had himself been a great jumper, decided to go to that event on skis over two Alpine passes from Val Gardena. When I was asked to come along, I was thrilled.

The events in Cortina were the first where I saw ski jumping and I was immediately hooked. People jumped 50 or 60 meters at the most and the style was altogether different from today. After take-off they bent forward from the hip and rotated their arms to keep their balance in mid air.

In the winters that followed, I practiced jumping whenever there was some free time in the snow. I used a step in a slope or built a small jumping hill with a few bricks of snow. That's what I did with a couple of schoolmates during my first winter in boarding school at Neubeuern. We shoveled a lot of snow on a pile of branches just above a steepish slope. It raised the take-off about three feet and we could fly for nearly twenty meters and still land on the steep part of the slope. The first day we did not jump very far. The next day it was snowing and I thought the run in would be much slower. So I went a good bit higher and when I jumped, it took me much further than I intended. I crashed into the flat at the bottom and broke an ankle and a thumb. The thumb, I remember, was much more painful than the ankle, but the ankle was not set right and some years later I had to have an operation. Jumping, I decided, was not worth the risk. But the unfortunate jump that made me focus on downhill skiing was not the last one I took.

Going fast over a rise in the ground, you can often not avoid being lifted off, and if the slope is steeper after the rise, you may be in the air for quite some time. If you have been used to jumping, this does not make you uncomfortable at all. You take it in your stride so to speak—as long as there is a slope to land on after the rise. Shortly after the war, when I had taken up skiing again, I went for a day's excursion with friends to the Val Gardena. By then there were cable cars and gondolas that took you up to where I remembered climbing as a boy with my mother; and there were new trails cut out of the forest, where one had never gone before. One was called Ciampinoi. It faced north and there usually was still a lot of deep powder snow. Starting at the top, that day, above the tree-line there were only a few tracks, but it seemed obvious where you had to go. Coming to the first trees, the tracks went through them, one here, one there. I saw a nice band of untouched snow on the left and took it, intending to turn round a tree to join the other tracks. In the middle of my turn I was in the air. Coming from above in the deep snow, there had been no hint that the slope dropped away as a precipice just behind the tree.

I was flying, having a bird's eye view of a few pine trees on a very steep slope. The first thing that came to my mind was how wrong films were that showed people screaming when they realized that they were falling. You couldn't do any such thing. There was an instinctive reaction to fill your lungs with air and hold it. I was sailing down, holding my breath and my position, hoping that I would not hit a tree. And I didn't. Well, almost. The end of my right ski must have hit a branch, so that the point of the ski was sharply pushed down, but it was high enough, so that the ski could come up again for me so I could land on both. As I was later told, the rock face was ninety feet high. As I landed a good bit further down on the steep slope, I must have fallen well over hundred feet. Although I landed in five or six feet of soft snow, it was a terrific thump and it winded me for a minute or two.

When I had dug myself out of the snow, my right ankle hurt, but I could stand on it. I looked up and saw the small heads of my friends high above, gingerly looking over the edge of the rock face. I made my way to the other tracks and waited for my friends to come down. They were more shaken by my jump than I, but when they saw that I was quite alive, they relaxed and we went down to the village and had some Glühwein before we drove home. The chap at the inn said that the place where I made my jump was called "Mäuerl" (little wall) and that there usually was a warning before it, but the last snowstorm probably blew it away. I thought he was a bit casual about my adventure, but the villagers, I knew, considered all skiers to be mad anyway.

Having been enormously lucky, I very much appreciated the experience. I was going to be careful not to repeat it. It also provided an unexpected relief. I had sometimes worried about being afraid of death. Now I had learned that it was by no means what worried you most when you realized that some action you had embarked on was likely to get you there.

Salzburg 1950

A letter from Shelah Richards told us that she was going to bring a Dublin theater group to the Salzburg Festival that summer and wouldn't it be nice to meet there. From Meran it would be an easy drive and I liked the

idea because apart from meeting with Shelah it gave me an opportunity to
see my old friend Fery again.

The play Shelah directed was scheduled towards the end of the festival
and we timed our visit to take in both. The play was one of John Synge's
masterpieces and although the Salzburg audience was presumably
unable to appreciate the remarkable quality of Synge's language—a kind
of Gaelic English—it was quite a success. The next day there was a cock-
tail party in the ball room of the festival and Shelah took us along as her
guests. The ball room was enormous and at one end there was a broad balcony above it, rather like the dress circle in a theater. A band was playing
and people were beginning to dance. Shelah pointed out Marcel Marceau,
who was dancing with a very pretty girl. As they were passing close to us,
a big man stopped them. He was at least a head taller than Marceau and
twice his size all round. He wanted to cut in and dance with the girl.
Marceau stepped aside and with a little wink to his girl conceded her to
the big man. Then he strolled past us and stopped directly under the balcony. He looked up to it and then down again, as though he were gauging
its height because he wanted to jump up and get a hold on it with his
hands. It was clearly impossible. But Marceau's show was convincing,
and when the big man came dancing around, he left the girl standing and
placed himself beside Marceau, looking up at the balcony and obviously
thinking that he had a better chance. Marceau smiled at him and went
back to dancing with his girl. It was a superb performance, but no one
besides Shelah and the two of us noticed it.

"Marceau," Isabel said, "used his skill as a mime to generate this experience for himself and for his girl friend. Just like a great painter, who
creates with the skill of his hands what he wants you to see."

"Or a good actor," Shelah added. "who creates a reality with the very
same means that we use to create our ordinary one."

* * *

Fery no longer lived on the Mönchsberg. His mother had died before the
end of the war, and he and his brother could no longer afford to keep up
such a large place. His brother, who was the elder and therefore had
control over the inheritance, had had the idea to turn it into a hotel. For a
start —and this was a much worse idea—he wanted to try a restaurant. So
a lot of money was spent making the necessary changes. Then a cook was
hired. He was Italian and had very good references. For the beginning,
Fery and his brother were going to serve as waiters.

One of the first evenings a foreign guest asked whether he could have
Salzburger Nockerln, a regional sweet like a bulging, self-supporting

soufflé. It was not on the menu, but the guest said that as they were in Salzburg, they surely could make it. Of course, said Fery's brother and went to the kitchen. The cook had never heard of Salzburger Nockerl, but after a rough explanation of what they looked like and how they tasted and that they consisted largely of beaten white of egg, he was ready to try. Fery's brother had been emphatic that they must be very light and fluffy. So to make sure that what he produced would stand up by itself and match the description he had been given, the cook added a little baking powder to the mixture. When he took the Nockerl out of the oven and placed them on a dish, they certainly looked light and fluffy; but as Fery carried them to the guest's table, he noticed that they were still growing. The guest looked at them in surprise and said:

"I didn't realize that they were alive!"

There were other unforeseen events and the restaurant did not make it. The property was sold, and Fery, who had always played with cars, found a job in a big garage.

He also recounted the following. After the allies liberated Salzburg, a man telephoned him.

"Do you remember," the man said, "that shortly after the Germans marched in here, someone stopped you in the street and warned you about your phone?"

"Yes," Fery said.

"That was me. I was employed by the telephone company and when the Nazis took over, they called you to say that there was something wrong with your phone and they were sending someone to repair it. And I was sent to put a bug in it. I had been in the communist party and knew about your father. So I decided to warn you."

"I remember it very well!"

"Now I'm in trouble. They are denazifying everyone in the company and the fact that I used to be a communist doesn't help at all. Could you put a word in for me with the CIA?"

"Of course," Fery said, "and if there's anything else I could do, I'd be delighted — you may have saved our lives!"

"Thanks, but if I can keep my job, I'll be all right."

Fery's intervention somehow denazified the man and he was able to keep his job.

I asked Fery if he was happy with the job in the garage.

"No," he said, "I'm about to leave. In fact you were lucky to have found me here. I'm disgusted with the whole situation. The denazification was a colossal hoax. They plagued all the small people, the workers like the man who warned me, but many of the ones who had important jobs, still have them today, as though they had never worked for the Nazis. It bothers me every day. My mother is dead, my brother adapts to anything, I have nothing to keep me here and at the end of the summer I'm going to Africa to see if I can't find something interesting in that new world.

"If you want to write articles from there," I said, "I can probably print them in the *Standpunkt*—not that you could live from it, but it might start you off as Africa correspondent for bigger papers."

I gave him our new address and hoped to hear from him. But I never did. I often thought about him and in the end I concluded that, having lost their place on the Mönchsberg, he probably wanted to forget all about his former life.

Bérénice 1953

As the daughter of one of those landed families in Hungary, who had everything except cash, Bérénice had grown up close to horses, the stable boys who looked after them, and the women and men who worked the land. She developed not only affection and respect for them, but from the peasants—who, unlike the mountain folk in the Austrian empire, had a great love of song, dance, and fun of all kinds—she acquired a great deal of know-how and practical wisdom.

Her parents had early on launched her education by teaching her English, French, and German and then letting her loose in their library. It contained not only all those notorious French novels of the 17th and 18th century that bourgeois parents (if they happen to have them) anxiously lock away from their children, but there were Montaigne, Pascal, Rousseau, and all the poets from Villon down to Beaudelaire. There were also a great many medical books in English and German which an uncle, who had left the countryside to become a surgeon in Budapest, had bequeathed to the family.

At seventeen, Bérénice was a lean, long-legged filly with bottomless black eyes and a conspicuous aquiline nose. One might not have called her beautiful, but her appearance and the way she moved and spoke were striking and tended to become attractive. By then, her reading had given her a hankering for the wider world. It was not that she had got tired of the Hungarian plains, the peasants, and the horses. She loved them as she loved her parents, but she wanted to see for herself the kind of people and the settings she had read about. She was not in the least impatient, but she was waiting.

In the summer after the First World War had ended, an old acquaintance of her father's came as a guest to spend a month in the country. He hailed from the part of the Austrian empire that Hungary lost to Czechoslovakia when both were made independent states. Baron B was a big, good-looking man with impeccable manners. He was a master at choosing the right clothes for every occasion and he radiated that air of unshakable self-confidence that professional diplomats acquire even if they have few other skills. He had been in the Austrian diplomatic service and the posts he had held during the twenty years of his preceding career had never demanded anything beyond the ability to represent—and representing was what he did under all circumstances and without any conscious effort. Apparently he had done it so well and innocuously in several languages that the newly created Czech Republic was only too pleased to take him over as a diplomat.

Besides his manners, the Baron had another accomplishment. He played excellent bridge, and his dispassionate explanations did more to teach Bérénice the finer points of the game than the impatient instructions from her parents. His cool detachment did much to convince Bérénice that the Baron was a suitable vehicle. She guessed (and later experience proved her absolutely right) that his amiability and good manners would not disintegrate, no matter what the pressures might be. Such steadfast dependability, she decided, made up for any lack of originality. At the end of the four weeks they were engaged to be married.

When we met Bérénice in 1947, she had been the Baroness B for twenty-five years, but had not seen her husband for almost a decade. He happened to have been on a mission to London when Hitler marched into Czechoslovakia. Like so many others who had an international style of living, the Bs had been denounced as enemies by a Czech Nazi. Bérénice and her daughter, who was then about eighteen, were arrested in their home in Prague and sent to a concentration camp. The Baron tried everything to get them released, but as the member of what had become a government in exile he had no power. Then war broke out, and there was nothing more to be done.

For the first year of captivity Bérénice and her daughter were together. Then they were sent elsewhere and separated. Bérénice did not see her daughter again. Towards the end of the war she was liberated by the Soviet army and spent another year in a Russian camp. Some months after the war had ended, she was released and put on a train with Italian prisoners who were being sent home. The journey took several weeks and she became friends with Federico Brandi, an army doctor, whose family had been killed in the bombing of his home town in Tuscany. He had no wish to return there but wanted to be in Italy. Bérénice clung to the hope of somehow finding her daughter, but Prague was not where she wanted to be and Hungary was under Russian occupation. So she stayed on the train. When it stopped at Bolzano, Federico said:

"Let's get out here."

He had been to the neighboring town of Meran and knew it as a place where, during the days of the Austrian Empire, many had found refuge after falling into disfavor at the court in Vienna. Meran was an old spa and tourist center, and he thought that with a bit of luck a doctor could make a living there. And he was right.

Bérénice became part of his practice. Her knowledge of languages was a great asset, and so was her familiarity with the aging Austrian aristocrats, who had settled there before and during the war to end their days unobtrusively and peacefully. She also remembered some of her medical readings, and with Federico's help she became an efficient nurse and learned to do most of the analyses he needed in a laboratory he managed to assemble in a backroom.

They made no secret of the fact that they were living together. They were attached to each other by a loyalty more conspicuous and more profound than mere love. They had found in each other a reason to live when their former worlds were gone, but in the background there was always a shadow of sadness.

Some people showed surprise when they heard that the Nazis had sent her to a camp.

"But you are not Jewish," they said.

She gave them a cold look.

"It's a sad thing that the hundreds of thousands of socialists, anti-militarists, and my gypsy compatriots Hitler killed seem to be forgotten."

She also confided to us the pain she felt when someone asked whether she had children.

"If I say Yes, it's not true for the present, if I say No, it's not true for the past. Either way it hurts."

Federico Brandi was a good doctor and his fees were modest. His fame spread by word of mouth. A friend told us about him when we were in a panic. Sandra, who had just had her second birthday, had swallowed a pebble. She came running to us, crying.

"I drink it," she said, "the red one!"

It took us a long time to understand. She had been playing with a treasure of colored stones she had collected at beaches. She dropped one into a cup and later did not notice it when she filled the cup with water. The red pebble was her favorite. It was about the size of a thumb nail, the edges worn off, almost like a marble. It had gone down with the water. We had visions of her getting horrible cramps and dying.

Dr. Brandi took Sandra and us to the hospital to have her x-rayed.

"Don't worry," he said while we were waiting, "quite large things can pass through us. I knew a woman who swallowed her three rings when she was arrested. They didn't harm her at all." After a moment he added: "But of course with the latrines in the camp, she had no way of retrieving them."

He asked us what we were doing in Meran and I told him that we had recently come there from Ireland and that I was trying to live in Italy for a while, as a freelance journalist and translator.

When we finally got to the x-ray machine, we saw the pebble. It had already gone through Sandra's stomach.

"She'll be quite all right," he said, "Give her a lot of solid food and on no account a purgative. Call me when you have found it in her pot."

For two days we could not think of anything else.

"Don't you want to go to your pot?" we asked Sandra every half hour. Then, at last, it was there. Isabel called Dr. Brandi and Bérénice answered.

"You must be relieved," she said, "I'm so glad – one always expects the worst when things like that happen."

Isabel asked whether we should pass by to pay or would they send us their bill. Bérénice hesitated for a moment.

"Why don't you come to tea on Sunday afternoon. I would love to see Sandra once more – without her pebble."

We quickly became friends and saw quite a lot of B & F. They were attractive people. There was no nonsense in the way they treated each other and there was no nonsense in their friendliness towards us. They looked at the world with a cool detachment that was rare and refreshing. It was clear that B was fascinated by Sandra because she reminded her of her own little girl. And Sandra loved visiting them because B had two love birds that freely flew about the apartment and sometimes settled on her shoulder.

Occasionally we would pick B & F up on a Sunday and drive up one of the Tyrolean valleys to look at Gothic frescoes in little churches or at the glaciers. Once Federico said to me:

"You know, all these ruins of castles and the gaunt mountains are the Middle Ages to me. They are beautiful in their way, but very stern – the hills of Tuscany, where I grew up, breathed the free spirit of the Renaissance, a spirit that is no more."

"We have another freedom," I said, "don't we? Look at where we are."

He nodded, but his smile was sad.

A year or so later, Bérénice's husband, the Baron, retired from his job at the embassy in London and came to live in Meran. His relations with B & F were perfectly friendly but not particularly close. He had got used to living by himself and felt perfectly at ease among all the old aristocrats who vegetated in Meran; and as a good bridge player, he was in constant demand.

One day, Bérénice called and asked us to come by. She had a surprise for Sandra, she said. When we got there, a white animal was hopping about the living room. When it sat up on its haunches, which it did every now and then, making a noise like an asthmatic struggling for air, it was almost two feet tall. It was so large that it took me some time to recognize it as a rabbit. Sandra, of course, was enchanted with it, even though it was too heavy to pick up. It was called Daisy, Bérénice said, and could be fed on lettuce or just grass. She was sorry, but we couldn't stay for tea, because she had a lot of work to do.

There was no way we could have persuaded Sandra to say: no thank you. So we took the rabbit and left. The first few days at home were not too bad. Mehitabel, of course, was not pleased by this addition to the family but merely kept her distance. Daisy slept quite a lot, but when she didn't, she wanted attention. She constantly followed someone and at every stop she would sit up and make her suffering noise, wanting to be picked up. She often did this behind you, so that, when you stepped back, you stumbled over her. It soon became too much even for Sandra. And there was something else. Almost at every step, Daisy produced a little pellet from her rear end, a light brown bean, quite dry and harmless, until you stepped on it and ground it into the carpet. Someone constantly had to follow her with a brush and pan. The moment came, when we all agreed that we couldn't stand it any longer.

We went to see Bérénice and asked where Daisy had come from. Why, she asked rather coldly, and I explained as tactfully as I could that we wanted to return her.

"How can you do that," she said, "Sandra loves her!"

She stared at us with belligerent disapproval. Then her expression faltered. She turned to the window and raised one hand to her forehead, as though she had suddenly woken up.

"I am so sorry," she said, looking out the window with unseeing eyes and tears began to run down her face.

Isabel stepped forward and put her arm round Bérénice's shoulders — somehow she had grasped what was going on. "It's not your daughter," she said.

Bérénice straightened herself and tried a smile.

"I don't know why — Sandra does not look at all like her, but from the very beginning she made me remember — and the thought of hurting her just overwhelmed me."

Bérénice dabbed her eyes with a handkerchief, looked at Isabel and smiled.

"A cup of tea? Isn't that what settles all problems?"

She went to put on the kettle in the kitchen and I asked Isabel, how on earth she had guessed.

"I saw it in her eyes, many times when she looked at Sandra. And I have never been able to look at Bérénice without thinking of the daughter she lost. It's a wound that does not heal."

Bernard Berenson 1953

The first comprehensive Picasso exhibition after the war took place in Milan around 1952. By then I had about two years experience as "cultural" editor of the *Standpunkt*, the weekly published in German in Meran, and I had begun to feel quite relaxed about writing lead articles on topics that were considered my field. The Picasso exhibition clearly was an occasion not to be missed.

Milan had not been heavily bombed during the war but the archbishop's palace, right in the center, had suffered a hit that destroyed two thirds of the enormous ballroom. It had been as sumptuous as Versailles. But now one end wall was missing, more than half the arched windows were shattered, and broken caryatids and fragments of other decorations were scattered on the floor. In a moment of true inspiration, the organizers of the show decided that this was the place for "Guernica" and Picasso's equally large war panel. Both were hung on the one remaining side wall and a path was cleared on the floor, so that people could walk along without stumbling over stones and mortar. It was a brilliant idea. The two paintings are effective no matter where you see them, but with the debris of pompous statuary and stucco columns scattered below them on the floor they were overwhelming.

When my review appeared, Hanna Kiel, a German art historian, whom I had frequently met at newsworthy events in Florence, wrote to me asking if I would mind if she showed my article to Berenson.

"Mind?", I wrote back, "I'd be delighted!" Bernard Berenson, after all, was reputed to know more about art than anyone and to get an opinion from him was a rare privilege.

Hanna Kiel had moved to Florence when Hitler came to power, long before the war. She had no reason to emigrate, but she was a good German and could not stomach the direction German politics was taking. She lived in La Capponcina in Settignano, a little villa that D'Annunzio had decorated in Art Nouveau for Eleonora Duse at the beginning of the 20th century when they had their famous love affair. Hanna had no sympathy for D'Annunzio's nationalist/fascist undertakings, but she was an art historian and it delighted her to live in a house with such flamboyant historical memories and decor.

When the Nazis marched into Italy she became one of the handful of people who managed to keep Berenson hidden and in good health through the years of occupation. She was now translating some of his writings into German and had sent me a few excerpts for publication in the *Standpunkt*. She reported that "BB" had found my review quite acceptable and asked her to bring me to tea the next time I came to Florence.

Berenson had discovered, researched, catalogued, and thus made respectable Siennese and Florentine painters of the late Middle Ages and the early Renaissance. In the process he accumulated quite a fortune and he shrewdly invested it in the Villa I Tatti, a 16th century manor on a large slice of land in Settignano, the community below the hill of Fiesole north of Florence.

At his tea parties the guests assembled in the lobby and waited until BB, close to ninety then, at the arm of one of the loving ladies that took care of him, descended the wide staircase. There was no fanfare, but it still felt much like Queen Victoria's tea parties. When Hanna Kiel introduced me, he said:

"Hanna translated your Picasso review for me and I found that I agree with some of what you say; maybe we could talk sometime when there is not such a crowd."

He gave me a crinkled paper smile and focused on the next guest.

The next guest happened to be a dowager from the conservative section of Florence society. She clasped Berenson's bony fingers in both her hands to make sure he wouldn't move on before she had finished with him. She wanted to hear what he thought about a startling news item that, to the embarrassment of the Vatican, had occupied the press for days.

"Isn't it wonderful," she said, "that our Holy Father has had a vision of Jesus?"

Berenson looked at her for a moment, tilted his head, and asked:

"Did he say what school of painting his vision represented? Was it Flemish, or Byzantine?"

* * *

The opportunity to talk with BB came during the following summer when he, like many of the rich Florentines, had escaped the heat of the city and spent some weeks in the hills at Vallombrosa.

"Thank you for coming," he said, "I get bored up here with nothing to look at and no one to put down." As an afterthought he added: "Not that I'll put you down—I did like your Picasso review. You brought out the fact that the revolution in art was breaking down all rules and that, in the long run, this will be self-defeating. There is no art without rules. That is what I would say, but I don't discuss modern art. Let's take a little walk before we have tea."

I was, of course, enormously pleased, but as he did not want to discuss modern art I did not really know what to say next. I did not feel up to discussing old masters. I knew that Venice was preparing a Giorgione exhibition and I asked BB whether he would go to see it.

"I don't have to," he said, "they sent me the proofs of the catalog. There are four genuine Giorgiones, the rest are by apprentices, with or without him, and by imitators."

We walked on a gravel path in the garden below the small villa. BB put his hand on my shoulder whenever we came to a step, but his walk was amazingly steady for such a frail little man. Looking down the Arno valley, there were several hills staggered on either side and with the hazy summer air each was set behind the other like the scenery on a stage.

"For a visitor," I said, "this is well worth looking at."

"Yes, but I have little time for landscapes—it's their interpretation by painters that interests me."

I had begun to notice that the summer air was also full of mosquitoes and they were concentrating on me rather than on the wizened man beside me. It distracted my attention and from the rest of our conversation I only remember that what BB said fitted well with what I had read about him: he had an uncanny eye for distinguishing painters and characterizing what set them apart. But he was not happy with his fame as art historian and critic. He wanted to be remembered as a writer and realized that this he had not achieved.

Marilyn Monroe 1953

In the fall of 1953 we saw, for the first time, Hollywood's "blonde bombshell". What she evoked was different from the sultry, sexy mood a trailer and the rest of the publicity had led us to expect. Far from generating seething erotic dreams in the public, the auditorium resounded with giggles and merry laughter.

The film in which Miss Monroe showed her world-famous female attributes was called *Niagara* and did indeed crush any lascivious expectations. Yet, Miss Monroe was certainly an exceptional girl: as a living advertisement for a particularly vitamin-rich baby diet, for a gentle soap, or for a curves-generating hormone pill, she could not be bettered. Never had any star looked so healthy and so thoroughly hygienic.

Were we Europeans since Baudelaire really so decadent that we could savor flowers only if they had a touch of evil? Or is it that people in America are trying to market sex-appeal in a plastic wrap and to pasteurize all that might be erotic? In this film, the camera sweeps to and fro between the thundering waters of the Niagara and the pneumatic charms of Miss Monroe, suggesting that both are irresistible forces of nature. The powerful images of the waterfall leave no doubt about it; but the cuddly girl remains a well-nourished child that knows about love, let alone passion, as much as Walt Disney's *Sleeping Beauty*.

Discord 1954

During all the time that Isabel and I were together there was only one occasion when the harmony was broken. As in other years around Easter, we had climbed from Meran to the Similaunhütte in order to spend a week making excursions in the Ötztal Glaciers. On the first day we went over the Hauslabjoch to the Vernagthütte, from where we planned to climb the Wildspitze. The descent from the Joch is an easy one, and as it was our first that year we took our time. There was one small stretch where the sun had not yet touched the snow and it was icy and felt like a grating iron under your skis. Isabel began her first turn and sat down. She got up, tried again and sat down. Cesare, who was always tactful, went quickly ahead and waited at the bottom of the slope.

"Try to remain flexible and don't stiffen your legs," I said to Isabel; "you don't have to make turns, you can just slide down sideways."

It was no doubt the rattling of the skis that upset her. Every time her skis began to slide, she sat down, and I got irritated.

"Like a bloody beginner!" I said after the fourth or fifth time. "If you don't pull yourself together, I can't help you."

I joined Cesare and waited. After a while she managed to come down and we went on. All that evening Isabel remained rather wordless. She was obviously very cross with me. It had never happened and I didn't know what to do about it. The next morning I tried to make peace, but it didn't work. She did not want to talk to me. As we climbed, of course, we would not have talked much anyway.

There was one place where we had to take off our skis because the last bit up to a ridge was so steep that you had to make steps like stairs for your feet. As always on such occasions I turned to Isabel and took her skis to put them on my shoulder with mine.

"Thank you," she said and for the first time she looked at me. When we reached the summit of the Wildspitze, she, too, was overwhelmed by the view, but she spoke only to Cesare. I took my Leica from my rucksack and shot a few pictures. I was looking through the viewfinder and was about to make a step backwards when I froze with shock. I suddenly remembered where I was. I was standing at the edge and behind me the east side of the Wildspitze dropped down almost vertically for several hundred meters.

Half the way down to the Vernagthütte the route of descent follows a broad back from which we could see several of the peaks we had climbed in the past. I took out the camera again to take a few shots with a long-focus lens. I left it hanging round my neck while I went on to choose a place from which I could photograph Cesare and Isabel as they were coming down. Without stopping, I turned round to look back — something one should not do when going faster than walking speed. Before I knew it I was flying head first into the snow. As I picked myself up, Isabel and Cesare had stopped beside me and were laughing themselves sick.

"This should teach you to have some sympathy for beginners," she said still laughing. Then her expression changed. "Your lip is bleeding!"

I had just noticed it and also that the corner of one of my teeth was broken off. Apparently the nine-centimeter lens had been slammed on my mouth. Well, it wasn't too bad. The lip soon stopped bleeding and I was immensely glad that Isabel was speaking to me again.

In bed that evening she said:

"I don't know what happened to me yesterday on that stupid slope. I had ..."

"I should have taken you by your hand, the way I did with Sandra when she was beginning. Instead I lost my temper. That was bad."

"Does your lip still hurt?"

Etruscan Fantasy 1954

In the early 1930s my parents had made a summer trip to Florence where my father spent a few days photographing. One of his most reproduced pictures, a shot of the roofs of the Uffizi Gallery, was made in those days. My mother, who did not always feel like accompanying her husband on his photographic explorations, used one of the days to visit an Italian tennis friend of hers, whose family had a villa not too far from Florence. It was my first experience of Tuscany and I have never forgotten it. The villa had been built by Brunelleschi and it made a profound impression on me. It was a hot, breathless day and what struck me most was that there was a constant cool breeze where we were sitting in the courtyard. My mother remarked on it and her friend was obviously pleased.

"They were pretty good architects in the 15th century, they knew all about air currents and how to generate them."

On the drive I saw for the first time the landscape that taught the great painters how to structure backgrounds. The vineyards and the olive groves, in which cypress trees stood where the painter's sense of space required them, were the same that Signorelli and the other early masters of the Renaissance had` painted. Of course I did not see it in these terms, but it made a deep impression on me.

Twenty years later I was a journalist and constantly in search of subjects that did not involve politics. My views were much too far on the left for the editors I had contact with and I had to limit myself to topics that were politically more or less neutral. There were several Etruscan excavations going on at the time and that was something I could concentrate on. I read up what there was to be read and, having been educated about painting by Isabel, I felt confident writing about the Etruscan findings. The frescoes in Tarquinia and the other burying sites were for me an expression of the same joyous sensuality that I saw in the works of Matisse. It was, of course, quite impossible to know how the Etruscans themselves might have viewed their paintings; for us, however, their attraction had to spring from our interpretation.

On one of our visits to Vulci we were shown a big vase that had just been found. The director of the excavations explained that the decoration and its inscription made it clear that it was a prize from the Olympic games between 550 and 480 BC. Apparently an Etruscan athlete had won it and taken it home.

We went on towards Orvieto where we wanted to spend the night. After a few kilometers we came to a small place the name of which was given as Commenda. I was startled because my mother's maiden name was Kommenda and the similarity made me think. Apparently this small town in the heart of Etruria had nothing worth looking at and the Guide Michelin did not even mention it. But there was a pleasant baroque church and in it a plaque that commemorated the death of Lucien Bonaparte. What he had done for Commenda was not mentioned. Lucien, who had some disagreements with his brother, had lived for several years in Viterbo and had died there. As it is barely thirty kilometers from Viterbo to Commenda, it's very possible that Lucien got there for some reason or another.

"Just imagine," I said to Isabel, "Lucien Bonaparte, riding about in the landscape loses his way and stops at a peasant's house to find out where he is and how he can get back to Viterbo. The peasant shakes his head and explains that he is in Commenda and has a rather long ride home. He should take a rest and have a glass of wine."

That's how the story began that I then spun out at leisure. Lucien liked the wine and asked the peasant if he could bring him a little barrel of it to Viterbo. The peasant had never sold much of his wine and was greatly flattered by the request. When he brought the barrel to Viterbo, Lucien paid him and had him given a good meal. It was the beginning of a pleasant, more or less regular connection, but it turned out to have tragic consequences for the peasant. When Lucien, in spite of their earlier differences, went to help his brother during the "hundred days" of his return to power, the peasant was branded as *Napoleonista* and shunned as a traitor. Life in the small town became more and more unpleasant for him and he decided to leave Italy. He went to the Austrian Burgenland and was able to buy a small vineyard with the money he had from the sale of his farm in Commenda. His experience with vines in Tuscany quickly brought him success and he soon became a well-known wine producer. As he had a long Italian name that was difficult to pronounce in German, he changed it to Kommenda, which he spelled with a K.

That is how I thought I might have acquired an Etruscan great-great-grandfather.

Farewell to my Father 1955

Like other summers, we went to visit my parents in 1955. It was a pleasant week and this time the weather was perfect throughout. Every day we drove a few miles up one of the mountain roads and went for a hike in the forest or above the tree line. I enjoyed plodding along with my father and it reminded me of the times before I had been sent to school. My father, it seemed to me, had not changed at all. He took the same gentle interest in the flowers and the beetles we came across. The only difference was that he no longer carried a camera. When he and my mother had come to Ireland before the war, he stepped out of his photographer's career and never shot another picture. I often wondered how it was possible that he never showed the slightest regret.

On these walks above Château d'Oex, I usually kept up with my father while Isabel and Sandra walked with my mother. One day I asked him whether he didn't feel an itch sometimes to look through a view finder and press a shutter.

"No," he said, "when I think of a camera I see things the way they looked through my 'putting-off' glass—do you remember?"

I had forgotten about that, but now it came back. He used to carry a small beveled square of blue glass in his pocket. When he was hesitant about something he saw, he took the glass out and viewed the scene through it. The blue glass made everything look drab and uninteresting. He saved a lot of film that way.

After a while I said:

"You know, these days when I am writing bits and pieces every day, I'm doing something I learned from you without knowing. Now that you have reminded me, I realize that the way I scan the things I have to write about is very much like your blue glass method. But that's not all. I think I also learned from the way you speak that stories get better with the things you don't tell."

He looked at the distant mountains with a rare expression of contentment. Then he turned to me with a smile:

"Are you sure you didn't learn that by yourself?"

* * *

In November of that year my mother called and told us that he had suddenly died. It was a shock, because he had seemed so sturdy and well in the summer. But I thought how much worse I would feel if we hadn't had that little conversation.

Ischia 1956

"How come you called your dog Angelo? I didn't think you had much faith in angels?"

"I don't," said Hanna. "It was to remember Angelo Poliziano, my favorite Renaissance man. In case you don't know, he was a friend of Lorenzo il Magnifico, was chosen as the tutor of Lorenzo's son, and became famous for his poetry, his Latin translation of the *Iliad*, and acute observations about classical authors that were later considered the foundation of scientific philology. Like many other great thinkers, he has been pretty much disregarded by today's teachers. Your lesson for the day!"

"Hanna, I can't tell you how delighted we are that you are coming with us on the trip to Ischia," said Isabel. "we'll discover treasures that we didn't even know existed!"

We were getting into my car in front of Hanna's home in Florence. My car was a Fiat 600, the smallest four-seater that existed, with an engine in the back. Isabel and I had managed to put all our things in the boot in front and Hanna placed her large, almost spherical duffle bag on the back seat beside herself. When Angelo jumped up on her lap, she very decisively put him on top of the duffle bag and told him to stay there. He was a middle-aged, silver-grey Sealyham terrier with impeccable manners. His eyes — or rather what you could see of them through the fringe that hung over them — could look unbelievably soulful at times and wickedly knowing at others. He always seemed to grasp what Hanna wanted before she said it. On the entire trip, which took us four days because we were stopping to look at all the places that Hanna recommended, Angelo kept to his patch behind my head. It was the beginning of July and getting hot and we had the windows rolled down in both doors. For the first hour Angelo stretched his head out the window, but then he got tired of the rush of air. He inched forward a bit and rested his chin on my right shoulder. I was flattered by this demonstration of trust and patted his head with my hand. He acknowledged it with a deep sigh and relaxed. After half an hour I began to feel the weight of his head, and when we stopped for lunch, there was a wet patch on my shoulder, his sweat and mine.

The first night we were going to spend in Rome and Hanna guided me to the place where she always stayed on her visits to the city. It was not really a hotel but a trattoria with four or five rooms. She had booked a room for us ahead of time and saved us the trouble of going to a tourist place that would have cost infinitely more. It was simple but clean and friendly. The couple that ran it treated Hanna as though she were part of their family. Hanna asked the woman whether she could use their phone and disappeared into the back of the house, while we were shown to our room. We had barely opened our suitcase, when Hanna knocked at our door.

"I hope you don't mind," she said, "but we've been invited to dinner with friends of mine."

"We, too?" I asked, "Isn't that unusual?"

"They are unusually nice people—and you'll love the pictures they have."

I managed to find a parking place not too far from the house Hanna was taking us to. We climbed two floors and Hanna rang the bell at a sumptuous wooden door. There was no elevator, but it was clearly a very desirable place to live. A spic and span maid opened the door and led us through a sliding wrought iron gate that would have stopped any burglar who might have managed to break down the outer door. We stood in a large hall that was lit by lights trained on paintings. Facing us was a large rectangular canvas, a scene on the San Marco Square in Venice.

Isabel looked at me with her eyebrows going up.

"Is that what I think it is?" she said to Hanna.

"You bet!" Hanna said, and then she turned to greet the lady of the house who had come swishing along a corridor. She told her our names and added: "They are the right sort, they instantly recognized your Canaletto."

Our hostess smiled and shook hands with us and Isabel explained that we were on our way to a holiday on Ischia and were not dressed for a formal visit.

"Good God," she said, "don't worry! We're never really formal—and certainly not when Hanna is here. She always says the most outrageous things!"

The Contessa Bondone was a good looking woman in her sixties, slim and sprightly and with a tinkling laugh that was perhaps a trifle too ready. She took us to the dining room and explained that her husband—"as so often"—was away on business. Hanna had explained to us that he was what she called a power broker in Roman politics and had great influence because of his personal connections. He carefully avoided an official position himself. He could not, he apparently said, keep up with the rapid changes of direction in Italian politics. It was for him that Hanna had been scouting around for pictures. She certainly had done a great job. The dining room was devoted to the Venetian mannerist painter Magnasco. There were three beautiful little landscapes of his. We had never seen so much of his work together.

"How did you manage to find them?" Isabel asked, "there cannot be many of them lying about since he was discovered in the twenties?"

"We thank Hanna for all that", said the Contessa.

And Hanna explained:

"I spent a whole summer before the war, digging about in the crumbling villas of the Venetian hinterland and though I didn't make millions, like Berenson in Tuscany, it provided me with a reasonable basis."

We had a very pleasant dinner. We talked about the Venetian painters and I mentioned Giorgione's Madonna at Castelfranco as one of my favorites. Why? asked the Contessa, and I answered that I thought it was the most beautiful portrait of a painter's lover. The contessa was obviously puzzled and I explained:

"I owe this to our friend Benno Geiger, the man who helped a lot in the discovery of your favorite, Magnasco. He told us that on the back of the Madonna at Castelfranco there was a ditty that earned her the nickname *Amorosa*:

Vieni, o Cecilia,	Come, oh Cecilia,
Vieni, t'affretta	Come and don't tarry,
Il tuo t'aspetta,	Yours is waiting,
Giorgio	Giorgio

I was enchanted with the idea that Giorgione saw his lover as the mother of God."

* * *

The trip to Naples was hot and our enthusiasm for all the treasures of unpublicized art that Hanna was ready to show us diminished rapidly. We had deliberately not taken the direct route along the coast but gone inland to the Abruzzi, hoping that it would be relatively cool in the mountains. But it was not, and the going on the small provincial roads was slow. Angelo and I sweated a great deal, and we were all glad when we could finally turn down to the sea and the port of Naples.

"Too bad we're not getting further south in the hills here," Hanna said. "There's a village above Sorrento with a Romanesque church that has a Madonna in it that is really a Greek sculpture of Ceres from about 200 BC. A farmer must have plowed it up in the Middle Ages and because their church was poor and had no decorations, they painted proper clothes on Ceres and adopted her."

The early Christians were practical people. When they built a cathedral in Syracuse, they used a Greek temple. One can still see bulges, both inside and outside on the walls of the main nave, where the temple's columns are. I always thought it symbolic of two opposite attitudes: the Greeks, open to the world of sensory experience, the Christians, afraid to look at it.

We found our way to the docks and I enquired where I might find the ferry that would take us and the car to Ischia. When we came to the place I had been told, I thought I must have misunderstood. There were two boats, not much larger than those we had rowed in on Lake Garda, with a small cabin at their stern. One of the men who had been sitting on the quay came to the car before I had got out.

"Ischia?" he said, turning it into a question, and I nodded, "But we want to take the car, too!"

"No problem," he said, "three people and the car." Then he laughed and added: "And that includes the dog."

I looked at the boat and then at the car and shook my head.

"Don't worry, we do it every day. Your car is like a bicycle. Yesterday we took a minibus with six people! They'll show you a picture in the office where you have to pay." And he pointed to a doorway. Above it there was a board saying *Traghetto per Ischia*, which does indeed mean "Ferry to Ischia".

I saw the picture, but I still was profoundly worried, especially about getting the car on the boat. As it turned out, it was quite easy. A kind of platform was fixed to the back half of the boat, extending a good three feet on either side, and another, smaller one was laid from the quay to it.

"You can leave everything in the car," said the man and got into it. As he carefully inched it on to the boat, I saw it dive into the Mediterranean. Angelo stood between Hanna and myself and was, I think just as worried as I. For four days the car had been his second home and he felt he was losing it. When it all had gone without a hitch and we were asked to step into the boat, he was reluctant to be picked up by Hanna—but what can a dog do? Which was very much what I thought.

In fact, it was a gentle ride of two hours, putt-putting along under a serene sky and on a gentle sea, watching the old volcano on the island come nearer and nearer until we could discern the little town and the harbor of Porto d'Ischia at its foot.

We stayed the night with Hanna in the house she had rented from an architect friend. After dinner, sipping the light white wine that came from the slopes of Epomeo, the old volcano, Hanna told us about the house. It had been built for Arthur Koestler at a time when he was in love with a woman, who, like him, was well below average height. Apparently he had quite a fixation about his lack of stature and insisted on having the doors in the house some six inches lower than usual. The architect was not pleased, but Koestler insisted. It was unfortunate, indeed, because Koestler and his friend separated before the house was quite finished, and he no longer had any desire to live on Ischia. After months of haggling, the architect was left with the property instead of being paid. He still had not got round to altering the doors.

The next day, we got into our car and drove to Forìo, a fishing village, where we had been told it was easy to rent a room in a fisherman's house. There was no hotel and Forìo had not yet been discovered by tourists; but it had a number of famous summer residents.

Like any decent village, it had a small intimate square, covered in part by the metal tables of the only café. Maria, the owner, was the matriarch of the village. She knew where everyone was and could get you what you needed. Through her I got an appointment with the manager of the little bank—which I needed to arrange for some money to be transferred from the north. Maria gave you food and drink, and if a couple needed privacy for an hour or two during the day, she had a key in her apron that fitted a bedroom in a house on the other side of the square. Her "Ristorante" was a large room beside the bar and her menu just right for evenings after a long day on the beach: spaghetti, fish, and scampi, and such vegetables as the fishermen grew in their little gardens.

Only two of the half dozen foreigners who spent the summer at Forìo came to eat at Maria's. The most regular was a middle-aged American widow, who had inherited a fortune from her husband and used this out of the way fishing village as a hide-out. She shunned society because she could not walk without a stick. But when she heard us talking English, she took to us and told us that she had broken her ankle in such a way that she needed an operation. The surgeon had botched it and there was nothing more to be done about it. We thought it might have had something to do with the high alcohol content in her system. She drank like a fish and had a wicked tongue. She was accompanied by a very tall young man, who could have been her son. He smiled ingratiatingly, but we never heard him speak. She laughingly called him "my great Dane".

When, on the first evening she started to talk to us, a rather riotous group, whose every second word was "fuck", entered the Ristorante, she said quite loud enough to be heard:

"Ah, there's Mrs. Auden and her flopsy bunnies."

The group took no notice and settled round a large table which, as we later realized, was always reserved for them. Auden, she told us, used to pay the Atlantic fare for young men who were prepared to accompany him.

The other famous people kept very much to themselves and hardly ever appeared in the village. The villa at the northern end of the beach belonged to William Walton, the British composer, who shared it with Fred Ashton, the choreographer of the Saddlers Wells Ballet. When they were on the beach, there was always a very beautiful woman—a South American, our informer told us—who spread a big towel when Walton came out of the water, so that he could discreetly take off his wet bathing pants. Ashton went knee-deep into the water and splashed himself, but never went further out to swim. Isabel and I were much impressed by how this austere group managed to create an invisible barrier between themselves and the rest of life on the beach, which mostly consisted of the two of us. There was something in the way they moved that discouraged approach and made it quite clear that you were not to trespass on their domain.

The other celebrity was the writer Alberto Moravia, who must have been in the middle of writing a new novel because he never appeared in public. I ran into him a couple of times at the post office, where I collected our mail. But though he politely acknowledged my letting him go in first, he did not encourage further contact.

We did not mind social isolation. Sandra was with my mother in Switzerland and this was the first time in many years that we were quite by ourselves. We enjoyed this togetherness, went snorkeling in the clear water along the shore, where you could see savage morays pouncing on their prey a dozen feet down in a fairy landscape of colors and shapes; and in between we baked in the sun.

* * *

Our landlady told us that on the way up the Epomeo there was a hot spring that had been made to flow into a large rectangular concrete basin. People went there and immersed themselves, because it was reputed to cure rheumatism and all sorts of diseases. We had read about this, because a few months ago a partially broken Greek frieze had been dug up there. It showed Diana holding the hoof of her horse under a spring flowing over a rock. The morning we came to it, the mountain was deserted. We hadn't met anyone on the way up and there was no one to be seen anywhere. We decided that it would be quite safe to get into the basin, because the flow of water was strong and surely had washed out all germs in the course of the night. The water was really hot and there was enough of it flowing past you to give you a gentle massage. The idea of bathing in a spring that Diana had chosen to cure her horse was enchanting, and as we continued our climb up the dead volcano we felt decidedly healthier and stronger.

The feeling lasted, and when we came home to Meran after this perfect holiday we felt confident that we could take on whatever was to come after the folding of *Standpunkt*, which had been our only source of regular income.

The Montesi Mystery 1957

Venice is an enchanting city. There are no cars or motorcycles, only pedestrians. From April to October there are millions of these, and ninety percent of them are tourists. They crowd Saint Mark's Square and block the narrow lanes and bridges everywhere, taking photographs. Most of them are unsuitably dressed and too illiterate really to enjoy the many layers that make up this unique city. Dozens of small restaurants have adapted to the invaders and serve food and wine that no Venetian would touch.

During those months, Venice is a mixed pleasure; but from November to March it is still as it was in the Renaissance and before, quietly sensual and infinitely mysterious. I had the fortune of spending two weeks there in the winter of 1957 and during those two weeks I saw something that happens only every third or fourth year: it snowed all night and the next morning three inches of snow covered the city under a luminous blue sky. The effect was unbelievable. The glistening whiteness on the decorated upper edges of the façades, on the ledges across them, and on the window frames turned the palazzos into frosted dreams. I walked through a fairy landscape, from my little *pensione* on the Ripa dei Schiavoni to the Rialto, and when I crossed the bridge to get to the *tribunale,* the old court house, the snow had all but melted away.

What had brought me to Venice was an event that, too, had the aspect of unreality. It was the trial that had arisen out of the Montesi scandal, a

festival of conjectures that had been celebrated by the public and dili-
gently nourished by the press of all colors for well over three years.

In the spring of 1953 the dead body of a 21-year-old girl was found on
the beach at Tor Vaianica, some twenty kilometers from Ostia, the port of
Rome. Wilma Montesi came from a lower middle class family. Her uncle,
Zio Giuseppe, was a government employee who had an illegitimate child
by the sister of his fiancé and was known as a womanizer. Wilma had
gone out with him several times and he happened to have bought a train
ticket to Ostia on the day of her disappearance. But, like in a well-
constructed thriller, this suggestive piece of information did not become
known until the end of the trial four years later.

Wilma's death was at first attributed to an accident. The investigators
concluded that she had gone to Ostia to bathe her feet because her mother
had told her that sea water was good for the sore she had on her heel. Presumably she had slipped from wherever she was sitting or stumbled if she
was wading. Once in the water, she fainted and drowned. Case closed.

But it sprang open almost immediately. From Ostia to Tor Vaianica it is
quite a distance, and no one believed that currents could have conveyed
the body so far to then deposit it on the beach without underclothes.
Besides, when a thorough autopsy was made, it was announced that she
was dead before being thrown into the water and that no rash or lesion
was found on her heel. It also came out that she died a virgin.

The story was a challenge to invent intricate theories. In a country rife
with political resentments and profound dissatisfaction with a government which, people felt, was run by United States money and the Vatican,
it was not surprising that wild rumors began to circulate, rumors that
incriminated those in power.

The rumors became solid enough for official reaction when the illustrated weekly *Attualità* published a story according to which Piero
Piccioni, the son of a minister, had taken Wilma Montesi to a hunting
lodge that was managed by Ugo Montagna in the vicinity of Tor Vaianica.
The girl fell sick, fainted, and died, probably as the result of taking drugs.
Piccioni panicked, and Montagna came to the rescue by depositing the
corpse on the beach later that night and making sure that there would be
no serious inquiry about the death. Enough was known about Montagna
to make this seem plausible. He was a Sicilian, seemed to have millions
that no one knew where they came from, and had close relations with
prominent politicians and top persons in the Vatican. He sometimes used
the title *Marchese di San Bartolomeo*, but it was said that he probably
belonged to the slice of aristocracy created by King Victor Emmanuel at
the airport before flying into exile. This picturesque character also had an
intermittent mistress to whom he occasionally gave largish sums of

money. Anna Maria Caglio was the daughter of a respectable family in Milan and she was just then beginning to get sick of the intermittency. When she read the article in *Attualità*, she concluded that Montagna's millions could only come from drug traffic and she became suspicious of his unexplained activities. Bit by bit she reviewed and, it seems, adapted memories of what he had said and what she had heard, and when she was questioned in the course of the investigations of the Montesi murder, she became the main witness for the prosecution. Piccioni was accused of "deliberate homicide" (which is different from murder) and Montagna and Polito, the head of police in Rome, were arraigned for complicity.

Communist voices called the Cabinet of ministers "a collection of pimps and scoundrels" and it came to the point that the entire Left demanded the resignation of the government. When Rome's chief of police actually did resign, the "marchese" Montagna was reported to say: "This may be the end of the world!" This was instantly interpreted as a threat to reveal more damaging details of the government's and the Vatican's corruption. Even the two usually more reticent papers, Milan's *Corriere della Sera* and Turin's *La Stampa,* were driven to comment that it was a trial, not just of the accused, but of the post-war Italian Republic. Anna Maria Caglio became a heroine, was likened to Joan of Arc and called the "Black Swan" or the "Daughter of the Century". There was the sincere hope that her revelations would help to expose the Babylonian corruption of the powers in Rome and the expectation that the trial would restore some faith in the government.

I timed my visit to Venice so that I would catch the week of Caglio's appearance as witness. Mario Tiberi, the president of the court, looked like a nobleman of the 18th century and commanded instant authority. A glance from him was sufficient to curb any histrionics on the part of a counsel, a gesture would restore silence in the court room, and his smile helped timid witnesses to get over their nervousness. He had a presence that could not be disregarded and it was he and he alone who managed to maintain a minimum of decorum during a trial that was repeatedly threatening to turn into a farce.

The judge began his questioning by telling Anna Maria Caglio that she had made many statements that had nothing to do with the trial and that she must now focus on things connected with Wilma Montesi.

"When did Montagna mention her to you?"

Caglio wore a simple but certainly not cheap black dress. She did not hesitate and spoke quietly and with the accent of the self-conscious members of Milan 's café society. Montagna, she said, mentioned the name Montesi when the death of the girl was in the papers. Piero Piccioni was a scoundrel, he told her, he had had an accident. He, Montagna, had had nothing to do with it.

As a witness, Caglio was not the least bit nervous, and I was impressed. A cool cat, I thought to myself, I'd like to talk with her. After the proceedings at the Court House ended for the day, I made some inquiries. It was easy to find out that the Black Swan was staying at the Bauer-Grunwald. I bought a dozen very pretty roses and took them to the concierge at the hotel. I wrote "Best wishes!" on one of my visiting cards (in those days I still had engraved ones with just my name) and added a note that, as the correspondent of a Swiss weekly, I was asking her for the privilege of half an hour's conversation. Later that evening I would telephone to find out when it would suit her. I thought it was best not to suggest in any way that she could decline my request.

When I called, she had left a message with the concierge: she would see me the next day at four in the afternoon.

I actually had more than an hour with her, but in the end I still did not know what to believe. She seemed perfectly straightforward and uninhibited but gave me nothing really solid.

"I had the bad luck of falling in love with Montagna," she said, "and when you're in love with a man, you don't spend your time collecting evidence against him. When I became suspicious of some of his mysterious activities, I made the mistake of challenging him before I talked to anyone else. So all I have now are memories, and they don't seem to be worth very much in court."

Her memories, I thought, were rather malleable material and she seemed to adapt them as needed at the moment. As the examination continued, she got caught in serious contradictions.

The trial went on for another two months and, as I read the reports, it never got closer to facts than I had in my interview. There were all sorts of suggestions and colossal accusations, made not only by Anna Maria Caglio but also by a Jesuit priest and other apparently respectable people. But none of them produced anything that gave the prosecution solid ground to stand on. The suspicion about Zio Giuseppe never became more than a suspicion. In the end, Tiberi, the head of the judges, clearly irritated and dissatisfied, declared that the charges had to be dropped. The mystery about the death of Wilma Montesi was never resolved. The reputation of the politicians in Rome sank lower than it had ever been, because people thought, not without justification, that parts of the accusations had to be true.

The next year, when another scandal was occupying the press, I had a drink with an Italian colleague and we mentioned the Montesi Affair.

"Indeed," he said, "ever since then I've wanted to ask you: How did you manage to get that interview with the Caglio? She'd given a press conference earlier in Florence, she had released innumerable *memoriali*, but none of us could get near her during the trial."

"Well," I said, "what would you do if you wanted—something you've probably never done—to ask a girl for an innocent favor?"

He looked up to the ceiling, one of those common gestures of mild despair:

"Flowers, of course ... A journalist might offer her money. The fact is, you just aren't a professional!"

Avalanche 1957

On one of the holidays I took from the editorial office every spring, we went skiing into the Ötztal glaciers. By car we drove up to the end of the Schnalstal, some twenty miles from Meran and almost a thousand meters higher above sea level. From there, as several times before, we climbed about another two thousand meters to the Similaun Hütte, one of the oldest refuge huts of the Austrian Alpine Club. These "huts" were in fact run like very simple country inns. You could sleep there, take a shower, and get simple but excellent things to eat without bringing your own food. The clothes you had to take for a week in the high mountains and all the gear you needed—rope, ice pick, skis, and all that went with them—were a heavy enough load, especially if you were totally unfit after working a year at the typewriter. A couple of years before, a cable had been stretched from the Hütte down to the end of the little valley through which you approached. There you could put everything you didn't need for the last two hours of the climb into a wooden crate that was pulled up mechanically from above. It was a godsend; not only for the way up, but also for going home, because the way down from the hut was tricky and one didn't want to be loaded down with too heavy a rucksack.

It was the last week in April, and the four of us, Isabel, Sandra, our faithful skiing companion Cesare, and myself, had started out on a clear summer-like day, but when we reached the Similaun Hütte it was snowing thickly. The next morning it was still snowing and looked as though it would never end. The whiteness outside was impenetrable, and there was nothing we could do. In the afternoon we decided to move down the glacier to another Alpine Club establishment, the Samoar Hütte, which was much larger and more comfortable. It was an easy way, because you didn't have to see anything to find it — as long as you kept going downhill you had to arrive at the Samoar Hütte. I had done it many times and only had to watch that none of us ever lost sight of the others.

The first rule in the mountains is never to take any risks. Two days later I learned that risks could arise from one moment to the next. We had had another snow-bound day and then woke up to a cold, clear morning with all those beautiful peaks around us, looking as new and untouched as though they had been made during the night. The easiest and closest was the Kreuzspitze, which rose directly behind the Hütte. By eleven o'clock we had climbed three hours and were about one hour below the summit. Suddenly I noticed that it had become much warmer. The Föhn had come, that famous warm wind from the south, and the temperature had risen far above freezing point. I should have become aware of the change at once, but as the work of making the track had started me sweating earlier, I hadn't. I realized that with a foot of new, unsettled snow, it would be very foolish to go on. The new snow was bound to get heavier with the change of temperature and that meant that it might start slipping on the older layers. We quickly decided to get off the mountain and I chose what seemed the safest possible way down: keeping to the edges of slopes, where much of the new snow had been blown off by the wind. But there was one biggish slope we had to cross, because the edge we had been following down ended in rocks and we had to reach the other side.

"I'll cut across this slope at a reasonable angle," I said. "Wait until I'm on the other side. When I wave, you Sandra come at the same angle, just below my track. And then Isabel, again parallel just below Sandra's track, and finally Cesare."

I pushed off and went at a comfortable speed, looking up at the slope above me whenever I could, in case something was breaking there. I knew that if it did, it would come down as a "Schneebrett", which is a layer of snow moving as a whole and only slowly cracking and crinkling as it moves. With any luck you can get away from that sort of avalanche if it doesn't cascade over rocks. When I reached the other side, I waited for a moment. Nothing moved and my track did not close. So I waved, and Sandra came safely across and then the other two.

From there we had a relatively safe route and we lost no time skiing down to the Hütte. As we took off our skis, I looked up to the Kreuzspitze. Our tracks were neat and clearly visible in the midday sun except for the diagonal ones crossing the slope — the Schneebrett had come down after all and swept them away. It could not have been more than a few minutes after we were there.

"Why did you make us go in parallel tracks?" asked Cesare, "I would have thought that's more dangerous than just making one track."

"Well, one could argue about this for a long time. I think that once there's a cut through the slope, a second one below it makes little difference. But I had another reason. If Sandra had come in my track, her skis would have run much faster and, to slow down, she would have had to get out of the track and make a new one above mine, which would have carried her much further up the slope. I wanted to avoid that. Board avalanches may be tripped in two ways: a track across the slope may rob the layer of snow above it of its support, in which case the upper half of the slope will begin to slide down. That is what we didn't want to happen. The other possibility is that the track cuts the cohesion of the snow below it with what is above, and then the lower half of the slope will take off, which would probably not have worried us at all."

I had once seen this happen to a friend of mine before the war. He was leading and making the track as we were climbing. Having reached a kind of shoulder, we could either follow that shoulder straight up and then cross above the slope to the point we were aiming at, or we could cross the slope at a comfortable angle and get there directly. He chose the second way and started into the slope. He had gone barely ten meters when we heard that soft ominous sound that makes a mountain skier's marrow curdle. It's a hollow kind of plop, like one heavy cushion falling on another. It's horrifying only if you know what it means. It means that a whole layer of snow is settling a quarter of an inch. In a more or less flat hollow, it feels like a little earthquake; if it happens to be on a slope, it will begin to move. In our case, it was as though the carpet had been drawn from under my friend's feet. The carpet was the snow he had been standing on. A crack had quickly spread from the points of his skis to the other side of the slope and a thick layer of snow below it began to move. It did not move very fast, but it moved steadily and because the slope fortunately did not end in a precipice, the board avalanche came to a gentle stop in a hollow some fifty meters further down. My friend, who had lost his footing at the very start, had slid half the way down, until the slab of snow he had been standing on disintegrated under his weight. The layer of snow above the crack his track had caused had not budged and looked as though the cover of the slope had been cut from it with a knife.

When the four of us were having supper that evening in the Samoar Hütte, we noticed that the two men at the end of the table were speaking English. There weren't many other people and we could not help hearing what the two were saying. As I listened, I realized that the older man was an Austrian guide, the younger one was undoubtedly British. It became clear that they had made excursions together at previous occasions. At some point the guide asked the young man about his mother.

"She's fine," he answered, "she still lives in her cottage on the West coast of Ireland and goes to Dublin only for the first night of a play."

I couldn't have been surer who his mother was, if he had mentioned her name. There were not many women living in a cottage on the West coast who would go to first nights in Dublin—it had to be Da Barnett and we knew that she had had a son when she had been married to Lord de Ramsey.

I could not help smiling and said:

"You must be de Ramsey's son."

He was obviously startled.

I am," he said, and looked at me with raised eyebrows—as much as to ask, and who are you?

I said, "I hope you'll forgive me," and explained that Isabel and I had lived near Dublin during the war and had come to know Da Barnett because we were friends with Sheila Richards and Denis Johnson.

"We'll have to drink to the happy coincidence!" he said, and we began a long evening of Enzian schnaps and reminiscences.

He was very impressed when we told him that we had bicycled round the South of Ireland and visited his mother on our way up the western coast. It was a funny story. I remembered her cottage when we arrived for a couple nights in Galway. I found out her address, but no phone number was listed. So I cycled out the few miles to the cottage. It was late afternoon and no one answered the doorbell. I left my visiting card and the name of the hotel we were staying at. The next morning there was a message inviting us to tea.

"I don't think I ever knew your full name," your mother said, "I knew you as Isabel's husband. When I found your card last night and saw the name, I thought a U-boat commander had passed by."

We had a delightful evening and stayed up much too late. De Ramsey did not mind, because they were on the way down to Sölden and it didn't matter when they left the hut the next morning. We much regretted this because we would have liked to make an excursion together. But he said he had to get back to London.

We felt a little jaded the next morning and went to the Hauslabkogel, an easy two and a half hour climb. On the way down we had another surprise. The last slope before you reached the bottom of the valley was a lovely one. You could make as many turns as you liked and then take it straight for the run home to the Samoar hut. I took the last quarter of the slope straight and came out into the flat with a certain speed. Suddenly my skis stopped and I fell forward, straight on my face. There was a run of melting water under the surface of the snow and it stopped you as though you had hit a patch of sand. I got up and frantically waved to warn the others. They were so pleased to see me fall at last, that it never occurred to them that I was trying to tell them something. One after the other they came to the same spot and fell on their faces. No one hurt anything and we laughed a lot about our wet pants and prepared for the Hüttenwart's question, where we had taken a bath.

Federico Fellini 1958

Rome, Fontana di Trevi, one hour after midnight. The Tramontana, the raw wind that descends from the Apennines, is blowing through the city once more in this April that seems to be unable to get rid of winter. A glittering spray of water covers the brightly lit marble landscape that forms the heroic background of the large, semicircular basin of the fountain. Spectators, hundreds of them on the narrow old piazza in front of the fountain, are squeezed between the stands of spotlights and hugging their overcoats.

"Let's shoot it!" says the director, barely raising his voice, and silence spreads around him. He creeps from behind the camera to let the camera man take the seat at the view-finder. While the technicians get ready for their routines, he slowly paces up and down, a giant of more than six feet, his wide-brimmed black hat pressed low on his forehead and his chin buried in the woolen scarf around his neck. His face is in the shadow, only his large attentive eyes catch a spark of reflected light. As the take begins, he straightens up, tilts his head a little and pushes back his hat. His face is now in the reflected light from the illuminated fountain and it shows that he is living through every detail of the scene that is being played.

Anita Ekberg, the Swede with the golden mane, steps like a true daughter of the Rhine into the basin and wades, up to her hips in the water, towards the glittering cascade. The temperature of the water may be a little above 40 degrees [Farenheit] — the spectators shiver and their heads creep lower into the turned-up collars of their coats. Alone the director smiles as though he actually felt the sensual touch of tepid water. And what the blond woman in the shoulderless evening gown enacts is indeed the thoughtless exhilaration of a hot summer's night. Even her partner, Marcello Mastroianni, who, given his southern background, is hardly used to cold water, finds unsuspected reserves of self-control after the

first shock, forgets his goose-flesh, and splashes almost as gaily and uninhibited as the Nordic Anita in the icy water.

The lips of the director mouth every word of the dialogue spoken by the
actors; his shoulders, his arms, and his hands indicate their movements
and actions much as a conductor shapes the sounds that issue from the
orchestra. Suddenly he interrupts the scene. With a couple of steps he is at
the edge of the fountain and … No, he does not go further. At his first film
he might well have stepped in the water himself, to demonstrate what he
wants the actors to do; and the telling point is that his collaborators would
not be at all surprised if he did it today.

"I have worked with quite a few directors," a woman of the team said to
me afterwards, "but for none of them would arrived actors have taken
such an icy bath."

"Why do they do it for Fellini?"

"Indeed, why? We are all asking ourselves that question. He has, of
course, his very own charm — and he never screams at people …"

"Except about ridiculous, trivial things," the assistant director interrupts, "and no one takes that seriously, because we all know that it's just a
way of relaxing."

"… but charm and patience is something others have, too. That's not it. I
think it is because everyone feels that Fellini's work makes sense and that
is the reason why he will not make any compromises. It is something so
rare in the movie world that you can't help getting enthusiastic about it."

The film Federico Fellini is making at the moment is good evidence for
the author/director's independence and consistence. La Dolce Vita (the
title is not easy to translate, because it intends something between the
sweet and the heedless) is to be a mosaic of postwar society, a society that
tries superficially to overcome the shock of two world wars by surrender-
ing to an unbounded euphoria. It deals with a subject that, in spite of
Fellini's recent worldwide successes, was rejected by a dozen producers.

"Love, work, catastrophes, ecstasies — is there anyone today for whom
they have a deeper meaning? One lives on the surface, in the foreground
and one takes great care not to turn one's head; the background is apoca-
lyptic and under the sweet, heedless life gapes a vast emptiness."

In the conversations we had during whatever pauses there were, Fellini
more than once returned to this point.

"Don't misunderstand me, I am not criticizing, I am not starting a
polemic, I merely show the dolce vita as I see it: pleasant, enchanting, decorative, and noncommittal. But here and there are cracks in the smooth
surface and the emptiness seeps in. And this emptiness is not altogether
negative — it is also a waiting, an indefinite waiting. One might say, it's a
religious matter."

"And what would have to happen to shake our society out of its stupor?"

Fellini looks at me in surprise. Apparently he forgot that I was there and talked to himself. A friendly, benevolent smile spreads over his face and in his dark, always observant eyes there is a flicker of irony.

"It seems that I have again said more than I should. I am not a revolutionary and I do not moralize. I merely try to show life as it is—it has to speak for itself."

"But apart from the film, in the life you actually live, in politics ..."

He cuts short my question by exaggerating one of those Roman gestures: he hunches his shoulders, lowers his eyelids, and pulls down the corners of his mouth: "I?—how would I know about that? I am myself in the middle of the dolce vita!"

Speaking with Fellini, one quickly realizes that he does not consider films a weapon but exclusively as artistic expression. Much as he avoids putting his most essential fundamental ideas in words, he endeavors to build his films on the visual and to eschew anything literary.

"Films are a more complex but also a more complete language than literature. Don't take this as a judgment of value. It's a technical observation. A writer may go to New York for three months and write a novel that takes place there. He can make do with a small selection of characteristic ideas and aspects. A film, in contrast, consists of images, and in images the characteristics can hardly ever be reduced to a few. If I show an American, it is not sufficient that he wears American shoes—he has to wear shoes that are characteristic for a certain type of American; he has to have his tie knotted in a certain typically American way, and he has to use certain specifically American words. In short, he has to be characteristic in every conceivable way. In order to get all that right for a particular country, you have to have lived there all your life. My 39 years in Italy are often not enough for me to be certain."

Fellini's focus on the visual, on what he himself has seen, is no accident. He started his artistic career as cartoonist for *Marc'Aurelio*, a weekly of cartoons and satire. As graphic artist and journalist he managed to get through the years of war without ever taking a weapon in his hands. After the liberation of Rome, he and a friend opened a little shop in the Via Nazionale, where allied soldiers could get either a portrait or a caricature of themselves. His radio program "Federico e Pallina", which for the first time made him known to a wider public, also consisted of caricature-like sketches in which he developed the tragicomical character that was later played by his wife Giulietta Masina in *La Strada* and *Le notti di Cabiria*. His first film was *Luci del Varietá* (Footlights of Vaudeville) made in collaboration with Latuada; and then came the first film of his own, *The White Sheik*, again a caricature, a satire about the heroes of American comic strips.

"Almost every frame in his films is autobiographical, something that he has lived through or at least witnessed," explains Guidi, Fellini's faithful assistant. "He has an album of impressions in his head which he pulls out when he needs them. And he's constantly collecting more. He is interested in everything and wants to know everything — his curiosity is without limits. If two blocks away from here there should be a car accident, he would run there to see how it happened and why. If I tell him that our janitor's wife has a dog, he wants to know what the dog looks like and what they feed it. He's not particularly interested in cars or dogs, but one day he might make a film in which someone gets run over by a car or a janitor's dog has to be fed."

For a similar reason, Fellini works as little as possible in a studio. If it's at all possible, he shoots his film on location. If the script requires an apartment, Fellini does not, as do most directors, get an architect of Cinecitta to build one, but he goes and looks for one in the proper quarter of town. This, of course, is mostly cheaper, but that is not his main reason.

"A good architect and I, we could build many of the characteristic things we need into an apartment, but, you see, in a genuine one I always find things that neither the architect nor I would have thought of. Often they are little things, but sometimes they are big surprises that throw an altogether different light on the scene. In all cases they are stimulating, lead to new ideas and above all away from the artificial and from the cliché."

His collaborators confirm it. Working with Fellini, they say, is always an expedition into the unknown, a continuous improvising in which, however, the ultimate goal is very well defined. Fellini spends many months of meticulous work on his scripts. Each scene and each shot is sketched out. At the moment of realization he tends to stick with the script, but the particulars that establish the individual characteristics of the scene are improvised from step to step.

These particulars are the stuff with which Fellini builds his worlds. He strings them together without forcing or distorting them, so that the viewer has at first the impression of random accidents; but after a while they coalesce into a panorama. The unshakable belief in mankind and an unprejudiced humanity are natural and unforced in Fellini's work. In the murky, the somber, even in the murderous mechanics of everyday life he spots human aspects and uncovers glimpses of joie de vivre and heart, where no one suspected them. The stark realism of his presentation thus merges with the fairytale. And hand in hand with this affection for the wondrous reality of human life goes the hatred of pretence and hypocrisy and all that is pharisaic.[1]

---

1   Published in the Swiss weekly *Die Weltwoche* on May 29, 1959.

Chapter Five

1959–1966

The First Research Contract 1959

Shortly after the foundation of the Centro di Cibernetica at the University of Milan, Ceccato went to a Congress on communication and language in London and met Colin Cherry, one of the foremost experts on communication theory. Cherry took some interest in Ceccato's ideas and told him that he would have difficulties getting them accepted if he did not show some practical applications. The best chance he had was the area of machine translation which was becoming fashionable at the time. The Americans, Cherry said, had lots of money for translation research because they desperately needed translators of Russian scientific journals. He suggested that Ceccato send a proposal to the research centers of the US Air Force or Navy.

As I later realized, this was one of the very few occasions where Ceccato followed someone else's advice. He drafted a proposal and asked me to come to Milan in order to prepare an English translation. It was a good thing that, thanks to the translations for *Methodos*, I had some experience with Ceccato's style, because translating his ideas into English was a tricky affair. He constantly invented new Italian expressions and one had to try to make them comprehensible in English.

It was, I think, something of a miracle that his proposal was accepted after some to and fro correspondence with an Air Force research office. The reason was that Ceccato's submission came at the very moment when projects based on traditional language theory had failed and the new gospel of Chomsky's transformational grammar had not yet spread. Two years later, an approach that started from semantics rather than syntax would not have had the slightest chance, in spite of the fact that the syntactic attempts at translation were not yielding any successes at all.

What also surprised me was that in all the correspondence that settled the number of employees, their salaries and working hours, as well as details about the location, access to computers, and the exact extent of the project, there was no request for a professional evaluation of the people who were to do the research. The project was to produce a method of mechanical translation from Russian into English, but the positions for Russian speakers were left open.

The first task, therefore, was to find persons who spoke Russian as well as English and seemed to have a certain talent for semantic analysis. That is to say, they had to have some skill in pinning down the meaning of words, a skill that is not spread very wide. I was sent to Vienna to hunt for someone at the universities there. After three days I was put in touch with a young man who was fluent in Russian and German and also knew a little English. I tried to discover to what extent his linguistic knowledge was conscious. He seemed to be quite good at dissecting meanings, but a short interview is hardly sufficient to form a solid opinion. The young man seemed enthusiastic and was very willing to come to Milan for a month's trial. When he arrived, however, we quickly realized that his enthusiasm was due to the salary he was to receive rather than a fascination with semantic analysis. We had to send him back before the trial month ended.

In the meantime Ceccato, through acquaintances, had got to know a lady who had spent her early life in Russia, was now fluent in Italian and also knew some English. Her name was Elsa and when she came for a couple of days to find out what she would have to do, we saw that she had an excellent feel for the subtle differences between word meanings that bilingual dictionaries would usually give as the same. She was willing to take the job and her work was highly satisfactory all through the duration of the project.

One Russian analyst, however, was not sufficient for the amount of work that had to be done, and after several futile attempts a German professor sent us Sergej, a student who had grown up with both Russian and German and had precisely the sort of mind we needed. After a few months at the Centro, where Italian and English were constantly spoken, he had picked up an astonishing amount of both. So we now had two experts for Russian—but not without a hitch. Elsa's Russian was that of society in pre-revolution St.Petersburg. Sergej belonged to the postwar generation. The difference of language was considerable and our Russian experts consequently quite often had difficulties agreeing on the interpretations of meaning. This created trouble for me, who had to translate what they came up with into English. But at the end of the first year we gained another helper who was always able to level the differences between the two others. I don't remember how he came to us. He had Russian and English from childhood and was a student in London. His name was Nicholas Pasternak and he was a cousin of the writer. He was cultivated, sure of himself, and, though he did not take anyone at the Centro di Cibernetica very seriously, he became an excellent collaborator.

Before his arrival it had become clear that even two Russians were producing more analyses than I could transfer into English by myself. Margaret Masterman, who directed a similar research project at Cambridge University, sent us eventually a student who, as she said, was ideal for the work we were doing.

I have never forgotten the day of Jehane Burns' arrival. Ceccato and his permanent assistant Bruna Zonta, a Latinist who was always the last resort for us when we had questions of grammar, happened to have come in our "Language-Room" and we were having a fierce debate about something or other. The door opened, and in came a slender apparition in a plain black dress, a broad-rimmed Quaker's hat on her head and a black attaché case under her arm. A ghost could not have created more of surprise. Even Ceccato was speechless for a moment. But as the apparition was recognizably female, he recovered himself quickly and greeted her with the charm that so many girls found irresistible.

Ceccato's gallantry had a different effect on Jehane. Although she quickly learned to appreciate his exceptional intelligence, she never took him seriously as a man. This apparently had never happened to him, and it took several weeks before he gave up treating her as a possible female. After that, in a sexless world, they got on quite well with each other.

For me, Jehane became the most precious collaborator I could have wished for. Her sense for language and the formation of concepts, her literary knowledge, and her cool openness with regard to philosophical questions were the best testing ground I ever had. In addition, her father, a very successful engineer, who was considered a pioneer in the area of die-casting industry, had introduced her to the theories of mechanics, so that she had none of the prejudices against computers which, at that time, were still current among linguists. She was the ideal colleague, attentive, tactful, and always ready vigorously to defend her own opinion. I am immensely grateful to her that she later agreed to collaborate in my own projects in Milan and in the United States.

A Poet's Daughter 1959

The slopes on either side of the Etschtal, the valley of the river that is called Adige in Italian, are spattered with castles all the sixty miles from Meran down to Verona. Many of them are spectacular ruins on inaccessible spurs, built in the late middle ages by robber barons who shared the spoils from attacks on the merchants who moved north on the only relatively easy way through the Alps. The barons used mirrors to signal to each other and to coordinate their ambushes. It was apparently a pleasant, if somewhat rugged way of life.

On a shelf of the steep slope rising north of Meran, there is Schloss Tyrol, the seat of the counts who owned the county and built the castle in the 13th century. It is well preserved and today contains an extensive museum. Halfway down the slope is an edifice of a different nature. Also built as a castle centuries ago, it was razed to the ground and rebuilt several times, the last time by a rich German before the First World War, who had the intention of turning it into a stronghold of the Freemasons. He also had an uncanny prescience of what Walt Disney was going to do to the concept of castle. The place was called Brunnenburg and he turned it into a strange concoction of slender turrets, steep gables, and perilous balconies, a vision of fairyland, not the kind of place you would want to defend if you were besieged. His money ran out before it was finished and it joined the many ruins that were owned by the county. After years of dereliction it was bought by the de Rachewiltz family.

Around 1950 we met Boris de Rachewiltz and his wife Mary, with whom we quickly became friends. Boris was a somewhat elusive man of many parts. He was known as an Egyptologist, had written an illustrated book about the sex life of the Sudanese. After he and Mary had restored and made partially habitable the Brunnenburg, he created and directed the Order of Canossa, a name that had many links to the middle ages and was able to attract Italian business men searching for social standing. We did not have much contact with Boris, but saw quite a lot of Mary. She was the daughter of Olga Rudge, a very successful concert violinist with whom Ezra Pound had a close relationship that lasted until his death. They met while Pound lived in Paris, but Mary was born in Brixen, a little town in the eastern South Tyrol. Because neither parent felt able to cope with a baby, they left her as foster child with a peasant family in Gais, an hour's walk up a little valley from Bruneck. Two or three times a year they visited her or took her to Venice, where they lived for some time, but in practice her parents were the peasant couple, who treated her as their own and from whom she learnt their Tyrolean dialect before she acquired standard German and Italian. In her mid teens she was sent to a boarding school in Florence, where she learned French and perfected her two languages and also English, bits of which she had picked up earlier from her father.

When we knew her in Meran, we did not know any of this history. She was a gentle, unpretentious, and altogether loveable person, who had an immense knowledge of English and European literature and a winning way of talking about it. The only background she ever mentioned was her parents life with literary friends and artists in Venice. She often spoke of her father and created the impression that he was an infinitely wise, benign man — quite unlike what he was reputed to be. We got no inkling that she had grown up on a mountain farm and was a native speaker of the local Tyrolean dialect.

In 1958, when, after thirteen years in an asylum in Washington, Ezra Pound was released and expelled to Italy, he came to stay for a short while with Mary at the Brunnenburg. One day we were invited to tea and I was looking forward to hearing what he had to say about his days in Paris and his friendship with Hemingway. We had been sitting in the living room for a little while when he came in. He barely grunted something when we were introduced and lowered himself into the chair that had been waiting for him. He looked like the portrait I had seen in a newspaper: A tight-lipped mouth in a wilderness of scrub and a pair of piercing eyes, so fierce that you expected a wisp of smoke to rise from what they focused on.

"These are not my cookies," he said taking one and leaning back in his chair.

Mary made conversation with us and tried to involve him, but he did not respond. When I got a chance I turned to him and asked about Hemingway and Joyce in Paris. His death-ray eyes turned on me and he muttered:

"They called us Hem and Ez."

A dry snort followed, and that was all he uttered that afternoon. On the way home we wondered how Mary managed to bear with him.

* * *

Now, fifty years later, I have begun to understand. Having seen a recent photograph of the Brunnenburg that did not at all match my memory, I searched on the Internet and found that it was completely restructured in the 1970s and now houses the Ezra Pound Center for Literature. In the course of further exploration I came across Mary's book *Discretions* and ordered it. It is an unusual and thoroughly charming memoir, published in 1971 under her married name, Mary de Rachewiltz. It is unusual because it contains words and sometimes passages not only in German, Italian and French but also snatches of phonetically transcribed Tyrolean dialect and some of them are not translated. Readers, therefore, will encounter difficulties. Although my knowledge of the mountain peasants' dialect in the South Tyrol is somewhat limited, I felt privileged understanding practically everything.

"Discretion" is a complex word. It can mean thoughtfulness, circumspection, carefulness, judgment, as well as reticence. It's choice as title shows the profound knowledge of English Mary had acquired alongside the mastery of her two earlier languages, German and Italian: all the meanings of "discretion" are manifested in her writing. On the surface, the book is a remarkable document of the human adolescent's power quickly to acquire several languages and to grow into cultures as different as that of mountain peasants and intellectuals of the Western civilization. Underneath it is a moving document of an extraordinary mind that was capable of neutralizing staggering contrasts in the construction of her world. The mere fact of growing up with two sets of parents, radically different except for their affection, but both visible, tangible and active as sources of often incompatible experiences, would have been enough to send most children into some form of neurosis. But Mary's adult persona showed no scars and what she wrote in her memoir indicated no trauma.

Not that there are not traces of melancholy in her writing, but she had an extraordinary capability of dealing with the incompatible. To adapt, after a childhood in a mountain village, to the social ambience of Venice and the bohème in Rome, to function in her late teens as nurse in a wartime hospital in Cortina, and above all to reconcile without resentment the spell of her father's genius with his anti-Semitism and fascist leanings, required a truly uncommon flexibility. Ezra Pound emerges from her description as a thoroughly honest man with an encyclopedic mind but also some incurable blind spots. His respect for Mussolini, for instance, was apparently never tarnished by the gruesome invasion of Abyssinia. But the account Mary gives of her life makes clear that it was not lack of discernment, but a depth of good sense and a fundamental equanimity, rare indeed among humans, that allowed her to keep her balance.

After my own seven years as a farmer in the Wicklow hills, I would like to think that it was the years before her teens, spent shepherding sheep on the slopes around the mountain village of Gais, that gave the unruly poet's daughter her infinitely benign attitude towards life.

Dottore and Mehitabel 1959

When Mehitabel had been with us for a couple of years, a friend came to have tea with us and presented Sandra with a pitch-black poodle puppy. Although an enlargement of our family was not really what we had intended, once Sandra had seen the black puppy, we didn't have the heart to say no. It was supposed to be a small poodle, but it kept growing and growing and ended up a sturdy middle sized one. At first, Mehitabel was not at all pleased. But as Sandra carried the puppy about much of the day, she realized that she would have to put up with him and quickly began to teach him that he had to keep his distance. When he rushed at her in an attempt to play, she would give him a quick little smack with her paw, not too hard, but sufficient to discourage him. I don't think he ever understood that his form of play was considered uncouth by her, but in time he learned to restrain himself and to approach her slowly and with a certain circumspection.

When winter came and the stove in our apartment often seemed unable to produce sufficient heat, Mehitabel discovered that the poodle, who by then was larger than herself, provided more warmth than the stove. So the two took to sleeping together like an amorphous bundle of black fur. From then on they lived in perfect harmony, fed together, and both sat up on their haunches when Isabel had been whipping cream and let them lick the whisk.

I was working as a journalist during those years, and it was taken for granted in Italy that anyone writing professionally would have a doctorate. But as I did not have that qualification, I was always a little embarrassed when that title was attributed to me. So when we had to choose a name for the poodle, who indeed seemed to be quite intelligent, I suggested we call him "Dottore", so that at least one member of the family would have full right to that form of address. It had no consequences as long as we lived in the country in the South Tyrol. But this changed when we moved to Milan. The first time we took a walk in the streets of our neighborhood and called "Dottore", because he had run too far ahead, practically all the men in the street turned to see who had called them. Most of them laughed when they realized for whom it was intended, but some, I am sure, were shocked by such brazen blasphemy. From then on, the cars were not the only reason that made us keep Dottore on a leash when we took him out for a walk.

Dottore had very thick black fur. When it got hot in the summer, we used to trim it — not in poodle fashion but simply all over. Our efforts usually left him a little ragged and when we moved to Milan, this was not good enough. We had him professionally trimmed at a place within walking distance from our flat. Once every year he was taken there. To get to the place, one had to turn left half way down the street that led to the little park where we took Dottore when there was no time for a longer walk. The second time we took Dottore to be shorn, he began to pull on the leash as we approached the first crossing where we had to turn left. He desperately wanted to cross to the other side of the street. But I turned left, and he reluctantly followed. At the next block, we had to cross the street and turn right. Again he pulled to go straight, and it was quite a struggle to make him follow. The moment we reached the sidewalk, he sat down and looked at me with an unforgettable expression: Don't you realize, he seemed to say, that we don't want to go *there*?

Much later, at the University of Georgia, when I was introduced to animal psychology, I learned that it was unscientific to attribute intentions, values, or anything like reasoning to animals. Their behavior, Professor Skinner had declared, was determined by the environment and the histories of their reinforcement and was invariably the result of a particular organization of muscles. It took me some time to understand what was wrong with that notion. Then I remembered the experiences with Dottore, and it became clear that it was not only inadequate but, indeed, unscientific.

Dottore had obviously associated the unpleasant procedure of being shorn with the itinerary that led to it. But the way he manifested his aversion, the things he did to show us that he didn't want the procedure to be repeated, were forms of behavior that he could not have learned from the one experience at the particular place. He clearly had the capacity to categorize experiences as unpleasant and then to use avoidance maneuvers he had acquired elsewhere. In other words, he had certain values and tried to act on them in ways that were available to him. It is no advantage to science to deny the fact that on Dottore's scale of values, being shorn was at a low level and that he was able in some fashion to foresee that unpleasantness lay at the end of this particular itinerary.

If one said this to an animal psychologist, he would smile condescendingly and discard it as anthropomorphic fantasy. He would be profoundly shocked to hear that all his scientific models, from the theory of evolution to the behaviorist learning theory based on stimulus, response, and reinforcement, are no less human conceptual structures built on human experiences according to human ways of thinking. Whatever humans see, think, or plan is inevitably in the one form accessible to them, i.e. the human form.

Taxes in Milan 1959

While we lived in Ireland, I had no personal income and the only taxes due were paid by the farm. I don't know how it happened that in Meran, where I did receive a salary from the *Standpunkt*, I never received a tax bill. I also did not try to get one. I have always had rather strong socialist convictions and in principle had no objection against taxes. But knowing about the chronic disorganization of government affairs in Italy, I saw no reason why I should draw attention to the fact that I could be considered a prospective tax payer. The customary way was that they came to you, not you to them.

In Milan things were not quite as happy-go-lucky. The city had reduced its labor by splitting the tax problem in two. They farmed out the collection of taxes to a private firm that every year had to hand over an amount fixed according to the number of inhabitants; and what they collected over and above that amount they could keep as profit. The city provided the *finanzieri*, a sort of financial police as a stimulus for reluctant payers, and helped the firm to keep track of newcomers.

Not six months had passed after our arrival, when I got my first summons to the tax office. I did not really know what to expect and therefore was not unduly worried when I was shown into a waiting room half full of people. Every now and then a name would be called from a door at the end of the room, and someone would get up and disappear through it. As no one came back from there, I assumed that there was another exit, either into freedom or into prison. Eventually my name came up and I walked into a big room with a desk and the big man behind it pointed to the one chair in front of him . While opening a file, he said in a friendly almost fatherly way:

"How do you like Milan, Signor de Glasersfeld?"

Careful! I thought to myself and said:

"Well, I haven't been here very long, but it seems a nice place."

"You are a foreigner, are you not? But you have a job with the university, at the Center for . . .?"

He clearly wanted me to say it, because it was an unfamiliar word.

"Yes, the Center for Cybernetics."

"Right. And you are also a member of the Foreign Press Association," he said with a smile, "a second source of income."

I could hardly deny it and I told him quite truthfully that I wrote four feature articles a year for a Swiss weekly and received two hundred francs each for them.

"Do you really want me to believe that?" he said.

I told him that I could show him the bank slips and added that, as he could surely imagine, it was not very easy to live in Milan on so little, if you had a wife and a teenage daughter.

"I should have guessed you have four times as much; but you're a new Milanese and we'll let it pass. You'll get our bill in a few days. A rivederci, next year!"

The next year I came armed with bank balances and letters from my Swiss paper. After quite a struggle we managed to agree on a modest increase, which I could cover, because by then I was selling articles to other foreign papers as well, which, I made sure, were not reflected in my bank balances.

People were called to the tax office in alphabetic order and consequently you saw more or less the same faces there every year. I had noticed an elderly gentleman, whose name had a "de" before it and came just before mine. His clothes were remarkable. He wore the same jacket every time, a beautiful Scottish tweed, frayed at the cuffs and the button holes, almost transparent at the elbows, and so adapted to his bony shape that it seemed a second skin. His grey flannels, too, looked as though they had been worn for decades and on his feet he had the old boots of a farmer. One year I came to the waiting room a little early and took the seat beside him. He turned to me and said:

"You're not Italian, are you"?

I was startled, because he said it in perfect English. I told him I was not, but that I worked at the university.

"Ah," he said, "that explains it, you don't know the ways of our tax collectors. Your shoes look practically new!" And he explained to me that the clothes he was wearing were what he called his tax-outfit.

"They are like children," he said, "if they see anything new on you, they think you must have had some extra income. Do you know that they go to every first night at the Scala and note down what jewels the women are wearing? Then they compare their notes with those of previous years, and if there is anything new, they raise the taxes for the woman's companion, whether or not he's her husband."

Just then his name was called, and of course I paid more attention to it. I asked a friend if he knew who that was, and he did. It was the name of a count whose family owned a whole street in Milan ever since the days of Lodovico il Moro in the 15th century.

Closed Houses 1961

When the sale of my parents' house in Meran was finally concluded more than three years had passed since our first visit there after the war. The dentist and his family had moved out but it took quite some time before the lawyer who handled the sale for my father was able to find a buyer. In the meantime my mother had been there once more to select things she wanted to keep and had taken them with her to Château d'Oex. We now had the problem of getting rid of the furniture and what else was left. An acquaintance suggested that an auction would probably be the easiest way and she knew a Frau Schindel who did that sort of thing professionally.

Frau Schindel came, looked at everything and was enthusiastic.

"You have a fine lot of things," she said, "and you'll be surprised how well they are going to sell, especially the rubbish that's in the attic. For God's sake, don't throw anything away, not even broken things. We put all that into large boxes, call it 'mixed treasures', and you'll see how people will bid for it, even if none of it is any use."

Frau Schindel organized the auction with the zest of a general going into battle. At least two days, she said, there would have to be an open house for people to view things, and one had to watch that nothing was stolen. She had three daughters, and if we could supply two other guards, we should be able to manage.

It was a fortunate coincidence that Ruth Childers, the oldest of Erskine's children, who had the same name as her mother, was staying with us just at that time and was delighted to help with the preparations for the auction. Bit by bit we brought everything down from the attic and distributed it in different rooms. Frau Schindel instructed us how to arrange things "to their best advantage". She seemed particularly fond of china and always asked where it came from. I explained that as my parents had lived in Munich for many years, they had bought much from the manufactures of Nymphenburg and Rosenthal.

In a corner of the attic we found a dusty old trunk. We had some difficulty easing it down the steep ladder. When we opened it and unwrapped
the tissue paper of the parcels it contained, it revealed an astonishing collection of old-fashioned dresses, some of them obviously for formal evenings. Isabel instantly knew that they were from the years around 1910.

"Unbelievably elegant," she said, "look, there's even one from Jean
Patou!"

Evening clothes, Frau Schindel said, were eye catchers, and we should
spread them on separate hangers in the entrance hall. We followed her
advice, though we could not imagine that anyone would be interested in
the fashions of 1910.

The viewing days came and there was a guard in every room. Nevertheless two small objects were stolen. But the auction was so successful
that we quickly forgot about them. Everything was sold. The china that
Frau Schindel with great emphasis announced as "Nymphenthal und
Rosenburg" reached fantasy prices and the "mixed treasures" all found
enthusiastic buyers. What baffled us the most, however, was that none of
the antique dresses was left. I asked Frau Schindel who on earth could
have bought them.

"Well," she said with some hesitation, "I hope it won't offend you, they
were all bought by the brothel-keeper, the 'Puffmutter' of the *casa chiusa*."

The official name of the state-run brothels in Italy was *casa di tolleranza*,
house of tolerance or sanctioned houses, if you like; but in everyday language they were called *casa chiusa* — which always seemed absurd to me,
because I had noticed that, especially in southern Italian towns, the brothels were the only houses with the front door wide open in the middle of
the night.

* * *

When we had moved to Milan, we discovered that, quite close to where
we lived, there was on Saturdays the famous *Mercato di Senigallia*, a very
superior kind of flea market for tools and antiques. As our furnishings
were far from complete, we went there quite often. On one of our first visits I found an ashtray that was cast in a pretty golden bronze and had
along its edge a naked lady stretched alluringly on a wave. It was clearly
from the best period of *art nouveau* and certainly worth more than the man
would ask for it. As I gave him the money, he said he had two more that
were exactly the same. I asked what he wanted for all three and the price
he mentioned was too tempting to be refused. He went to a box behind his
stand and we bought the three of them.

"Did they all come from the same house?", I asked.

"Right," he said and laughed, "from the *casa chiusa!*"

A little earlier, Senator Lina Merlin, a heroine of the Italian resistance, had managed to get a law passed that abolished the state-brothels.

We often laughed about the exchange that had taken place: we sold my mother's evening clothes from the end of the *art nouveau* period to a brothel and then acquired our charming ashtrays from another brothel.

Our Manual Computer 1962

Although we were quite unaware of it, our American adventure began five years before our move, at the International Conference on Machine Translation of Languages and Applied Language Analysis 1961 in Teddington, a suburb of London.

Ceccato, the director of the Cybernetics Center in Milan, had been invited to present his work at the Teddington conference and he wisely decided to take along the two English-speakers of his team, Jehane and myself. Ceccato's French had been characterized as understandable only if you knew the Veneto dialect of Italian, and though he read English quite well he had been reluctantly convinced that he could not speak it. Jehane and I read a paper each and I presented Ceccato's paper and helped out in the discussion.

Harold Wooster, who was at the conference as observer for the Air Force Office of Scientific Research in Washington, which he directed, apparently became interested in our papers. To find out more about our work, he asked Jehane to have dinner with him one evening. After the conference she maintained contact with him and sent him whatever papers we wrote.

The American money that financed our work at the Center for Cybernetics came from an altogether different Air Force office and the contract terminated at the end of 1961. About a year later I received an RFP (request for a research proposal) from Wooster's office. I went to Ceccato, thinking that he would be delighted to have a chance to continue the work we had started, but after some hesitation he declined. This left me with a problem. As a private individual I could not administer a research project. If the Center for Cybernetics would not do it, I had to find some other institution. Fortunately Paolo Terzi, who ran the Institute for Engineering Information (IDAMI), had been a frequent visitor at our work place at the university and had become fascinated with the kind of language analysis we were doing. He was an engineer and had done some extraordinary things, among them the design of an airscrew for fighter planes that became the direct ancestor of the one used in the RAF's famous Spitfire. His most recent exploit was an automatic sorting system for punched cards that delivered them into a set of pre-established boxes. He jumped at the opportunity of housing a project in the area of cybernetics and we wrote a proposal for a system that would enable a computer to extract the meaning from English sentences. The project was to be administered by his institute. Jehane and I would do the language research and Terzi supplied Brunella, a young Italian who spoke English, as secretary/coordinator. We still needed a computer programmer and Terzi put me in touch with Pier Paolo Pisani, who directed the computer center of a large industry in Milan and who, he thought, might be able to suggest a suitable person to us.

When I met Pisani, I explained to him what we were hoping to do and showed him my notes about the procedure that would have to be programmed for a computer. My notes were sketchy and rather vague in some areas, but he at once got the drift and seemed fascinated.

"What sort of salary do you have in mind?" he asked and I told him what we had planned. "I'll see what I can do", he said, "and I'll let you know when I have something."

He called the next day and said:

"I would like to take the job myself, if that's all right with you."

I was flabbergasted. His salary as the director of a computer center had to be much larger than what we could offer (I later found out that the company had paid him almost four times as much). Of course he noticed my surprise and explained that he had been bored to tears by the tedious, repetitive things commercial outfits wanted from their computer and he was dying to get into something more challenging.

When the proposal was accepted we started to prepare our premises. Terzi's IDAMI Institute was housed in a 17th century palazzo in the very center of Milan. It had a large portal and a spacious courtyard with space for more cars than the IDAMI staff and we would ever have. Sumptuous stairs led up to the floor that was Terzi's. The space allotted to our project was what had originally been the ballroom, an enormous space with a high, domed ceiling and huge windows at both ends. It was about thirty by eighty feet. The windows at the far end were boarded up and, as we discovered the first time it rained, the roof above them had several leaks. It was summer then, and it did not damp our enthusiasm. When it began to get cool, Terzi and Piero suspended infrared radiation heaters from the ceiling above our desks and they kept us comfortably warm while the rainwater was dripping into buckets, far away at the other end of our "office".

One of the difficulties we foresaw for our work was the insufficient access to large computers, which were still rather scarce in those days. An arrangement had been made with one of the banks to let us use their computer every now and then at night. It wasn't the computer Piero would have liked for this work, nor did we believe that the arrangement would last forever. It was clear that we would have to test parts of the analysis procedure all the time, before further steps could be designed. To have to postpone testing until the late evening, meant that we would have been held up every day. So I suggested that we should simulate our tests by hand on a static, non-electronic representation of a computer. There was only one way to do this. We fixed six or seven sheets of plywood like a steep extended drawing table along one of the long walls and covered them with graph paper. On the graph paper we drew a grid of half-inch squares so that we had columns and rows along the entire surface. It was our representation of the bytes of a computer's workspace. For more than two years we simulated the computer's operations on this chart by moving colored thumbtacks. It was, of course, a slow process, but the fact that you had a visual representation of what was happening was a great help both in finding errors in the flow of operations and in designing new subroutines. In that way it saved a lot of time and I don't think our progress would have been faster if we had had a real machine.

It seems that no one else had thought of such a method to design and debug procedures without the complication of a computer language. When a group of researchers from the University of Texas Linguistics Institute visited us later, they could not believe their eyes. They insisted that we show them how we worked with our thumb tacks on the giant panel, and one of them took photographs so that they could show the strange European invention to their colleagues at home.

None of us had been quite sure that the analysis system would really work. So we were greatly relieved, when it ran flawlessly through its first demonstration. It captured the possible meanings of sentences up to twelve words and was considerably faster than all the other ventures at the time. It produced *all* the meanings and there was as yet no attempt to select among ambiguities. This was the main problem of all automatic systems. We had ideas of how to approach it, but in the 1960s computers were just too small. Even at the end of the decade, when we were working in the Unites States with the largest machine in existence, it was not nearly large and fast enough to operate with the network of conceptual relations that would have been needed. It no doubt could be done now on the

Macintosh on my desk, but I would have to learn programming and it's much too late for that.

First Taste of America 1963

My first experience of America was organized by the official from the US Air Force Office of Research in Washington, who was looking after the project I was to direct in Milan. The cable that announced the project monitor's visit brought a surprise. It said that SHE would arrive at such and such a date and gave her name as Rowena Swanson. The only project monitor I had so far experienced was the one who supervised Ceccato's project. He was a skinny little man, trying so hard to be knowledgeable and serious that he couldn't ever get himself to smile. I don't think he ever understood what we were struggling to do. Rowena was the opposite in every way. She knew what she was talking about, was ever ready to laugh, and had grasped a great deal about our work even before she came to talk to us.

Rowena was the second in command at the US Air Force Office of Scientific Research in Washington and was responsible for half a dozen projects directed by Warren McCulloch, Heinz von Foerster, Gordon Pask, and others who were among the first cyberneticians. Some of their writings I knew, but Rowena thought it important that I meet them to discuss our project and perhaps get some advice.

A few weeks later I received a call from the US Consulate in Milan asking me to present myself and my passport at such and such a time. I had always been somewhat nervous of authorities and it was not without a tremor that I went there. But I need not have worried. Thanks to my Irish passport everything went perfectly smoothly. I was told that I would be traveling on a military plane to McGuire Air Force Base in New Jersey and would there be advised how to get to Washington. My marching orders would be sent to me about a week before departure. I said thank you and wondered whether I should try a military salute. But I decided to let sleeping dogs lie and left in a neutral civilian manner.

Of course I wondered what my "marching orders" would look like and when they came, I was a little disappointed. They consisted of a batch of about two dozen sheets, stapled together and each containing the same information: who I was, who sponsored my trip, why I was making it, and where I was to go. A quite informal cover sheet instructed me to hand over one of them at every stop of the journey.

As it happened, the only opportunity to hand one of the sheets to someone was at the air force base where the plane from Milan took me. The flight was altogether uneventful. As I realized later, when I was flying across the Atlantic two or three times a year, it was by far the most comfortable one. The plane was not a military one but a loan from an ordinary airline and airline planes in those days were a good deal roomier than they are today. Besides it was almost empty and I had a whole row of seats to myself. When we landed and I stepped down the ladder there was no one. A vast expanse of tarmac, a few planes scattered between me and the horizon, and not a soul to be seen. I asked one of the chaps who came down the ladder behind me whether there was any building where travelers should go. Just like the dervishes in the Arabian desert, who always know where Mecca is, he pointed in the direction in which I should walk. I thanked him and picked up my bag and, sure enough, as I passed the plane that was standing a hundred feet from ours, I saw a flat building in the distance. Having little experience with airports, I kept looking above and behind me while I walked, because I didn't like the idea of a plane landing on top of me.

The building seemed deserted and it took me some time to find an office with someone in it. I respectfully waited in the open door and the man behind the desk looked up and said "Hi". It was the first time I heard that salutation. Thinking that it might be an exclamation of surprise, I didn't move.

"Come in!" the man said, "You just arrived?"

I proudly produced my marching orders, hoping they would prove that I wasn't an enemy invader. The man barely glanced at the batch, tore off the top sheet, and said:

"OK, you can go."

No questions, no customs inspection. I was stunned and, of course, delighted that it was so easy to enter the United States. But, to get further into them, I needed some information.

"Excuse me," I said, "I'm supposed to go to Washington. Would you tell me how I could get there from here? Is there a bus or something?" And as an apology I added, "It's my first trip to the Unites States."

"No," he said, "there are no buses, but I can call a cab. He'll take you to Trenton and from there you have a train."

"Thank you, that would be great."

"OK," he said, "there's coffee at the end of the corridor and the cab will be at the door you came in. It'll take about twenty minutes."

I thanked him and proceeded to the end of the corridor. When I saw that the coffee was in what I was used to calling a slot machine, I cursed myself for not having brought any coins. I took my bag and waited outside the door.

When the cab came it was mid-afternoon. To be at the airport in Milan at 7am I had got up at 5 and I thought I had better get a good night's sleep before arriving at the Research Office in Washington. I asked the driver if he could take me to an inexpensive hotel in Trenton. He turned to me and said the names of three or four. As I didn't know any of them, I told him it did not matter to me, but if there was one near the railway station, it would be convenient for me.

"You're not staying with us?" he said and grinned. He had a somewhat rectangular face, with a broad jaw and the beginning of heavy jowls.

"I'm afraid I have to go to Washington."

"Don't blame you," he said, "people don't stay in Trenton unless they have to."

I am sorry I did not record the name of the hotel he took me to. It remained unique in my American experience. It was an old townhouse full of worn Victorian furniture and a pervasive smell of mustiness that even an open window could not abate. I was surprised but had no objection when I was asked to pay in advance. I took the key I was given, found the room, and put down my bag in a little space left between the huge furniture. I opened the window and went down again to ask for a place where I could get something to eat. Two blocks down the street, I was told and though I had never heard the expression "block" in a similar context, I guessed what it meant and found the café without difficulty. The menu was not very extensive, but even so there were things I could not understand. It didn't worry me because I had long ago decided that for my first meal in the United States I would have a hamburger, something I had heard of and was curious to taste. I ordered it, and when the waitress asked what I wanted to drink, I said I'd like some tea.

When the hamburger came, I recognized it from descriptions I had been given, but no one had warned me about the size. It was sitting on its plate, as thick as my biggest dictionary, and I was wondering how one would ever find a way of biting into it. However, when I touched it the problem disappeared: it was like sponge rubber and a little pressure flattened it to half it's height and made it almost accessible to a normal mouth.

When the waitress brought the tea, I was startled as I heard the tinkling of ice cubes as she put it on the table. Living in Italy, I was familiar with *caffé freddo* but of iced tea I had never heard. But I thought to myself, "in Trenton with the Trentonians", and embarked on yet another new experience.

I slept for almost twelve hours, which eliminated any jet lag I might have had. But my troubles were not over. I had an electric razor, but when I tried to plug it into the only outlet I found behind the bed, my plug did not fit. It never occurred to me to ask about this before I left. I tried to solve the problem by using a couple of paper clips to make a connection, but there were so many sparks that I was afraid the hotel might catch on fire. So I went out to have breakfast unshaven and spotted a barber's shop on the way. I got an excellent shave by a man who talked to me incessantly although of course I did not dare to make it a conversation while he was wielding the cutthroat razor. But I had time to study his face and was astonished how like it was to the taxi driver's of the day before. It was the same rectangular shape with a broad jaw and heavy jowls. Maybe they are brothers, I thought but did not pursue with a question.

Not wanting to risk further adventures, I went to have breakfast at the place where I had eaten the night before. I ordered two fried eggs and *hot* tea. The waitress said: "Sunny side up?" It sounded like a question, but I had no idea what it meant. The waitress noticed my hesitation and, wanting to help, she said: "Or lightly over?" But as I had never heard of fried eggs being turned over, it was no help to me. In fact, I became embarrassed by my ignorance and quickly said, "Sunny side". When the eggs came and the yokes sparkled brightly at me, I suddenly understood what the foreign expressions referred to. I therefore remember Trenton as the starting point of my induction into American English.

I had no difficulty finding the railway station but noticed that here one said "railroad" instead. I bought my ticket and, when the train came, settled into an empty compartment and promptly went to sleep. I was awakened by a gentle tap on my shoulder. "Your ticket please," said the conductor. I looked at him as I pulled out my ticket and couldn't believe what I saw: the same rectangular face, a broad jaw and heavy jowls. I had heard it said that all Chinese look the same to a European until he has lived in China for a year or two. I had not expected to encounter that problem in America.

Condolences 1964

The year began badly. In the first three weeks several wives or husbands died and their respective widowers and widows, mere acquaintances of ours, considered that Isabel and I deserved to be told of their bereavement. After the second of these calls, we became somewhat reluctant to pick up the phone. It seemed an epidemic. And what can you say on such occasions? If you barely knew the people, your sympathy is at best generic and impersonal and you feel inadequate.

"It's awful," I said to Isabel, "we sound just like everyone else."

She thought for a little while and then came out with a startling suggestion: "It's all stock phrases—your computer could answer those calls, couldn't it? A sort of ELISA for condolences?"

ELISA was a program Joe Weizenbaum had written. It mimicked a psychoanalyst, and it did it so well that most people who were introduced to it, thought they were talking to a real shrink.

We played with the idea for some time, but there was a difficulty. The people who informed us of the death did not usually begin with this piece of news. They first talked of other things. It would be embarrassing if they said for instance, I was frightened to death by the storm last night, and the computer cut in with a condolence. There were all sorts of distinctions and judgments involved that the computer could not possibly make. So we decided to give up the idea. But try though we did, I never got rid of the feeling that what we said on those occasions was like a computerized condolence script.

The Wiener Memorial Meeting 1965

Established Science always tends towards a certain dogmatism. In the United States this tendency is so strong in psychology and the other human sciences that it makes one think of religion. Revolutionary ideas are suppressed as long as possible. Thus it came about that an international memorial celebration of Norbert Wiener, the founder of cybernetics, took place in Italy and not in Massachusetts where he had lived and worked. The Memorial Meeting was organized by the University of Genoa and brought together cyberneticians from all over the world.

Rowena had come with Warren McCulloch and made sure that Jehane and I were invited. The talks were given in a huge auditorium. In those years scientific meetings were still a very formal affair in Italy and the European professors dressed as though there were going to a funeral. Until late in the afternoon of the first day, a team of mechanics was working in a corner next to the dais, struggling to install a computer that should provide a direct connection with the Massachusetts Institute of Technology.

During one of the lectures a voice from the computer corner interrupted the speaker. "That's not so!" The voice came from a young man with an open shirt and sneakers, who stood on one of the packing cases. The young man was Seymour Papert, who was responsible for the computer connection and, as one of the best-known cyberneticians, also took part in the congress.

After each talk there were a few minutes for questions. One of the speakers said that cybernetics would do for thinking what the sewing machine had done for sewing. The comparison had been made several times in popular accounts and I thought it was an irresponsible distortion. As the speaker ended, I raised my hand and because it seemed to be the only one, the chairman waved me to the dais. It was the first time I attempted to speak to an auditorium and I was terrified. I remembered the autogenic training and it was a great help. There was a big blackboard and while I was looking for a piece of chalk I took a few deep breaths and stopped shaking. The comparison with the sewing machine is misleading, I said, and drew a diagram on the blackboard, first of how the thread goes to and fro when a seamstress is sewing, and then how two threads interlace when the machine does it. The result of the procedures is often quite similar, but if you look at the relevant operations, they are different.

As we were going to lunch, McCulloch said to me:

"I like your pragmatic view — like the plywood computer Rowena has told me about."

It was a compliment that gave me encouragement for many years to come.

Across the Atlantic 1966

One of the conditions I had made for our move to the United States was that we go by boat. I had several reasons. One was that the move was such a monumental change for us that completing it in a matter of a few hours seemed quite unacceptable. If we went by freighter, we would be on the way for about a week and could perhaps prepare a little for the culture shock. Another thing was that on a freighter we could take all the stuff from our office with us and I could also bring my Alfa Romeo, a car of which I had grown exceedingly fond. The transport would cost practically nothing and our tickets, too, were much cheaper than if we had gone by air. This was probably what inclined the Air Force Office to agree to my condition. They thought it was a strange choice, but they had nothing against it, provided we continued working while we were on board. Of course we would, I said, and mentioned that in this way we avoided any jet lag that could have incapacitated us for a week, if we made the journey by plane. But as I had thought of the sea journey as a well-deserved holiday after the continuous work of the past three years, we created an "Atlantic" folder while we were packing the files at the office and put some unfinished things in it that had never been mentioned in our reports. There is no shortage of interesting sidelines in a research project involving uncharted areas like ours which, because of the general lack of time, never get pursued; and those are things that would seem quite suitable to think about while lolling in a deck chair on a ship.

We booked our passages on an Italian freighter that left from Genoa and would deposit us in Fort Lauderdale in Florida. It was the most convenient landing place, because our destination, the little town of Athens was in the bordering State of Georgia, a mere 600 miles north. Everything seemed to be going smoothly and we looked forward to the trip. Little did we know what the Atlantic Ocean was like in mid-November.

Though the Mediterranean was its customary blue and barely rocked the ship with its gentle swell, Piero and Brunella began to feel queasy the moment they stepped on board. Isabel and I, who had weathered seven-week journeys to and from Australia, told them that it was quite normal and they would get over it in a day. They bravely stood on deck as we pulled out of the harbor at Genoa and kept a stiff upper lip until we passed Gibraltar. Then all hell broke loose, they retreated to their cabins, and we barely saw them for the rest of the trip. I felt awful that what I had planned as a holiday for them had turned into suffering.

I had lived through a storm in the Indian Ocean on the way home from Australia, but that was on a passenger liner. I had no idea what it would be like on a small freighter, and a practically empty one at that. It danced on top of the waves like the proverbial nutshell. If you stood at the back of the deck, to which I ventured once, it felt like being on a gigantic seesaw. When it carried you to the highest point and you looked forward, the top of the ship's chimney was below the horizon, as the ship plowed down the steep slope into a valley of water. At night you had to brace yourself with your feet at the corner posts of the bunk in order not to slide out. Isabel and I slept just the same, but we shuddered to think what it was like for Piero and Brunella. Sea sickness, fortunately, seems to stop as quickly as it starts. The mere thought of approaching land made Piero and Brunella feel better and by the time we had got through the customs procedures at

Fort Lauderdale they were almost back to normal. They went off to rent a van to transport all our things to Athens. In the meantime I discovered that the boot of the Alfa had been cleared out. All we had carefully packed there was gone, including our treasured Swiss down sleeping bags and my made-to-measure ski boots that were among the first to have an inner as well as an outer lacing.

"It often happens," said the official to whom I complained, "the men who load the car have to be given the keys and they take advantage of it. But don't worry, it's all fully insured."

This was little consolation for things that I could not replace in the United States. But as it happened, I had no opportunity to use ski boots during the next twenty years.

Brian Dutton, a professor from London's Birkbeck College, who had sporadically worked with us at IDAMI was now to be a permanent member of the team. Brian's field was really medieval Spanish poetry, but when he discovered that the work we were doing fitted with his second interest, semantics, he decided to join us. He had arrived in Athens a few weeks earlier and rented a big flat for all of us to stay until we found our own places to live.

Athens was a small town in Georgia, some sixty miles east of Atlanta, the State's capital. It was the seat of the University of Georgia, but we were not directly affiliated to the university. A separate administrative entity had been created to run our project and our only link to the university was a contract that gave us unlimited access to their computers.

The office where we worked the first few weeks was provisional. It was a tiny house with trees around it, which, after the smog in Milan, we thought was wonderful. The office furniture that had been bought for us was large, solid and looked very expensive. It surprised me, because we had always tried to keep the "overheads" included in our contract as low as possible. A couple of years later I found out that the professor, who was the administrator for our move, was also the agent of the furniture manufacturer who had supplied our office.

One day when I pushed back in my chair, which ran on heavy casters, there was a crunching noise and I fell backwards. The floor had crumbled. I was glad that the chair was solid, because the high back prevented my head from hitting the floor. The next time the professor came, he looked at the ragged whole in the floor and said:

"Termites. They're all over the place."

We tried to remember this and stepped carefully about in our office, as though we were on very thin ice, until we eventually moved out of the reach of termites and onto the seventh floor of a bank building in the center of town.

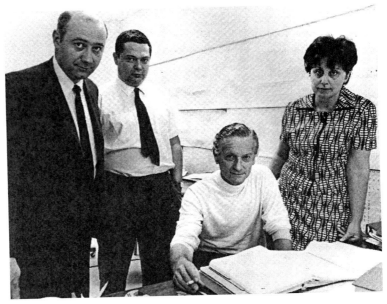

Our Research Group 1968
Brian Dutton, Piera Paolo Pisani, EvG, Brunella Notamarco

Lana and her keyboard 1974

In Heidelberg with Paul Watzlawick 1991

Honorary doctorate University of Klagenfurt 1997

Ernst von Glasersfeld and Josef Mitterer

Sandra 1 and Sandra 2 1952

Granddaughter
Sandra Ceccarelli 2006

Charlotte von Glasersfeld 1998

On my private ski slope behind our house in Amherst 1998

At the back of our house with a burnt-out tractor 2004

In Heidelberg receiving the Gregory Bateson Prize 2005

Chapter Six

1967–1972

Settling on the Oconee River 1967

Looking for a flat turned out to be disappointing. Being a university town, Athens had many student digs but few more comfortable apartments. After three weeks of searching we had not seen anything we liked and were getting disgruntled. I mentioned it to the university person who managed the agreement we had with the computer center and who had been helpful in other matters.

"Why do you want an apartment?" he asked, "it would be much better to buy a house."

It was an amazing suggestion and I said: "Well, you know, we're not exactly rich."

"You don't need a lot of money. You put down ten percent of the price and then you make monthly mortgage payments that will be less than the rent for a decent apartment — unless you choose a very expensive house."

"That would be wonderful," I said, "but all we have is about four thousand dollars, and that, surely, would not be enough."

Not to worry, he said; most houses in Athens were well below forty thousand dollars. He gave me the address of an estate agent and in the next few days we were shown more than a dozen houses. There wasn't one that we were enthusiastic about. But we had noticed that there was always a For Sale sign on the front lawn and we decided to spend the week-end driving around to see if we couldn't find something ourselves. I don't know how many times we stopped, walked round a house, and discarded it for one reason or another. I suppose, when you have to invest your entire nest egg for the first time, you tend to be super careful.

One afternoon we found it. It was a low, part two-story house, standing between tall, straight Georgia pines. It had a nice open space at the back, bordered by more pines and an enormous hickory tree, beyond which there was an embankment and a slope down to a river that had the American-Indian name Oconee. The house even had a terrace at the back from which you could see the flowing water. We were enchanted, but the more we liked it, the more we feared that it would be outside our range. The agent named on the For Sale sign was not the one we had visited and we wondered whether this would be an obstacle.

We rushed to the estate agent on Monday morning. He called the other agent and after a lengthy conversation, which we couldn't follow, he hung up and told us that the house was indeed on the market, that he could manage the sale, and that the price was $32,000. We were amazed. This was quite a bit less than most of the houses we had seen and discarded. We liked the look of it, we said, but of course we would have to see inside. A visit was arranged and the inside was not at all disappointing. What clinched it for me, was that there was a large basement for a workshop with windows giving on the back lawn. After we signed the contract, the agent told us that the house was only ten years old. The lot had been vacant for quite some time. The previous owner had won it in a game of poker, but had left Athens soon after the house was finished.

"A game of poker," said Isabel, "seems a good background for us."

Before we moved in, I asked our administrator what I had to do to get electricity, phone, and gas connected. He told me that there was no problem; all I had to do was telephone the companies. I did this the next morning, and that very evening we had it all running, including water. I couldn't believe it. When we moved to Milan, it took five weeks to get a phone connection, even though I was an accredited foreign correspondent; and each of the four services required long forms to be filled out and a substantial deposit. America, I thought, made some things in life marvelously simple.

The house was on Riverhill Drive, a street that went down a hill to a barely noticeable little bridge and, curving slightly to the left, past our house and the well-kept lawns of our neighbors. One afternoon, about a month after we had moved in, I opened the front door to go to our mailbox at the edge of the road. A car came careening down the hill, a little too fast. Having made it across the bridge, it jumped the curb and tore across the lawn in front of our pines and then hit a big one of our neighbors. A big young man in shorts and with a crew cut and the kind of neck that characterizes football players got out. He went to the front of his Corvette and saw the considerable damage the impact had done to the car. His hands went up to his head in an eloquent gesture of desperation. He let out the primordial scream "Oh, shit!" and it reverberated through the suburban stillness.

Our neighbors, an elderly couple, had rushed out of their house when they heard the crash and were looking in consternation at the car glistening in the sun right in the middle of their torn-up lawn. At the young man's scream, the white-haired gentleman took a step forward and sternly said:

"Watch your language, there are ladies present!" — We clearly lived in a very respectable neighborhood.

Later in the summer, we realized why the lot had been vacant for a long time and why the house was relatively cheap. When the Oconee river was in flood, it came right into the basement. We were shocked. But then we said, two feet of water won't do much damage, once you expect it and have arranged things accordingly. So we continued to enjoy the house and when the floods came, we pretended that we were in Venice and that it was quite normal to have deep water under our terrace.

Years later, reading the first lines of Joyce's *Finnegans Wake* to a friend, I heard myself saying:

"... nor had topsawyer's rocks by the stream Oconee exaggerated themselse to Laurens County's gorgios while they went doublin their mumpers all the time "

There was the OCONEE, which runs through the little town of DUBLIN, a few miles south of us, in LAURENS COUNTY, GEORGIA. Given that almost thirty years earlier we had moved to Ireland at least partly because of Joyce's *Ulysses*, it was a strange coincidence to find ourselves now settled on the Oconee of *Finnegans Wake*. For Joyce, the river was another incarnation of the mother goddess Anna Livia, because, like the Liffey, it flows through a city called Dublin.

Work Ethic 1967

If I had occasionally heard the expression "work ethic" before coming to the United States, I had interpreted it (rightly, I think) as referring to the rules governing one's labors and the quality of the work one undertakes. Now I realized that it also had another meaning here: it referred to a sacred obligation to make money irrespective of need. It was considered important for children to learn this early; boys earlier than girls. Not child labor, of course, but making money just the same, even if the parents had tons of it. A favorite was to get them the job of distributing newspapers. It was apparently considered a safe employment and sometimes it was made even safer.

When we started living in our new house in the very respectable River Hill development near the Oconee River, we noticed a big white Cadillac that rolled along our street every noon, at walking speed. Every hundred yards or so, it stopped. A little boy jumped out with three or four newspapers, put them one by one into the mail boxes along the curb, and got into the car again.

We wondered what character-building effect this procedure could have.

"Did he contribute some of his earnings to the upkeep of the Cadillac when he collected his salary from the paper at the end of the week?" Isabel asked. And who would be paying income tax on the boy's earnings? We felt pretty sure that parents did not worry about such particulars, but we thought that they should be important features in the learning of work ethic.

Girls, although they mature more quickly, enter the work force later. It's when they go to a university that they often have to earn pocket money as waitresses or hostesses in a restaurant. There is the peculiar belief that the young can learn the value of money if they earn it. Rich parents will buy their teenagers expensive cars but force them to make spending money by taking jobs that can hardly be considered educational. When I was young, parents who could afford it, sent their teenagers to stay with a family in some other country, where they might learn another language and get a little bit of polish and experience of a wider world. But foreign languages and polish do not count for much in the United States.

Exploring the South 1968

I had become friends with Charles Darby, the head of the university's Department of Psychology, after the first talk I had given there, shortly after we arrived in Athens. He invited Isabel and me to dinner and it was my first experience of a professor of psychology. It was a rather misleading experience. Charles was a totally open-minded person, he distrusted most of the standard theories in psychology, had more interest in animals than in people, and though he was an experimentalist he believed that it was more important to teach students to question ideas than to prove them. He liked what I had said in my talk. Especially my arguments against Chomsky's notion that language is innate.

"To say that something is innate," he explained, "is to shut off research because you don't know how to tackle it."

He, too, was interested in cars. He had an Austin-Healey and was thrilled when he saw my Alfa. One week-end we drove to the nearest mountain road in the Georgia Mountains and swapped cars. It was the beginning of a lasting friendship.

One day early that summer he asked me if I would like to drive to New Orleans. There was a psychology conference there and he and Barbara would like to drive down in his Austin-Healey; but he had never taken it on such a long drive and he wondered whether I would come along in the Alfa. Isabel and I loved the idea.

The speed limits were not taken seriously in those days and trying to keep two cars together on a five hundred mile trip is always a diversion. And driving through Alabama and Louisiana one needed some diversion. The interstate highway goes straight for countless miles and there is nothing to see. The country lies flat like an ironed sheet. Once it was agricultural, but now that the government was paying farmers not to grow certain things, there was little but weeds. Even more of a shock for a European were the scattered homesteads one could see from the road. They were slums, rural minislums, I said to Isabel. There was often a tractor rusting where it had broken down in a field nearby, a battered refrigerator lying on its side near the shack, and other derelict stuff strewn about. No attempt to grow anything; yet, in the south-eastern States things grow practically by themselves. When I mentioned it to Charles, he said:

"If they don't buy it in the supermarket, they think you cannot eat it."

I thought of Southern Italy. There, too, people were poor and lived in the simplest kind of houses. Yet there were flowers around them, and always a well-tended vegetable garden. It was indeed a different culture. But later I realized how superficial such culture is; the Calabresi and Sicilians brought little of it with them when they immigrated in the United States.

The two mornings at the psychology conference were an unforgettable experience. I had been to one or two linguistics meetings in Europe but had never seen anything like this. It took place in two giant hotels that were barely a block from each other. There were more than 800 psychologists (today there are several thousands at such meetings) and between the two hotels there was a band of endless to and fro traffic, just as with

ants when they are moving to a new heap. The lobbies were full of psychologists hurrying from one lecture to another, deadly earnest and per-
petually worried.

"Do they ever have fun?" I asked Charles.

They might, he said, but not at meetings like this. You went there to
advance your career or to solidify your position at your university. Pre-
senting a paper meant a line in your curriculum vitae, and you needed
lots of lines to get promoted; and graduate students had to collect them to
get a teaching position when they had finished.

The second evening, Charles led us to a place a little outside the city. It
had obviously been a country manor. It had tall white columns framing
the entrance and a valet offered to take our cars to the parking lot at the
back. I declined. I let Isabel get out and wait with Charles and Barbara,
while I followed Charles' car being driven by the valet. It wasn't that I was
afraid they would dent my car, but to start the Alfa you didn't pump the
accelerator several times, as was then customary with American cars. If
you did that, you flooded the engine, and then it was hell to start. As I got
out, I heard the valet say something to the attendant at the back. It
sounded like Italian.

When we trooped in, we were directed to the end of a long line of waiting guests. It seemed an extremely busy place. Waiters were speeding
about like commandos, balancing trays in a showy fashion and looking
thoroughly Italian. Our progress was slow and it was difficult to maintain
a conversation as we had to stand in single file. After a while I turned to a
waiter who had been blocked by traffic just beside me.

"Will this take forever?" I said. "We are very hungry."

I said it in Italian, and it struck the poor chap like an electric shock. He
gave me one quick, frightened look and hurried away. Within two minutes the *maître d'* came and took us to a table.

"What on earth did you say to the waiter?" Charles asked when we had
settled down. I couldn't help laughing.

"It's not what I said, it's that I said it in Italian. He obviously thought we
were high up in the mafia."

And Charles confirmed that New Orleans was one of their centers in the
United States. The restaurant must have had some real mafiosi clients
because the food was excellent.

We had heard so much about the Charm of the city of New Orleans that
seeing it was a bit disappointing. Visually, the balconies with their
wrought iron banisters are the only thing one remembers. The architec-
ture in general is not particularly striking and the layout is not designed
to provide vistas. Only the food was memorable and a wonderful change
from the drab eating places in Athens and along the highways. The repu-

tation of the city, we thought, must be based on the restaurants and the music it had generated. But Charles' enthusiasm for everything was contagious and altogether we enjoyed the trip enormously.

As a result we were delighted when Charles asked us to join him on another excursion. His plan was to charter a sailing boat at the port of Fort Lauderdale for the relatively short crossing to Bimini, the closest island of the Bahamas. The island is a thin strip of sand, he explained, some five miles of beach with palm trees and a couple of small hotels at one end. Hemingway spent a lot of time there, he added, and that was all the advertising we needed. It was for a long weekend and, to have more time at Bimini, he and Barbara would fly to Fort Lauderdale late on Friday afternoon and start out on the boat in the evening. To save money, Isabel and I decided to drive to Fort Lauderdale by car and to meet them on board.

I had done a little sailing with a friend in Zürich, whose father had an eleven-and-a-half-meter boat that had a cabin with four bunks. The boat Charles had chartered was much larger. It had two cabins below deck with proper double beds and two smaller cabins as well as a common area with a kitchenette. It also had a captain called Lenny, who at the moment was drinking beer with Charles. Eventually the boat was untied and Lenny maneuvered it out of the harbor and well out into the open sea. There wasn't a breath of wind.

"There'll be no sailing tonight," Lenny said, "you'll be ok running with the motor. Just keep her going straight east/southeast. I'll go down and snooze a little. Be sure to call me if a wind comes up!"

Charles settled himself in the cockpit and in a little while Isabel and I went to our cabin. We were quite tired after the long drive. We wanted to sleep, but the cabin was murderously hot. We took a blanket and went up on deck. Charles was comfortably ensconced at the helm and we told him that we wanted to sleep up here where it was much cooler than in the cabin. It was a clear night and lying on our backs we had a wonderful view of the stars. Even the North Star, which the haze lying over land makes almost invisible, was clear and sparkling.

It was still dark when I woke up. I looked at my watch and saw that I had slept for nearly four hours. I stretched, looked up at the stars, and saw that they had turned a good bit. I couldn't locate the North Star. I remembered where it had been relative to the yacht's mast, but it wasn't there. That's odd, I thought. As far as I knew, the North Star shouldn't have moved much as the earth turned; but I found it in a rather different place. We must have changed course, I said to myself and looked for Charles. There were several cans of beer on the deck in front of the helm, which was gently turning to and fro with the slight swell of the sea. Charles was lying along the seat, fast asleep. When I woke him up he was shocked.

"We're off course, you say? I must get Lenny!"

It's lucky, I thought, that there aren't any rocks between Florida and Bimini; we could have had a pretty crash. But the crossing only took a couple of hours longer than expected and that was all. Once ashore we had a great time. Bimini was actually a British possession and the absence of billboards and other outdoor advertising was a visual reminder of it. There were barely a hundred inhabitants, I guessed, and Charles seemed to be having a beer with all of them. Isabel and I fled quickly from all this socializing and disappeared with a sandwich along the five miles of beach. The water was clear and blue, just like the Mediterranean. There wasn't a soul anywhere and the palm trees provided some shade if you felt you'd had too much sun.

It was probably the most restful holiday we ever had. On the way back we took the little plane that linked Bimini to Fort Lauderdale and drove home during the night to avoid some of the murderous heat. After two days in Athens, at close to a hundred degrees saturated with humidity, we could hardly imagine just how comforting the air, the sun, and the sea had been.

End of a Life 1969

At the end of April 1969 a research report was due that was to account for what we had done in our first two years in the United States. We had done a lot during those two years, but being constantly involved in struggling with particulars that had to be worked out, I had several times postponed writing the report about the overall procedure. I finally began to think about it in February and decided to do it on week-ends. This had the advantage that I was alone in the office and could not be involved in other problems.

When I came home, late on the third Saturday of that March, I noticed that the mail had not been taken out of the box near our front door. This was odd, because Isabel usually picked it up early in the afternoon. The door was still locked and the house seemed empty. I looked into the garden, but Isabel was not there. I found her upstairs, still in pajamas, on our bed. She was dead. Whatever hit her must have been so sudden that she could not reach the phone on the bedside table.

I stood at the window, looking through the tall trees at the quietly flowing river. I didn't see any of it. I was stunned and there were no thoughts in my paralyzed mind. I don't know how long this lasted. Eventually I called the only doctor we knew (he had treated my mother when she had come to visit us that summer), and he came almost at once. (Only later did I realize what an incredible exception that was. Doctors do not make house calls in the United States—and on a Saturday!) It was an embolism that killed Isabel, the doctor said. It seems, it can be as fast as switching off a light. This was a bit of consolation, but as there had been no warning, nothing could lessen my pain.

I still cannot write anything sensible about the days that followed. Our daughter had flown over from Italy and I took off a week from work. We drove south to see a piece of Florida where there were exotic water birds and alligators. When we came back, I threw myself into writing the report and it was this, I think, that saved me. It generated some continuity when everything else had crumbled. Isabel and I had been together for thirty-two years. Nothing seemed to make sense now that I was alone.

There is a strange form of pathology called *folie à deux* (e.g. the Papin Sisters, who, together, murdered their employer in the most atrocious fashion). Being young and in love is one thing; being able to maintain the enchanting relationship for years and years is quite another. It is a benign form of madness: it leads to the common construction of a joint reality. Nothing makes one more tangibly aware of this than the death of the partner. It is as though the scaffolding on which one has built one's everyday existence had suddenly collapsed. The fixed points of one's world, the support of one's attitudes, one's reasons for acting, and, indeed, for living, have vanished. What is left is a desolate vacuum.

Skunk 1969

I have been driving, maybe a hundred miles or more, eyes fixed on the black wet road, watchful of the wisps of fog that now and then flare up in the beam of the headlights. Suddenly I become aware of a familiar smell wafting in from the forest. Skunk, I say. Then I realize: there is no one sitting beside me. I am alone.

How many thousand miles did we drive together, Isabel and I? Many hours often without a word. But she was there, we were together and there was no need to speak.

I remembered watching a little boat, once. It was tied to a staunch wooden post, and whenever the breeze began to push it away, the rope was stretched out of the water and its weight was sufficient to pull back the boat. It was a gentle, mobile equilibrium. The boat was not immobilized, it was just kept safe.

I am alone now, I thought, drifting. There was no fixed point, no tie to keep me balanced. Where was I going? And above all, why?

I was driving north, all the way to Boston/Cambridge. There was a conference on the philosophy of language at MIT and I had registered weeks before Isabel died. A few days ago I had decided to go. I wanted to get out of the house. It was a good idea. In Cambridge I had an evening together with Ray Solomonoff, a young philosopher of science, whom I had met because he, too, had a contract with Rowena's office. He had never met Isabel, but late that evening, when we were drinking brandy in his flat, I couldn't help telling him that she had died barely a month ago. He was very good about it. He did not commiserate. He said:

"The problems of epistemology are probably the best to keep your mind off everything else. You're into them anyway, just keep going."

It was the most helpful thing anyone had said to me and I found myself following it as best I could. But even today a visual image, a sound, or a smell may tear the cover and kindle the awareness of what I lost.

Gripsholm and Upsala 1969

Twelve copies of the requested twelve copies of the "Final Report" of our research project were sent in good time to the Air Force Office in Washington. No one, as far as I know, has ever mentioned that report and all our ideas are molding away in some underground store of the Air Force. But Piero and I had worked very hard and after more than two years of uninterrupted work we felt we could do with a break. I had received an invitation to the International Conference on Computational Linguistics in Sweden and it seemed a good opportunity to relax. Talks we could give there were no problem because parts of our final report could easily be transformed into friendlier texts.

We flew to Stockholm and had a few very stimulating days. About a dozen listeners had come to us after our contributions and wanted to hear more about our work. It was a pleasant surprise and we spent much of the free time during the conference with colleagues who seemed to have no axe to grind.

On one of the free afternoons a boat trip to the ancient royal castle of Gripsholm was organized. Although the castle had been built as a fortress five hundred years ago, it was today, after many restorations and changes, a quite habitable building. It contained a wealth of good furniture and some remarkable pictures. Piero and I went our different ways and as I came into the library, I suddenly remembered that I had come across the name Gripsholm before. Years ago I had read that Kurt Tucholsky, who had died in a hospital in Stockholm in 1935, was buried at the castle. I found the graveyard near the castle's chapel and sat in the grass in front of Tucholsky's simple grave.

I remembered the pseudonyms Tucholsky had used — Peter Panter, Theobald Tiger, and the title of one of his books came to my mind: *Learn to Laugh without Crying*. I thought of Isabel and the countless bits of Tucholsky I translated for her and then of things I had just seen in the castle, things that we had enjoyed together. In one of the staircases there was Arcimboldi's portrait of Calvin, a malicious caricature composed of fish and other kinds of seafood. Arcimboldi, to whose work Benno Geiger had introduced us in Venice, had been our passion for a long time and Benno's book was always kept within reach. And in one of the large rooms of the castle there was a wall cabinet with a long row of hand-cut Baccarat glass almost identical with the set which had come down to me from the Bohemian origins of the Glasersfelds. When Isabel saw them for the first time, she said with that mischievous smile of hers:

"They alone would have been worth marrying you."

Suddenly it was all too much. The world of harmony and mutual understanding was gone and tears were running down my cheeks.

* * *

One of the people who had inquired about our work was the director of the department of computer science at the University of Upsala. He suggested that I drive to Upsala with him and his two colleagues in order to have a discussion there on our theory of language. He could not give me a fee for a talk, but he could promise a good supper and the fare to my plane in Stockholm. I could also sleep in his apartment and have breakfast before I left. I was delighted that someone took an interest in our work and accepted the invitation with pleasure.

Right at the beginning of the drive in his car, one of his colleagues said:

"Your method of reducing the syntactic links of language to semantic relations is a wonderful innovation but it won't cut any ice with linguists unless you can show a formalization."

"What exactly do you mean by formalizing," I asked.

"Well, something like the system of transformations in Chomsky's grammar."

"Something like his system of little arrows that hide the mental operations that would have to be analyzed if you want to understand the workings of language? That's not the kind of game we want to play. Is a computer program that brings the meaning of sentences to the surface as a readable output not formal enough?"

This started a debate among the three computer people in which I did not have to take part and which, by the time we arrived at Upsala, had not yet made clear what one actually had to do to formalize a theory.

My exposition of the pragmatic theory of language that we had begun to develop on the basis of Ceccato's ideas seemed to find some understanding and the leader of the group said on the next morning, when I was saying good bye, that they would write an article on the mystery of formalization.

Although I received several further communications from Upsala, the article on formalization was not mentioned again and I presume it was never written. Even today the question does not seem to have been fully cleared up, because every time a computer produces a proof that logicians or mathematicians had not been able to supply, it is considered illegitimate by the conservatives.

The Moon Landing 1969

When the first astronaut stepped on the moon, he said (we were told), that it was a small step for a man but a huge step for mankind. I was surprised when I read this. It is a neat statement and very different from what we heard when we watched the big event on television (a big step for us, too, because for the first time we rented a TV set). We saw some spectacular images of the uninviting moonscape, but the comments, on the whole, were of abysmal triviality. There were, for example, those anxious minutes while the space ship went round the dark side of the moon, when communication was cut and no one was quite sure what would happen.

"How was it?" the Space Center asked, when the rocket had safely emerged from the dark side. "OK," one of the astronauts said.

It was then that I thought they should have had a poet, or at least a slightly literary person, prepare a few comments. Circling the moon, too, was a big event for mankind. The other side was called the "dark" side because the moon never turned it towards the Earth and no one knew what it might hide. To hear the intrepid astronaut merely say that it was OK was a little disillusioning.

Einstein somewhere wrote that the mystery of the universe was that it functions according to laws that we could understand. I think this is saying too much. As I see it, the real mystery is that we are able to construct a relatively stable universe using concepts that we have created ourselves. We have no grounds for believing that these concepts have any application outside our domain of experience. The fact that they seem to work reasonably well in the world as we see it, does not mean that they have to work in the world as it might be before we interpret it in terms of our concepts.

The moon landing provided a good example of this. When the space ship was on its return journey, the news announced that Mr. Nixon, who was still president at that time, was going to welcome the astronauts when they landed. But then we were told that this could not happen; the astronauts had to be subjected to two weeks quarantine because they might have picked up some unknown germs on the moon. Why a quarantine of two weeks? Well, because two weeks was long enough for all the better known germs on this planet to manifest their presence. It was tacitly assumed that this rule would apply everywhere. But there is no reason whatsoever that it should. If there were germs on the moon at all, they might have had an incubation of two years.

It was an extreme example of the problem with conclusions from induction. Induction means that you review a set of experiences, find what they have in common, and formulate a rule that all experiences of that kind will have that feature. This is of course true for the past experiences, because you have examined them and found that they possessed that feature. But when you then categorize a new experience as a member of that same set, there is no reason why it should possess the particular feature. Inductive inferences are true for the experience from which they were inferred. They can be applied to future experiences, only if we assume that the world we experience will remain the same — but there is no way of knowing that it must.

Science, of course, makes this assumption all the time, and as long as it remains within more or less familiar areas of experience it works fairly well. Once it goes beyond our planet, however, there are no grounds for believing that the rules that seem to apply here must apply there.

So once you assume that there will be germs on the moon—an assumption without any scientific foundation—you might as well assume that their incubation periods are no longer than on Earth. It's not a valid inference for the moon, but what else should you assume? There is nothing wrong with it, as long as it is not thought of as an unquestionable fact.

Further Drastic Changes 1969

In November 1969, I received a call from the Air Force office. Things were going very well, they said, and I should visit them in Washington to discuss the future. Fine, I said to myself, I haven't taken a holiday for years. I'll go to Washington and then spend the Christmas week in New York. I had never been there and David Rothenberg, another researcher from Rowena's stable, offered me a place to stay.

In Washington, Wooster and Rowena were in good spirits. They would have more money next year, they said, our contract would be enlarged, and I could hire one or two more people. It was great news for me. Driving to New York I thought of things that we could now try to undertake, and for the first time since March I felt almost cheerful.

David had two apartments, one to live in and one as laboratory. There was a little bathroom, a tiny kitchen, a big couch to put clothes on in one of the rooms, and a mattress to sleep on in the corner of the other. He was working in acoustic perception and, being a musician as well, he was especially interested in musical scales. The two-room lab was full of electronic machinery, a big synthesizer, several tape decks and computers, transformers, and a network of wires connecting it all. David had hundreds of audiotapes from every corner of the world and one evening he let me listen to some classical Korean music.

"It's like Stockhausen in slow motion," I said. "The tones are others but I am unable to perceive any connection among them."

It's all a question of habit, he said, and started a tape with Rock and Roll, which sounded no less foreign to me. Music, I told him, practically ends for me with Mozart. It is my loss, no doubt, but there is nothing I seem to be able to do about it.

I stayed there for a week and had a wonderfully carefree time. David took me to several Christmas parties and I met many people. Some of them were scientists and we could discuss research. With the others I had little to talk about. Until I met Charlotte. We seemed to take an instant interest in each other and as the interest increased we spent much of my remaining days in New York together.

At one point I said to Charlotte, who had shown me some of the ceramic sculptures she had made:

"The University of Georgia has a very large Art Department and I know the head of the department quite well. He is Lamar Dodd, whom I consider the only real painter in the South. His department even has a foundry for casting bronze. Would you be interested in seeing it? I'm sure Lamar would let you work there for a few days. I have to drive back to Athens on New Year's Eve."

Charlotte, who had been making her sculptures on the kitchen floor in her apartment and kept clay at the bottom of the bedroom wardrobe, was visibly intrigued. I'll think about it, she said as I kissed her goodnight.

Five days into our acquaintance, the evening before I was leaving, she had made up her mind to come with me. By then I had met her sisters and their husbands and she told me that they were very against her coming with me, when she didn't really know who I was — I might be just another European scoundrel.

I thought of that as we were scorching down through North Carolina late on New Year's Eve. There were no speed limits then and the Alfa could do 120 miles an hour. Charlotte was sleeping in the seat beside me and I wondered how one could ever tell whom to trust. There did not seem to be a logical answer.

Charlotte had mentioned that if she drove south with me, she would like to see Savannah. That was where we were heading now. It was well after midnight when we reached a motel at the outskirts of the city. The next day we spent looking round. Savannah became my favorite city in the United States. It has 18th century squares and trim façades that could be part of Chelsea in London; and where there used to be factories, the simple brick buildings have been converted to house artists and crafts people. This has given the city a rather Un-American almost European feel.

Late that afternoon we drove to Athens and Charlotte entered our house. It was January 1st, 1970.

Three days later, I received a telegram from Washington. This had never happened before, even while we were in Europe. Communications were always either by letter or by phone. Now I had a telegram and its content was simple and shocking. It told me that contract number such and such (which happened to be mine) was terminated on December 1, 1969, and a final report was due by March 31, 1970.

Two weeks earlier, when I had visited the Office in Washington, I had been told how good things looked for the coming year. Now there was no note from anyone and no explanation.

I called the research person at the University, who, after all, was partly responsible for our being in Georgia. He had received a similar telegram but he knew a little more.

"It seems," he said, "the Air Force Office of Research will be closed in the very near future. Rowena and Harold Wooster are under investigation. ... Come to my office tomorrow morning. We'll see what we can do."

What the University of Georgia did literally saved our lives. The vice-president for research was able to find jobs for us in various departments and although the salaries were a little less than the Air Force had given us, we did not have to live through a month without one. We were lucky. Two years later the climate would have been different. As the president of the university was a political appointment of the State government, a different kind of person was chosen. Because big business had become influential, the university was turned into a PhD factory and research suddenly acquired a new purpose: to draw as many millions from the sponsoring government agencies as possible — never mind if it was neither original nor particularly interesting.

Piero Pisani was snapped up by the Computer Center, Brian Dutton's half position at the Romance Languages Department was turned into a full one and so Brunella, who had married Brian the year before, was not left in the cold. As far as I was concerned, I was told I could continue my work as a "research associate" in the Psychology Department. I had given a couple of talks in that Department during the past two years and was already friends with Charles Darby, its head. It was a large Department of fifty faculty members, experimentalists, clinicians, and social psychologists, but there was no one who specialized in language. At a time when the new discipline of psycholinguistics was becoming the fashion, it was an obvious lack. That my salary would be a little less did not worry me much, but I was terrified that I might have to teach. I was told not to worry.

* * *

That January brought another surprise. One morning, a few days before Charlotte was to leave, the doorbell rang and there were two men who identified themselves as FBI. Could they come in and talk to me, they asked. Of course, I said, and brought them into the house. They had some questions, they said, about the move of our research project to the United States. They asked who had initiated it. I fished out the correspondence file I had and produced the letter from the Air Force office that had started it all. I was glad I had saved all the correspondence. Their questioning was so naive that I quickly guessed what they were driving at. Someone must have suggested that our group was brought over the Atlantic because Rowena and I were having a love affair. Of course they didn't openly say so and I let them go on for a while with their oblique questions. Eventually Charlotte came into the room and I introduced her and said:

"We are going to be married shortly. I don't think that strengthens your case against Miss Swanson."

Then I turned to Charlotte and told her that the FBI apparently believed Rowena and I were having an affair, wasn't that funny? The FBI chaps were shocked by my bringing their quest into the open and one of them was obviously embarrassed and said:

"It could be *conscrewed* that way."

That was the end of their investigation of me. I signed no statement and they left. I am still grateful to them for having invented the verb "to "conscrew". It is clearly something the English language was lacking. It is an infallible tool to generate laughter when giving a talk.

Learning about Insurance 1970

My first experience with insurance companies in the United States stemmed from the time I had to insure the car I had brought over. I went to a company that had been recommended and showed them the policy I had in Italy. They said, yes, of course, they could give me the same sort of policy, but first I had to get a credit rating. I had no idea what that was. They explained that it reflected my reliability with regard to mortgage payments and other debts and that I surely had a credit card. But this was before we had bought the house and before I had adjusted to plastic money. To solve the problem, I had to go to Sears and buy something on the installment system so that I could prove that I had a debt. Not being great consumers, we couldn't think of anything expensive enough to buy. Then it struck us that a shortwave radio would enable us to listen to the BBC news. We had already realized that, for all the news media told you about it here, Europe was in another galaxy. The moment I could show the insurance people that I had an account with a negative balance, they insured my car. It seemed strange to me that you had to have a debt in order to be trusted.

I was, however, still a novice with regard to insurance. There was a hail storm one summer that I would not have believed possible if I hadn't seen it myself. There were hail stones the size of a tennis ball, and not just one, but hundreds. Many of them were not even round but just irregular lumps of ice. Cars that had been outside had big dents and the insurance companies paid for the repairs. A graduate in the Psychology Department had bought a big old Chevrolet a few weeks earlier for $250. His insurance now gave him a check for $350 to have the dents repaired — which of course, he didn't do.

A couple of days later, a man rang our door bell and said he was the adjuster from our home insurance and he'd come to see what damage we had from the hail storm. I said that I didn't know of any.

"Have you inspected your roof?" he asked, and when I answered that I hadn't, he said, let's have a look. He went to unstrap a ladder from his van and we both climbed up. He carefully examined the whole roof. When he came back to me he had two little bits of asphalt tile in his hand. They looked like broken off corners.

"You see," he said, "and there are a lot of invisible cracks."

"What should I do about it?"

"Best thing is to cover the roof with a new layer of tiles."

I was staggered. "How much will it cost?"

"I'll measure it. Then I can tell you. Anyway, we will pay for it."

I climbed down and told Charlotte that we were getting a new roof. A great idea, it'll keep us a little cooler in the summer.

"Do we need to do that?" she asked.

"No," I said, "but the insurance man thinks so — and they'll pay for it."

When he came down, he said it would be between eight and nine hundred dollars and he handed a card to me.

"These people are very reliable," he said. "Call them and tell them what color you want. We'll do the rest."

It was like Fairyland — I remembered an accident Piero had had a year or so before we came to the States. There was a traffic jam on the autostrada and he was waiting behind other cars. He was not moving but was hit from behind and pushed into the car in front of him. There was no question whose fault it was, but it took three years before he received about half of what the accident had cost him.

When I recounted our hail experience to a colleague at the university, he merely said that he was surprised that the adjuster actually gave me the business card of a roofing firm. Usually, he thought, they only mentioned it casually because they were anxious to avoid material evidence that they worked hand in hand.

It was an occasion for me to learn the deeper meaning of the adage: America's business is business.

Lana, the Almost Literate Chimp 1970

Charles Darby lived just a few houses up the street from ours and after Isabel died he and Barbara were among the few people I saw fairly frequently. One evening at his house, he introduced me to Ray Carpenter, one of the fathers of primatology in the United States. I had a great time talking with him because he was interested not only in apes but also in computers and wanted to hear all about our language analysis project. He had the background knowledge to understand what we were trying to do and he seemed sincerely interested. Later that evening, when we were leaving, he asked me if I played golf and I said that I was just beginning to take it up again.

"I'm not very good at it," he said, "but I like the exercise. Maybe you'll play with me some Saturday?"

I'd be delighted, I told him; all he would have to do was call me during the week.

He was, indeed, not a good player. But he liked the leisurely talks one could have walking on a pleasant surface and I liked listening to him. He was somewhat cranky and autocratic, but given his wide range of interests, he was hardly ever boring. Our Saturdays almost became a regular feature. When my research contract with the Air Force came to its abrupt end I appreciated his sympathy. It was all a question of money, he said. Ten years ago, Army, Navy, and Air Force were swimming in research money and had difficulty spending it all. That's why they were able to sponsor projects that had no direct connection to military matters. When Nixon became president, budgets were tightened in a spurious economy drive and the agencies had to limit their sponsorship to the strictly military.

One Saturday, later that spring, Carpenter came with an intriguing idea. The Yerkes Center in Atlanta, the first and foremost institute of primate research, was planning to investigate the possibility of communication between humans and great apes through a computer by means of a visual language. The great apes (gorillas, orangutans, chimpanzees), he explained, did not have the physical capability to modulate sounds very much and therefore would probably never learn a spoken language. But they were quick and clever with their fingers and Alan and Beatrice Gardner had successfully taught the American sign-language, the language used by the deaf and dumb, to a chimpanzee called Washoe. Washoe was in the process of becoming world famous. Linguists were in turmoil, because most of them wanted to believe with Chomsky that language was a human prerogative. Sign language, they said, did not have a proper syntax and therefore wasn't really a language. The Gardners, they suggested, were like parents with their baby: they saw and heard things that no one else could see or hear.

The Yerkes plan was to build a communication system with a simplified language, a keyboard, and a small computer. The computer would record everything the chimp typed on the keyboard and there would be no subjective bias as to what the chimp had or had not typed.

It seemed a great idea to me and when Carpenter asked me if I would like to design the special language and the computer system, I didn't hesitate to say yes. My only condition was that Piero Pisani would be part of the team because, although I had had a hand in designing computer procedures, I was not a programmer.

Before the end of the following week, I received a call from the Yerkes Center asking me and Piero to come to a discussion of the "Language Project". As far as the two of us were concerned, the meeting was a great success. The Yerkes Center would buy part of our working time from the University of Georgia (which I liked because it meant less teaching whenever I would be asked to give courses) and we would be completely on our own with regard to the design of the language and the computer program. At the end of the meeting we were introduced to the subjects of the research, which had already been chosen: a one-year old female chimpanzee called Lana and a female orangutan of the same age. I was instantly seduced by the orangutan's calm, soulful eyes that looked at me as she gently grasped a finger of my outstretched hand. It was as though she were sizing me up, far more knowing and thoughtful than a human infant. Lana, on the other hand was all action, with no indication of reflection, rather like a hyperactive child. Indeed, it soon became clear that they could not be taught together. Whatever gadget was shown to them, Lana would instantly appropriate it and consider it hers, while the orangutan would calmly sit and watch, as though she were trying to understand before touching. They would have needed separate treatment and therefore separate projects. The Yerkes people, who had far more experience with chimps, therefore decided to drop the orangutan and work with Lana only.

We had many more meetings to establish the details of the planned setup. A Plexiglas cubicle the size of a small room was to be built onto an existing wall that had a window to the outside. One of the Plexiglas walls was to be dedicated to the keyboard, a square unit of 25 keys, and there would be space for other units to be added as Lana got more proficient. Below the keyboard was a row of dispensers, activated through the computer; they would provide all sorts of food and it was hoped that Lana would learn to feed herself by means of requests typed on the keyboard. The dispensers could provide slices of banana and of apple, monkey chow, milk, and water, and there was the provision that, through the keyboard, she could ask for music or a film of primates in the wild to be projected. She could also request the curtain at the window to be drawn up or down.

Above the keyboard would be a sturdy horizontal bar that Lana had to hang onto in order to switch on the system. This was to keep one of her hands busy, so that she could not use both to press keys simultaneously.

It was expected that it would take several months to teach her to press keys, and it did. This was fortunate, because it gave me and Piero time to design the language and the program for the computer. Piero produced what in my view was his greatest achievement: he managed to squeeze a miniature replica of the system we had used in the Air Force project—a system that was based on 28,000 instructions—plus the necessary command module for the dispensers into the 4,000 machine-word memory of the small computer we were to use.

With the help of the primatologists I made a list of things that would presumably interest a young chimpanzee and could be available in the project. They were over a hundred. Twenty-five were to be put on the first panel of keys. Each key was to have an abstract design representing not a letter but the "word-design" for a single concept. I called these word-designs "lexigrams". Seven was the maximum length of a sentence. I wanted to use non-representational designs to emphasize their symbol-character and to prevent critical linguists from saying that Lana recognized them because they were just familiar pictures. It seemed a simple enough task, but there was a complication. Whenever Lana pressed a key, the respective lexigram had to be projected in a row of windows above the keyboard, one after the other from left to right. This would help Lana to see how far along she was in typing the sentence. It was necessary, too, so that messages could be sent from a keyboard outside Lana's cubicle for her to read.

Hal Warner, the in-house engineer at Yerkes, found the technical solution of the problem. Ten little projectors would contain simple design elements and project them as needed into the little windows above the keyboard. The lexigrams, consequently, had to be combinations of very simple design elements. I tried all sorts of basic geometrical figures look-

ing for a set that provided the greatest variety of combinatorial possibilities. I used Charlotte as guinea pig. As an artist, I thought, she would be a
good judge of which combinations were easiest to discriminate from one
another. She turned out to be a great help: Lana never confused lexigrams.
I formulated the rules of a primitive syntax that would govern which
lexigram sequences (i.e. sentences) were to be considered correct and
which mistaken. There were three classes of message: statements,
requests, and questions. Requests were differentiated from the others by
first pressing a key we called "please"; questions had to begin with a
question mark; and in order to know when to check the correctness of
Lana's typing the computer needed a signal to indicate the end of a sentence, like a period.

   Lana's training began with a panel of three or four keys, which enabled
her to learn in the good old "stimulus/response" fashion that if she typed
"Please give raisin", she would indeed be given a raisin. Then the configu-
ration of the keys in the panel was changed, and she had to learn that it
was the sequence of lexigrams that counted, not their position in the
panel. She also had to learn that it was always necessary to press the
period key at the end of a sentence. It took about four months and it was
hard work for Lana and the graduate students who every day spent several hours with her. But once she had learned these preliminaries, her
progress was much faster than expected. When she got the first
25-lexigram panel, she quickly learned to watch the row of windows
above the keyboard to check what she had typed. It took her no time to
find out that when she had made a typing error she could erase what she
had typed by pressing the period key. This made the computer cancel the
input because it contained an error; and it saved Lana the time it would
have taken to finish typing an invalid sentence. This, I thought, was a
good first demonstration that Lana's brain was capable of reflection.

   In the five years that I was involved in the Lana project she made it quite
clear that she understood the principle of symbolic communication, i.e.,
that by using symbols she could have some influence on what she was
experiencing. Unfortunately the director of the project was still greatly
hampered by the behaviorist doctrine that shunned the use of
"mentalistic" notions such as meaning, purpose, and intention. In order
to provide statistical evidence of her "skills", Lana was subjected to repetitive tests like a rat in a maze. The results were dismal. Because she was
not kept starving, like the animals in Skinner boxes, she did not care about
the reinforcement if the same problem was repeated four or five times.
Like a human child she lost interest and pressed keys without looking.
Her statistics therefore tended to be worse than those of rats.

On the other hand, she did things that no rat could do. When Tim, the graduate student who worked with her in these experiments, repeated the same question for the nth time, she typed: "Please Tim move out-of room." This was above all remarkable because Lana had encountered expressions such as "out-of", "in-front-of", and "behind" only in the context of boxes and wooden blocks on a table and the notion that her room was a kind of box you could "move out of" was entirely her own.

For conventional experimental psychologists such a reply, a repetition of which could not be forced by the experimenter, was purely "anecdotal" and had no scientific value. The fact that *understanding* in communication could not be tested statistically but shown only by the appropriateness of individual reactions or utterances, was not and, I believe, is still not wholly accepted by the profession. Consequently most of the things that persuaded me that Lana was well able to communicate by means of symbols did not cut any ice with the critics.

There were quite a few other examples of original, spontaneous, and appropriate utterances, but I'll recount only the one that I consider the most sophisticated. Among the things she could request were slices of banana. As bananas tend to be sticky, it happened that the arm of the dispenser that was to deliver them got stuck. One morning when Shelley, another graduate student, who regularly worked with her, appeared outside the Plexiglas cubicle, Lana, instead of waiting for Shelley to come into the cubicle to provide the day's first tickle, rushed to the keyboard and typed: "Please Shelley move behind room." It was a phrase that had never cropped up and Shelley had no idea what it could mean. Lana threw up both her arms in an unmistakable human gesture of despair (presumably acquired by observing her human keepers) and once more typed the same phrase. At that point Shelley happened to look at the array of dispensers and noticed that the one for slices of banana had got stuck. She went out of the cubicle and to the other side of the transparent wall – which from Lana's point of view could quite reasonably be called "behind room". Lana watched her clear the dispenser and immediately typed: "Please machine give piece-of banana."

Once I realized that Lana was indeed capable of forming concepts, I began to wonder to what extent they functioned like ours. I had some ideas of tests that might throw light on this question. Could Lana, for example, correctly answer: "Are bananas blue?" when there was no banana in sight. A correct answer of "no" would require a mental representation of banana that was independent of actual perception. I was also curious whether Lana classified objects and whether her classes were similar to the ones we tend to form. In short, as I was already deep into constructivism, I wanted to find out how Lana organized her experiential reality. There were obviously some solid parallels, but I thought it likely that there would also be differences (not as many, of course, as with a chimp who had grown up in the wild).

Though I mentioned the banana test to the director, there never seemed to be time to fit it into the schedule of experiments. Then, when a renewal of the contract with the sponsoring agency came up, there was the idea to try out the symbol keyboard and the computer system with autistic children. From what was known about them at the time, it seemed likely that they would become interested. I was enthusiastic about the idea and, with the help of Piero Pisani, I drafted a part of the proposal, adding a capability to the system that seemed essential to me: when the child pressed a lexigram key, a recorded voice would speak the English word through a loudspeaker. I saw no point in trying to teach an autistic child a symbolic communication system that did not in some way lead to the language she was to use later.

When we were shown the final draft of the proposal, the voice-part was left out. It would have added eight or nine thousand dollars to the total requested. It was too much, they said. The total was about a quarter of a million. I was furious and, as Piero had had his own disagreements with the direction, we decided to leave the project. The ironical sequel was that less than a year later the project director married a young cognitive psychologist who then did excellent work in the area of animal cognition.

Thoughts about Reason 1970

As we get older many of us male creatures develop troubles in our bladder or its neighborhood. Where we were used to experience pleasure there is now often unpleasantness. If you believe that the pleasures were sinful, you may consider these disturbances as God's punishment. But sooner or later this will raise some unanswerable questions. Why, for instance, should one think of the God who arranged all this as a loving God? Could he not have designed the body's canalization a little better? Or were there in the Garden of Eden earth quakes, hailstorms and floods? Did Adam and Eve have a navel? Were they stung by mosquitoes and had to avoid streptococci, influenza virus, and lice? Or did the loving God invent all these torture tools when He chased the creatures he had made in his image from the heavenly Garden? Was the "Intelligent Designer" so malicious as to create petrified bones and footprints of dinosaurs, animals that had not been created and therefore could hardly go extinct? And what on earth or better, what in heaven made Him think of the grotesque way He chose for us to procreate?

If you want to be a believer you must follow St. Augustine and say to yourself: the important thing is faith, not understanding. But this still leaves the question why God should have given us reason and made understanding so attractive.

I have never forgotten the pleasure I experienced when for the first time I solved a logical puzzle without help. The problem was: are there two people with the same number of hairs on their head? Bald pates were excluded. I don't remember how long it took me to realize that the number of people was very much larger than the number of hairs one person could have, so there had to be many with the same number of hairs; you did not have to count them. When I saw it, it was immensely satisfactory.

* * *

To see logical connections is always satisfactory, except when they imply unpleasant experiences. The conclusion that the 7:30 flight to London you had booked must have left when you get to the airport at 7:45 is logically impeccable but painful. The logical relations among abstract concepts, in contrast, do not imply immediate practical consequences and are always pleasant to see.

It is a great shame that the current methods of instruction do not exploit this effect more often. In middle schools, for example, pupils have to spend days plowing through the algebraic proof of Pythagoras' theorem without ever being shown the perceptual pattern that presumably provided the trigger for Pythagoras to formulate his theorem. The pattern constitutes a perceptual explanation and thus provides a sense to the algebraic proof which it otherwise never acquires.

Pythagoras grew up on the island of Samos. Art historians have lots of evidence that at his time there was a decorative pattern used in the whole

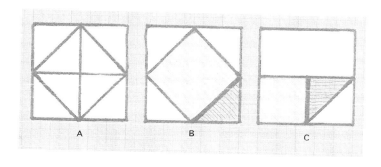

A   B   C

Greek domain of culture on tiles, vases, and even textiles. I imagine
Pythagoras sitting on his terrace one afternoon, drowsy but not quite
unconscious. It may have been the gently moving shadow of a branch that
drew his attention to the pattern of the tiles on the ground. He probably
had never examined it before, but now he saw that it was made up of triangles and squares (A). And as geometry was one of his interests, he
began to define the relations among the single figures.

He knew that the long side of a triangle is called hypotenuse and the
shorter sides cathetes. And now he saw that the square formed over the
hypotenuse of the four equal triangles in the corners of the pattern (B)
contained four triangles of the same size. He looked again and saw that
the square formed over one of the cathetes (C) contained two of these triangles. Consequently the square over the hypotenuse was as large as two
of the squares over the cathetes taken together. For Pythagoras the pattern
of the tiles was now infinitely more interesting than just a decoration, and
because he had his geometric interest he immediately wondered whether
this relation would hold in triangles that were not isosceles. The question
stirred him up and his sleepiness was gone. He got up and fetched a slate
and a stylus and began to draw. It did not take him long to discover that
four similar right-angled triangles could be arranged in two different
ways in a square, so that that the square respectively also contained the
square over the hypotenuse and the two of the ones over the cathetes. He
clearly had established a general rule—and Pythagoras found this so
satisfying that he spent the rest of life searching for such rules.

* * *

Of course reason cannot help us answer the big unanswerable questions,
such as the meaning of life, what lies beyond our experience, where we
came from when we were born, and where we go when we die. But reason
generates a network of relations among concepts that we have abstracted
from our experience and it makes the world we are experiencing far more
interesting than it would be without them. The domain of reason is the
domain of concepts; beyond them she is totally out of her depth.

Once, when I was very young and poetically inclined, I tried to formulate this in a sonnet:

> Tethered and blind,
> With futile tools
> We grope to find
> A soothing truth in rules.
> No one attains a rhyme
> to weave a world together,
> to last forever

against the blast of time.
From night to night
the ladder grows.
Thought upon thought
Into the darkness reason throws,
From nowhere to naught,
but a transient ray of light.

Where the incomprehensible begins only faith can help; and to a faith you
cannot be brought by means of reason.

Indiscretions about Saints 1971

Having come to New York for a meeting, I had a free afternoon and set out
to visit Giorgio Tagliacozzo, who taught Italian and Vico's philosophy at
Columbia University. He edited books about Vico, encouraged translations, compiled bibliographies of relevant articles, and was an altogether
delightful old gentleman. It was a lovely, clear day and I was walking to
Columbia. On the way, far up Lexington Avenue, I saw a big neo-gothic
church. As I came closer I read its name: Saint Vincent Ferrer. I was flabbergasted. San Vincenzo dei Ferreri was an ancestor of my faithful skiing
companion, Cesare Ferrero. I went into the church and found a postcard
to send to Cesare. His full name, which he never used, was so long that I
could never remember it all. He was a Marchese di Ventimiglia and his
family went back far into the Middle Ages. They had an estate halfway
between Mantua and Ferrara and in the 14th century they had somehow
become related to a Spanish Dominican friar, a famous preacher, who
traveled all over Europe and spent several years in Ferrara. Cesare told us
a story that shows that saints could also have a sense of humor. The official *Lives of the Saints* of course doesn't mention this. Vincenzo, it seems,
had a knack for working miracles and enjoyed it; so much so, that the
bishop told him to cool it.

Shortly after that episcopal order, friar Vincenzo was walking along a
street in Ferrara where they were building a house. As he came close to it,
one of the men, high up on the scaffolding, lost his balance and fell off.
Vincenzo stopped him in mid-air and said to a boy standing by:

"Quick, run to the bishop and ask if I may finish this miracle!"

* * *

After the war, when I was earning money as a journalist, I often used my Leica (and what I had learned from my father) to make pictures to include with my feature articles. One of these assignments was a portrait of the city of Piacenza. I spent a week there and heard a lot about Saint Columban, the Irish Monk, who had come to Central Europe with Saint Gall in the 6th century. I knew about him, because near Meran there is a small chapel that contains the oldest frescoes in the Alpine region. They were painted by one of the disciples that followed Saint Columban when he became *persona non grata* in Switzerland and moved to Italy. I had read up about Columban's journey and the pictorial evidence left of it in France and Switzerland. As I now visited Bobbio, the monastery he founded a few miles into the Apennines from Piacenza, I had what seemed to me a brilliant idea. A little book, I thought, a sort of guide with photographs of historic and contemporary sights along Saint Columban's itinerary, could sell quite well among tourists. It would also be great fun to produce. I had visions of the three of us spending a summer traveling with sleeping bags and tent from Auxerre and Annegray in the Vosges mountains of France to Sankt Gallen in Switzerland and then via Chur over the Ofenpass to the court of Milan and ending at Bobbio. I wrote a proposal and sent it to a couple of publishers, but they couldn't have been less interested. So there was no advance and no camping summer. All that remained of Saint Columban were the two stories I was able to work into my article on Piacenza.

When he came to Milan around the year 610, there were not many Christians in Lombardy, but the ruler's wife and some of her friends were among them. She took a liking to Columban and when Easter time came she invited him to dinner. Her husband benignly looked on her religion as a sort of extravagance. But he was not quite without malice. When he was told that Columban would come to dinner on Good Friday, he told his cook to serve fried pigeons, knowing full well that a Catholic could not eat meat on that day. When the birds arrived at the dinner table, Columban did not blink an eyelid. He simply performed a little miracle and turned the pigeons into a delicious pastry. It is said that this is the origin of the *Colomba di Pasqua*, the Easter Pigeon, which is traditionally made by the makers of Panettone at that time of the year.

Columban then moved to Bobbio and founded the monastery there. It was highly successful and soon there was a difference of opinion between Bobbio and the city of Piacenza as to where the border between the two townships should be. It was decided that it should be halfway. To determine that point, at the cock's first crow a dignitary would set out walking from Piacenza and Columban from Bobbio. Where they met, would be the border. It seemed a very reasonable settlement to Columban, but he had not yet discovered the trickiness of the people of Piacenza. They sent a secret agent to Bobbio, and at dawn before the great walk he let the monastery's cock into the granary so that he started feeding and forgot to crow. When Columban woke up, the sun was rising and though he went as fast as he could he met the representative of Piacenza before he was out of sight of the monastery. Maybe he just shrugged his shoulders and thought: Some you win, and some you lose; or, in a more saintly vein: Why should I worry about worldly possessions?

Teaching Psychology 1972

I had been hired as "research associate" by the Psychology Department of the University of Georgia, and this meant that my contract had to be renewed every year. In my second year, Charles Darby suggested that they make me "assistant professor" which would give me about seven years to work for a promotion to "associate professor" and greater security. It was not explicitly said, but I realized that as assistant "prof" I would not get away without teaching, but I thought I had better risk it.

The reason the department had taken me in in the first place was that they had no one who could teach anything about language, and that happened to be my expertise. Now, of course, they realized that this was not enough to teach introductory undergraduate courses in psychology; and in a way this saved me. I was scheduled to teach graduate courses of my choosing and co-teach introductory courses with another member of the department, and one third of my time was reserved for research. In the long run, this suited me very well. My co-teaching consisted in giving a few lectures on language and language acquisition at the right moment in a colleague's introductory course. At the beginning, this, of course, was terrifying because like every novice, no matter how many notes I prepared, I ran out of steam halfway through the allotted time. But after a few moments of panic, I learned to pace myself. With the graduate course it was much easier, because once you had assembled a suitable reading list, the course could be turned into a discussion, which you could start by asking the students about how they interpreted what they had read. And it was not too difficult to formulate the questions so that they were led to think along more adequate lines.

The teacher's role, I realized after a few years, had something in common with that of the dog that is indispensable when you have to drive cattle from one place to another in Ireland. The country roads there are separated from the fields by hedges; but every now and then the hedges have gaps to allow the farmer to get into the field with a cart. If you are alone, driving a few cows down such a road is impossible. You have to stay behind the animals to urge them on, and when the first cow comes to a gap in the hedge, she inevitably sees the nice grass in the field and goes through the gap. The others, of course, are only too happy to follow—and once the five or six cows are scattered in the field you have no way of getting them back on the road. That is where the dog comes in. With a little training he knows what to do. He stays ahead of the cows and when he sees a gap in the hedge, he just stands in it and barks until the cows have passed. A teacher cannot know where the students are going. He cannot give them what he would like them to think, but thanks to language he can stop trains of thought that he considers unhelpful. Maturana called this the orienting function of language.

* * *

When I became involved in the chimpanzee research at the Yerkes Center in Atlanta, this paid for another third of my time, so that I had to teach only one course per quarter. When I resigned from the Lana project, my colleague Charlie Smock asked me to join the Georgia Follow Through Program and the research on children's development of mathematical concepts became a replacement of the chimp research. I had no idea that this new focus of interest was going to determine my future. Throughout my time at the University of Georgia I was able to have external research projects that relieved me of one third of my teaching obligation.

It was Charlie Smock who introduced me to the theoretical world of Jean Piaget. Years before, when I was working at the Center of Cybernetics in Milan, I had read a reference to Piaget and had asked Ceccato about it. Don't bother, Ceccato said, he is interested in children. They had met several times and Piaget had made Ceccato one of the editors of his series of Epistemological Studies, a long chain of publications in which the various branches of Piaget's theory were described in great detail. I don't think Ceccato ever read any of them. He had taken an instant dislike to the man. In a way, this was a tragedy, because although Ceccato's ideas pertained to a lower level of analysis, they fitted well with Piaget's notions about cognitive development. The two could have been of great help to one another. I realized this when I started reading the many original Piaget publications that Smock had collected during his years at Geneva and I am eternally grateful to him for having given them to me.

Many times when I tried to explain some idea of mine to Smock, he would tell me that it was exactly what Piaget had said. This was a big encouragement for me and I avidly read the French texts. They greatly enriched my thinking and, no less important, provided a vocabulary that was comfortable for me to use.

* * *

From both the Charles (Darby and Smock) I got valuable tips about how to supervise students' master theses and dissertations. It was a very worth-while activity and I learned an enormous amount in my own way of thinking from the graduate students I had the privilege of teaching. The reason is that, once they have realized that you don't mind questions, they will ask about anything they don't understand. Your colleagues, who listen to talks you give in the department or at conferences elsewhere, are extremely reluctant to discuss things about which they themselves are not quite certain. Students' questions, on the other hand, often draw your attention to things that you have not expressed adequately or to holes in your reasoning. And the actual research they carry out under your guidance is often as much of a benefit to you as to them.

The research, for example, that Michael Tomasello and his wife did on the language acquisition of their daughter during the second year of her life not only provided him with a master's thesis as well as a doctoral dissertation, but was also of enormous value to me in that it supplied me with additional experiential material to underpin Piaget's theory of development.

Michael's PhD also did something for me of which I did not immediately become aware. Shortly after his graduation he got a job in the psychology department of Emory University in Atlanta. I was pleased because it meant that interaction with him would continue a little longer, but it did not strike me as unusual. After a few weeks, however, one of my colleagues took me aside and asked whether I had noticed that some of the behaviorists in the department had changed their opinion of me. I couldn't say that I had; but he explained that Emory was a private school and considered far more exclusive than Georgia University. No student of ours had ever got a job there. Your student now has, he said, therefore your colleagues think that you may be a professor of psychology after all.

Chapter Seven

1973–2009

Language and Thought 1973

Through Charlie Smock I came into contact with Les Steffe in the School of Education, who directed research on how to teach mathematics. He was intrigued by my ideas about language and asked me to join him in a project on children's acquisition of the concept of number. It was the beginning of a collaboration that lasted more than two decades and at once forced me to organize, formulate, and in some way justify thoughts I had been playing with for a long time.

Growing up with several languages, rather than with one, is fundamentally different from learning them in school or with the help of a primer. Growing into a language means that you pick it up in situations through which you are living, building up the meaning of words on the basis of what you are actually experiencing. When the teacher in a French lesson explains the meaning of a French word, or when you read its definition in a bilingual dictionary, the concepts the words of the explanation call up in you are inevitably concepts that you formed in the context of speaking English. They are frequently different from those a French child learned to form in his or her interactions with native speakers of French.

Living in more than one language, you cannot help becoming aware of the conceptual differences. The worlds described by different languages are hardly ever quite the same and sooner or later you stumble on the question which of your languages gives the right picture. It did not take me long to realize that this was a silly question. For a native speaker of English, the world English depicts is the only one he or she knows and there is no reason to suspect that it might not be the only one. Of course, one's friends and enemies sometimes see things differently, too, but one explains this as a matter of perspective (or stupidity) and it does not suggest that they see a different world.

Years of daily interaction with the speakers of different languages provide sufficient evidence that the worlds they live in are not identical. They are close enough for much of what they know to be compatible, but that does not mean that their worlds have to be the same.

It was this realization that triggered my life-long preoccupation with the theory of knowledge. My readings started with Wittgenstein's *Tractatus* and were accidentally directed by Joyce's *Finnegans Wake* to the Italian 18th-century philosopher Vico, who said that to know something means to know how it has been put together. This gave me the notion of construction that became the core of my thinking. It gave me a fruitful way of reading the Irish philosopher George Berkeley, to whom Gordon Glenavy introduced me, and it proved eminently compatible with the teachings of Ceccato with whom in one way or another I worked for almost twenty years. When I came to the United States and studied the works of Jean Piaget, I found that he had called his approach to children's cognitive processes and acquisition of knowledge "constructivism".

Piaget's statement that the mind organizes the world by organizing itself became the leading principle of my endeavors and much of my work consists in going to the roots of ideas that he left implicit — which is why I called it "radical constructivism".

With the notion of the mind organizing itself and its search for equilibrium, Piaget had anticipated the main concepts of cybernetics and I made it my business to interpret him from that position. A useful metaphor for the way we build up what we know is the course of a river. Its bed, that is where and how it flows, is carved out of the landscape by the force of the water and the fact that it cannot flow uphill. It is a cybernetic process in that it constantly generates a labile equilibrium between the force of the water and the constraints of the landscape. If the river were conscious of its flowing, it still could never get to know the landscape. It would become aware only of impediments to its progress. Thus I believe, as the sceptics have proclaimed for almost three thousand years, that we cannot come to know "reality", that is, a world as it might exist independently of us; we can only construct a more or less stable model of a world in the domain of our experience. How this experience is caused by something that lies beyond it cannot be grasped by our reason and must therefore remain the playground of mystics and metaphysicians.

I have often been accused of solipsism, that is the denial of a reality existing by itself. It's an accusation made by people who have not paid much attention to what I have said or written. I hold with Berkeley, who said that we cannot possibly know what the word "to be" or "to exist" should mean outside the domain of experience. I therefore profess agnosticism with regard to reality, but I do not deny it. The theory of knowledge I have developed is an attempt to show that all we know by way of reason can be built up from elements that we ourselves experience.

Our Lady of the Deep Snow 1973

My mother did not believe in frantic telephone messages. So when she broke her hip she waited until she was relatively comfortable in the hospital before writing us a letter. I called her the moment we received it, but she did not want to extend the conversation. As in her letter, she was mainly concerned that I shouldn't think she broke her hip while skiing. "I spilled some oil in the kitchen and promptly slipped on it," she said; "a stupid, avoidable accident." I asked her to let me know when they would allow her to leave the hospital. I wanted to be there for her first few days back in her apartment.

"It was so stupid," she said when I saw her. "It's been years since I fell on skis, and then I had to break a hip in my kitchen! I didn't believe it at first. It hurt, but I thought it was just a bad bruise and went to bed. The next morning I couldn't get up. They had to send an ambulance! Can you believe it?"

She quickly learned to wield her crutches like the athlete she was, and by the time I had to leave again (I couldn't interrupt the course I was teaching for much more than a week), she could balance on one crutch and use the other to push a chair where she wanted it. She moved so well that I had no qualms leaving her alone again with just Mme M, the housekeeper who lived downstairs. "Take it easy, when you start walking again," I said, "but do walk. Get Mme M to help you to get down to the street. Take your ski poles to steady yourself and go for a little walk. Not too much, but every day."

She was very good about it. She went a little further day after day but didn't overdo it. After six or seven weeks she wrote that she was going to use cross-country skis instead of walking. Some of the chaps from the village with whom she had been to the glaciers in the preceding winter said they would keep her company so that she didn't have to run alone. They had seen her ski in deep snow and had great admiration for her.

At the end of the winter she was perfectly fit again and there seemed to be no aftermath from the accident. But one evening during my next visit she shook her head and said: "I will not be downhill skiing again. You won't believe it, but I became not just nervous, I was downright frightened when my skis began to run a little faster on the cross country track. I had to brake on the slightest slope. I've lost my confidence because of that damned hip. It won't do."

She stuck with that decision during the next few winters. She went on the cross country track when her friends in the village told her that they would be there, too. I don't think she really enjoyed it, but she felt she had to keep fit. Her interest in life had been decimated by her accident. She saw it as a sign of incompetence. She began to decline. When she got faint at the age of eighty-eight, the nurse who looked after her wrote to me: "Almost every day she says that she's had a wonderful life but she doesn't want to go on living. Don't expect her to be here much longer."

The nurse was right. It came suddenly with spells of unconsciousness. By the time I got there, she was no longer aware of anything. She died the next day and left me trying to find a way to cope with it. For the second time the lid had clamped on a large section of my world. What, I wondered, are memories if they are only your own?

I arranged for the cremation, and the handful of people who had known her for years came to an informal gathering. There were two youngish men from the village whom I didn't know. They introduced themselves and explained that they had been running the cross country track with my mother. They had brought a bunch of flowers and the large note tied to them read: "Notre Dame de la grosse neige."

Getting US Citizenship 1974

In the 1970s the University of Georgia still had the old isolationist rule that foreigners could not be granted "tenure". If you didn't have tenure, the administration was under no obligation to renew your yearly contract. After our experience with the Air Force, I did not like that prospect and decided to apply for United States citizenship. When I mentioned this to Adrian, an art historian with whom we had become friends, he said that the arts department had advised him that as long as he was a British subject, they could not give him tenure. Like me, he did not have a PhD and shared my suspicion that this could be used at any time to terminate our employment.

"At first I was rather reluctant," he said, "but recently I have found out that I don't have to give up my original citizenship to get naturalized here. So I've decided to do it. Maybe if we apply at the same time we'll be summoned to the induction or whatever they call it at the same time. It takes place in Macon, the official capital of Georgia, and I've been told they do it in large batches. It would be fun to drive down there together, wouldn't it?"

Charlotte and I were delighted to turn a dreary chore into an entertaining excursion.

Driving to Macon with Adrian and his Junoesque companion Helena in his new BMW, we were in very good spirits. Part of the way we practiced the things we were going to be tested on. When our applications had been accepted we had received a little booklet spelling out all the things US citizens were supposed to know about their government and its history. Adrian and I were amused when we discovered that our native women knew almost as little about all that as we did. For the rest of the drive Adrian recounted his war experiences. He had been a bomber pilot, but after a year of flying almost daily missions, something gave way in him and he couldn't do it any longer. Seeing some of the planes that were flying beside him explode when they were hit by anti-aircraft shells, had gradually worn him down. He had something of a nervous break-down and decided to resign his commission in the RAF. But this was not possible. The only way out was to be demoted. He apparently succeeded in convincing the Air Force psychologists that he had to get out, and he was discharged with the classification "LMF" in his papers. He explained that LMF meant "lack of moral fiber". Turning to Helena, who was at least twenty years younger than he, he said:

"You'd agree, wouldn't you?"

She had been a student of his at the New England school where he had been teaching history of art. She was exceptionally good looking and interested in painting and in writing poetry. To keep their affair secret they had had to resort to unconventional means such as smuggling her out of his apartment in the trunk of his car. They had a cheerful relationship and she decided to come with him when he moved to the University of Georgia. But after a while she lost her interest in art and wanted to become a real estate agent. After they had amicably parted, he said to me:

"There I was, in love with a poet, and she turned out to be a realtor."

At Macon, all the applicants were interviewed individually. It was done alphabetically and Adrian's turn came quite quickly. When he came out he said:

"I don't think we took this lightly enough. Three questions I was asked, that was all."

As I had to wait until they had reached the letter V, Adrian, Helena, and Charlotte went off to get a coffee somewhere. They came back and I was still waiting. When my name came up and I appeared before the examining official, I was suddenly nervous. The instruction booklet had given the list of all the presidents of the United States and I certainly could not recite the whole lot of them. But I needn't have worried. Just as with Adrian, there were three questions: what does the government of the United States consist of (House of Representatives, Senate, and Supreme Court), who is the present President, and — to make sure that I knew some English — I was asked to recite the names of the days of the week.

Then came the solemn ceremony. We were led into a big hall where, collectively with some 300 Mexicans, Vietnamese, Greeks, and other immigrants we listened to the Oath of Allegiance and raised our hand in assent. At that moment the national anthem burst like thunder from loudspeakers and whoever knew the words began to sing.

As we left the building, three weathered Daughters of the American Revolution handed a little paper flag to every one of us. The stars and stripes were about two inches square and neatly glued to a wooden stick, a little thicker than a toothpick. Back in the car, I looked at this precious memento of the great day. On the wooden stick it said in neat, clear print: MADE IN JAPAN.

Reflections on Time and Space 1978

On some of my trips to Dublin, after we had settled in the United States, I visited David Berman, who taught philosophy at Trinity College, and I think it was he who suggested I look at some of the papers of the Irish mathematician William Rowan Hamilton which were in the Trinity Library. Most of them treated a level of mathematics that was well above my head. But I came across one that was philosophical and contained no formulas. I was attracted by its title: "Algebra as the Science of Pure Time". I found in it an invaluable hint about the conceptual construction of time.

Hamilton makes the startling observation that the concept of time is the result of projecting one series of experiences onto another. I thought it was startling, because unlike the modern physicists, who say that time began with the Big Bang, which gives it an independent existence, Hamilton suggested that it had to be conceived by a thinker, that is, some agent that deliberately projects and relates. Except for Wittgenstein, who casually mentions the same idea in his *Tractatus*, I don't know anyone else who shared it.

Berkeley, of course, said that time is "a thing of the mind" and Piaget makes the generic remark that "Time is nothing but the interrelating of the events that it contains". I agree, but this is not specific enough. I wanted to know how one could come to have the concept of time and was intrigued by the notion of projection. So I started from Hamilton's assertion and tried to think of how the projection of experiences he speaks of could be implemented in practice. A discussion with Charlotte's daughter Lisa, who is a dancer and very much aware of the problem of translating sensations into movement and vice versa, was of great help. For the notion of projection she immediately had a variety of applications, but what I needed was a way to describe what one had to do to "project". I suggested looking at the frame of the window in front of us and imagining beside it a vertical yard stick marked in feet. We noticed that our attention was either on the window frame or on the yard stick but could not be on both at once. We could, however, superimpose the attentional pattern of the one on the other; that is to say, you could begin to see the window frame divided into the sections of the yard stick, or conversely, the yard stick, disregarding the marks on it, as an unbroken whole. In other words, we were able to superimpose a different attentional pattern on an actual experience. This gave me an imaginable application of the kind of projection Hamilton had spoken of.

One night, lying in bed, I was scratching a mosquito bite on my left arm and it struck me that this was giving rise to two parallel experiences, between which attention can shift to and fro, like between the window frame and the yard stick. It seemed a promising idea and I played with it for several days. This is what I ended up with.

Rub one finger of your right hand on the bare skin of your left arm, from the wrist to the elbow. You have two sequences of sensation: one single source in your finger signals an unbroken repetition of contacts. In your arm, instead, a number of different sources signal points of contact with something. (Note that the sources by themselves cannot tell you what the contact is with.)

At first you may not find it easy to separate the two sources of sensation; but if you try it in bed, when the room is dark and there are practically no other perceptions, you will succeed.

In your finger, the point of origin remains the same, but in your arm, the point of origin changes. In both cases there is a sequence of experiences that come one after the other. These sequences are not the result of a medium that flows and passes, a medium like a river that carries experiences in and out of your awareness. The sequences are the result of the fact that experiences have to follow one upon the other because you cannot be aware of two experiences at once.

In the little experiment in bed you become aware of a succession of touched spots on your arm and of a repetition of contact made by your finger. These experiences differ in more than the places of origin. The sensations originating in the arm are perceived as qualitatively similar—a signal that something is touching the arm. As sensations they are not distinguished and therefore cannot, on this first level of abstraction, constitute a plurality. They are merged into a continuity. The sensations from the finger, in contrast, are not all quite the same, because of unevenness or hairs on the surface of the arm. Hence they tend to remain a succession.

This difference is crucial when the one sequence of sensations is projected onto the other. If a succession of discrete experiences is projected onto a continuity, the items of the succession articulate the continuity into discrete segments, each of which covers a certain stretch that can now be seen as 'duration', i.e. a portion of time. If, on the other hand, a continuity of experience is projected on a sequence of sensations, what leads from one sensation to the next can be seen as 'extension' and what separates them as space.

This can now be summarized: If an uninterrupted succession of differing sensations from one and the same source is linked to form a continuity, it gives rise to the concept of time; if, in contrast, a sequence of similar sensations from different sources is linked, it generates the concept of space.

If you accept this "explanation", it becomes clear that to say "time goes by" is not even a metaphor, it is a useless fiction. Time does not move, it's our experiences that, following one upon the other, necessarily pass.

Faux Pas 1980

During the three years that our project at the University of Georgia lasted, an additional contract with the US Air Force made it possible that Jehane, my original collaborator, could come to work with us for one month every year. Her help with semantic analysis was invaluable. She stayed with Isabel and me and we had a cheerful time together. When the Air Force contract was terminated, I did not hear from Jehane for several years. Then, one day she telephoned from California and told me that she was working with the architect Charles Eames and was just then helping him with the Copernicus exhibition in New York. Eames died shortly after this and Jehane wrote that she was staying another year to help his widow cope with the unfinished projects he had left behind. Again, there followed some years without news from Jehane.

Once more she telephoned, this time from Boston. I have great news to tell you, she said, and you won't guess what it's about. But as it is difficult to keep listeners in suspense on the phone, she quickly told us: she had got married, and her husband was the famous philosopher Thomas Kuhn. It certainly was astonishing news. I had not only read Kuhn's book about scientific revolutions, but also cited it frequently in my papers. When Jehane suggested that the next time Charlotte and I came to Boston we should visit them, I was delightedly looking forward to discussions with him.

It so happened that a linguistics conference in Cambridge provided a pretext to drive to Boston. I was far more interested in talking with Kuhn than in the papers at the conference. When we got to their apartment, there were drinks and for some time the conventional questions and answers. I noticed that Kuhn seemed to be a little nervous and absent-minded. Very soon he excused himself and went to the adjoining kitchen. Jehane explained that he had a passion for cooking and had decided to make a sauce hollandaise to go with the fish that evening, and sauce hollandaise was a rather tricky thing. The door to the kitchen remained open, and we caught glimpses of Kuhn feverishly dashing to and fro.

Jehane wanted to hear about Athens and what had happened since she had last been there, and we told her about the end of the research project and the generosity the university showed in taking over the entire team. When the dinner was served, it was quite excellent and we congratulated the chef on his sauce hollandaise. Jehane soon steered the conversation towards language and semantics and Kuhn mentioned the philosopher Jerry Fodor, whose presentation he had just heard that afternoon at the conference. Probably it was the presence of Jehane that somehow fostered the illusion of being at home. It never occurred to me that Kuhn and Fodor could be friends and in a moment of thoughtlessness I said I considered it irresponsible of Fodor to talk about "representations" without adding that they could never be representations of reality.

Kuhn dropped his fork and burst out:

"How could you say such a thing!"

He was so shocked that he got up and had to walk up and down behind his chair in order to calm himself. When he sat down again it was clear that there could be no more talk about philosophy.

It was the greatest faux pas that I ever committed. And I have not ceased to regret it. There was so much I would have liked to discuss with Kuhn, because he, too, has suggested in his book that a traditional epistemology was no longer acceptable. He was someone with whom it would have been enormously profitable to talk about unconventional ideas.

Sandra 1992

Our daughter Sandra had gone to elementary school in Partschins, the village in the South Tyrol where we lived in the Gaudententurm, the transformed "tower of revelers". The village school was half German and half Italian. In Meran, she then went to a small middle school that also dealt with both languages. From early on, she had been drawing a lot— Isabel helped her whenever she wanted help—and by the time she was ten, her sketches were not at all childish. Her interest, however, shifted to modeling and though we provided some clay, it was not an art form we could teach her. When she had finished the second year of middle school, it was clear that she would choose some artistic activity. Through my parents, I knew the well-known Tyrolean ceramist Maria Delago and when we showed her some of Sandra's drawings, she agreed to take her on as an apprentice. Isabel and I were going to look after Sandra's general education. As she was a voracious reader, this was not too difficult a task.

Three times a week Sandra rode her bicycle to the bus to Bolzano, the larger town twenty miles south of Meran. There she went to Delago's atelier and came home again at night. As an apprentice, it was her job to clean up the atelier and to function as a menial helper to the Artist. But in between, Maria Delago demonstrated and explained all the procedures that a professional ceramist uses and besides she introduced Sandra to the techniques of print-making and gave her critiques and advice for the drawings she went on making.

By the time we moved to Milan, Sandra had gone through a very productive apprenticeship, and when we showed a portfolio of drawings and color sketches to the people at the Brera Academy of Art, they let her enter their courses, though she did not have a high school diploma. She spent most of the day there and received an education that, as I realized later, was different from what she might have got in the arts departments of the universities of Georgia or Massachusetts. It was an education in classical drawing and painting, where teachers talked about methods and techniques, and the notion of creativity was mentioned only in the occasional lecture on the philosophy of art. When Sandra was eighteen, she could draw anything she wanted and decided to leave the Brera.

All along in the evenings, when we didn't go to the theatre—which during those years was quite enthralling in Milan—she had been typing away for hours in her room on the small Olivetti machine we had given her. Isabel asked her what she was writing, and Sandra said:

"I'm trying to write stories, but I haven't anything yet that I could show you."

Then she came home one evening and put a book before us on the table. It was a novel she had written and sent to a publisher on her own. Although we certainly never underrated Sandra's capabilities, this was a great surprise and we tried to celebrate it in an adequate fashion. The novel was no masterpiece and did not become a bestseller. It had nothing of the precocious maturity that, some ten years earlier, had given Françoise Sagan's first novel its international appeal. It did contain some good descriptions of people and situations—and Sandra said she was already making notes for her next book. Isabel and I were happy that she had found a satisfactory occupation.

Shortly after this, one of the big department stores in Milan gave her a commission to design a painted background for one of their windows. She produced a colorful fantasy landscape, and people liked it so much that she was given a second commission. What amused me was that the fee she received for each of them was larger than my monthly salary at the Cybernetics Center. It seemed that she would have no difficulty earning her living. But she took no further commissions because she married a rich young man and spent the next few months furnishing and decorating their luxurious apartment. It was the end of her artistic career. Before Isabel and I moved to the United States, Sandra left her husband and began to collaborate with a newly launched journal for art and literature. She became the companion of Franco Ceccarelli, the guitarist of the most successful rock group in Italy. With him she had a daughter, whom she called Sandra, like herself, and who today is a highly successful actress in Italy.

* * *

In the spring of 1969, after Isabel died, Sandra and Franco came to stay with me for a few days. I realized then that we had become strangers. A few months later, after a conference in Sweden, I visited her in Milan. She was running a little shop, a shop that I can only describe as Hippy-land. It was then that I started wondering why, after what to us had seemed an ideal childhood, she had become a dissident, a fighter against any kind of rules and order. A year later she was arrested and found guilty of possession and dealing in drugs. She was given a brief sentence and when she was released she left for India. There, too, she got into difficulties with the law and my only connection with her was through an extremely helpful woman at the Italian Embassy in Calcutta who had befriended her. After she returned to Italy, I met her for a day in Meran. She freely admitted that she was using heroin but was convinced that she had it under control. Indeed, when I met her in Milan a couple of years later, she seemed to be well in control of her life. It was the last time I saw her. Late on Christmas day 1991, her daughter telephoned to say that her mother had killed herself. It was the first and only time I was glad that Isabel was no longer alive.

* * *

Inevitably you ask yourself: What did we do wrong? Gregory Bateson, who knew more than most about the emotional traps in our minds, said it was an unwarranted presumption to claim responsibility for another's suicide. I had accepted this view long ago, and now it certainly was a help; but I still felt that, as parents, part of the fault must have been ours. I chewed it over during many a sleepless night. There was no trauma I could think of. We had always acted as a trio and Sandra was never left out in the cold. Yet I have come to believe that she must have felt lonely. The harmony that reigned between Isabel and myself was not something she could share. It was a harmony based on countless experiences and the gradual development of a common way of experiencing. Sandra had no such stock of past experiences — she was still learning to make them.

This, I think, made her sometimes feel like an outsider, and she resented it. There was no way she could side with one of us against the other. I had observed this in several households with children. They found and enjoyed occasions to play off one parent against the other. With us, Sandra had no opportunity to do this. It made her feel inconsequential, as though she did not matter to us. This was certainly not the case. But how do you show affection? A peck on the cheek and a hug are registered by children as conventional acts; they do not convey an intrinsic meaning. Hence the tendency to test the existence of a relationship by seeing what reactions you can cause in the other. In married couples this often takes the form of irritating the other in well practiced ways. In children it may boil down to generating annoyance.

It would be sad to conclude that a truly harmonious couple is a dangerous background for a child. I don't think this is a necessary conclusion. But children, I now believe, should get away from their parents before they reach puberty.

Heinz von Foerster 2002

I had the good fortune of knowing Heinz von Foerster for forty years. He was very much part of my life. His death left a big hole in my world.

The first time I saw Heinz was in the mid-sixties at a dinner at the California Institute of Technology in Pasadena. Rowena Swanson had taken me there on my first trip to the United States. Rowena was the courageous monitor of US Air Force research projects involving almost all the early cyberneticians. By supporting Warren McCulloch, Gordon Pask, Heinz, David Rothenberg, and others she contributed a great deal to the development of second-order cybernetics. Her policy was that cyberneticians should be acquainted with one another and discuss their work and problems as often as possible. The early cyberneticians were a very diverse collection of characters, and left to themselves, it might have taken them a long time to meet anyone who was thinking along similar lines. Anyway, for newcomers like myself being introduced to them was a great boon because it enabled me to step, as it were, into a movement that had already gathered momentum but would probably have remained hidden from me had I been left to my own devices.

I knew no one at that dinner in Pasadena and I felt awkward because my neighbors did not seem very responsive. I needn't have worried. In time I learned that scientists tend to concentrate on their food and don't say much when they are eating. We were well into the second course, when a bouncy figure came rushing in and everybody shouted "Heinz! Heinz!" They obviously all knew him and he presumably knew everyone. Later Rowena introduced me to him. I told him that I had read some of his papers and that ... but he interrupted me and said:

"So you may have been corrupted."

That was the extent of our conversation that evening.

My first opportunity to have a real talk with Heinz was when he came to the University of Georgia to present a paper. It must have been in 1967, just after we had arrived there. Rowena had the plan of making the University of Georgia into a kind of MIT of the South. It was the reason why our project had been settled there and she had told us that both Heinz von Foerster and Warren McCulloch were going to spend part of the coming years working there. Of course that never happened and our project was the only one that was for some time settled there.

I have no recollection of what he said in that talk of his, but he must have mentioned something about language that prompted me to button-hole him afterwards. It became a very long evening and a landmark for me. Heinz was the first scientist who encouraged my ideas about language. My ideas were diametrically opposed to Chomsky's, who was the infallible pope of linguistics in those days. Papers I gave at conferences were always being attacked; unreasonably, I thought, but nevertheless I felt a little lonely at times. Heinz's support was very important to me.

From then on, Heinz and I met fairly frequently at conferences and I don't remember where it was, but one evening Heinz mentioned something about his past in the Alps. Heinz was both a good skier and a superb rock-climber and we discovered that several of the mountain companions he had in the days before he came to the States, were people I knew because my mother knew them. She was also a great skier and often took me to races where she participated. I had in fact met some of Heinz's friends and we had a lot of pleasant memories to talk about from wonderful skiing excursions in the early 1930s. Indeed, we thought it quite possible that some time or other we were skiing on the same mountain on the same day, but never met.

From my point of view, Heinz has made three momentous contributions to our thinking about knowledge and science. His rediscovery of Johannes Müller's principle of "undifferentiated coding" was the first. It says that the signals produced by our sense organs differ quantitatively but are qualitatively all the same. As Heinz put it, they tell us how much, but never what. The qualities are our contribution. They are the basis of the differentiated experiential world we construct, but they do not carry information about an external reality. Müller's principle provides a comfortable empirical finding that harmonizes with a conclusion that is in any case logically necessary. From it derives the second foundational insight, the realization that, as Heinz said, objectivity is the delusion that observations could be made without an observer. This puts any form of realism out of bounds. All we can talk about and discuss is what someone has experienced, not a world as it might be "in itself".

Heinz's third contribution is the one that causes the most profound resistance against the constructivist way of thinking. It is the clear statement of the fact that, if it is we who construct our knowledge of the world and our ways of dealing with it, then it is we who are responsible for what we think and do. This does not entail that we are free to act as we like; but between the constraints that we encounter there are always possible choices and we cannot shirk the responsibility for what we have chosen.

Throughout the years we supported each other as well as we could. The line of thought we were developing was not at all popular. It still isn't.

Only recently, someone suggested on the website of the American Society for Cybernetics that it was time to replace constructivism with "constructive realism", a way of thinking that is quite incompatible with ours. Like so many, the writer had not grasped the basic principles of Heinz's and my thinking.

Given his third principle that squarely placed the responsibility for our actions on our shoulders, Heinz was preoccupied with ethics. Through the years he formulated some "imperatives":

1:   One should always say "I shall" or "I shall not" and never "Thou shalt" or "Thou shalt not".

2:   That you have to act in order to see.

This is an extrapolation from Piaget's analysis of perception. But Heinz exported it into the sphere of metaphorical seeing: to see that an idea is worth having, you must act to find out whether it is viable.

3:   A third one said that it was better to increase the number of choices rather than attempt to curtail them.

As I see it, this is fine as an over-all goal; but on the way, innumerable choices have to be excluded—otherwise there is no chance of getting where you wanted to be.

I do not want to repeat reminiscences that I have written about elsewhere. Heinz will be remembered by many who are still young today, for he had unbounded generosity towards students. He encouraged them endlessly, even if the ideas they were pursuing were incompatible with his own. A rare attitude among original thinkers.

To conclude this brief eulogy, I want to report a remark that characterizes Heinz's attitude and his unquenchable humor better than anything else. During his last year, I phoned him shortly after the amputation of his leg. I asked how he felt. "Better", he said, "because I know that I'll feel worse tomorrow."

Durrell on Love 2005

When I became literary editor of the *Standpunkt*, I broke the rule to review only books sent to us by publishers. My predecessor had stuck to this, largely because he did not read much that was not in German. I had no hesitation in reviewing foreign publications of which I was fairly sure that, eventually, they would be translated into German. For instance I wrote lead articles for my section of the weekly about the discovery and publication of Benjamin Constant's *Cécile*, an incomparable analysis of his affair with Mme de Staël, and a long review of Françoise Sagan's first novel, *Un certain sourire*. Thus it came about that I recommended the first two volumes of Lawrence Durrell's *Alexandria Quartet* as soon as they came out in English. I sent him the review and expressed the hope that he would write a book in which he would devote his extraordinary analytical skills to a happy love.

Novelists by and large have failed to do this. They usually state that A and B are in love with each other or simply describe them making it. There is hardly an attempt to show the reader why this should be happening. I felt that Durrell's subtle way of dealing with emotions might provide a way to show this successfully. I received a friendly letter in return, but as he said he could not read German, I cannot claim to have had an influence on his later work. But as I remember it, when I received *Clea*, the third volume of the Quartet, I thought he had done it, but I still had no idea how. Reading the book again, forty years later, I have the same impression. But I am far from sure how he succeeds in creating it. There are some points that now seem crucial to me — perhaps because I have reflected so much on my cloudless relation with Isabel. What develops in the conversations of Clea and Darley is the feeling that there are no things that have to be kept secret, the feeling that there is no need to worry about what the other might think of one's recollections. This creates a unique climate. Clea knows about Darley's love for Melissa (who died) and she knows about his painful passion for Justine. She accepts all that and more as part of him and his past life. There is no reason not to mention it, no fear that it might tarnish what they have now.

* * *

Since Isabel's death, I have often remembered a blissful moment when we lay entwined in bed, ready to go to sleep. Although it was pitch dark, she turned her head towards me.

"Do you often think of Lea?"

I was struck silent for a moment.

"Why do you ask? I haven't thought of her in years."

She gently put her lips on my mouth and gave me a sweet peaceful kiss.

"I wouldn't mind if you did," she whispered, "I know that I owe her half the fun we are having in bed."

It is the sublime confidence that nothing whatever can diminish a perfect fit. Once such confidence has grown, there is nothing you cannot talk about, nothing that has to be skirted.

Is it an accident that Clea was a painter, too? I would like to think that it isn't. Painters—the genuine ones, I mean, not the impostors who throw paint on a canvas in the hope that the manager of a gallery or a critic will find something fetching to say about it; nor the naïve dilettantes who intend to replicate on canvas or paper a piece of the real world. I mean the genuine painters who know full well that what they see is not a copy, but the fruit of their imagination. Their task is to produce an artifact that might engender a comparable image in the viewer.

* * *

I don't know whether rereading the book earlier would have helped me to recount events that might convey just how perfect my relationship with Isabel was. I have only been able to describe how I felt about it. Durrell gives the reader many hours of talk that preceded the union of Clea and Darley. Isabel and I, too, had many conversations before that night in Central Australia when we became lovers. And by "conversation" I do not mean the exchange of information but rather what seems to me the opening up of new vistas, new landscapes. that then become common ground. I see it as an exchange and mutual appropriation of images, views, judgments, and convictions that reveal one's stance in every sense of the word. In our case, we instantly liked where the other stood and wanted to find out more and more of that private world. In time, Isabel was able to introduce me to a far deeper understanding of art, modern and old, than I could ever have reached by myself; and I opened for her aspects of the rational approach that did not seem to contradict what she had come to believe. The miracle was that none of this led to friction, let alone conflict, but to the gentlest most rewarding form of compatibility.

A Dream about Numbers 2006

Last night I dreamt that I was talking to someone about the concept of number. It was a short dream, but unlike most others I remembered it very clearly when I woke up. I don't know who it was I was talking to. It wasn't someone I have ever known. That, I suppose, is not unusual. We often meet people in our dreams whom we have not actually met. The surprising thing was that what I said to that person was something I had never consciously formulated.

Ordinal numbers, I said, reflect a continuing pattern in space, cardinal numbers, a completed sequence in time.

I thought this was a neat, if somewhat esoteric way of saying something; Piaget had suggested it, but he, as far as I know, never made it quite explicit. It provides some reason for the fact that we can count objects in any order and come to the same result; and that we can then take this result as an indication of numerosity (i.e. how many objects there are, i.e. "cardinality") because we completed an ordered list of number-words. Ordinals, on the other hand, have a sequential experiential order before number words are joined to them. Apples lying on the table have no relation to ordinal numbers, it is our focusing on them, one after the other, that confers ordinal positions on them.

The experience startled me because it suggests that the unconscious can produce novel reflections that are perfectly valid on the level of conscious reasoning.

Paul Watzlawick 2007

Paul Watzlawick died in March 2007 at the age of 86. With him, I lost a dear friend and battle companion. My acquaintance with him began when, attracted by the title, I bought a paperback called *How Real Is Real*. I didn't have great expectations, but when I started reading it that evening, I was instantly captivated. It turned out to be a psychologist's compendium of experiments and observations that demonstrated to anyone who wanted to see it just how much the world in which people believe to be living is their own creation. I was teaching a course on constructivism at the University of Georgia and at once ordered Watzlawick's book for my students to read. It became a stock item on the reading lists I gave students, both in psychology and in linguistics.

When Heinz von Foerster invited me a year later to the conference on The Construction of Realities in San Francisco, I was delighted to have the opportunity of meeting Watzlawick in person. We became friends at once, not only because of the compatibility of our epistemological ideas but also because Paul, too, was used to living in several languages and we had a wonderful time unraveling some of the differences we had found between them. He had grown up in Austria, studied in Italy, later with Jung in Zürich, taught in San Salvador, and was now co-director of the Institute of Mental Research in Palo Alto and taught psychotherapy at Stanford.

As a result of the San Francisco conference he decided to edit a book and asked me to write the introductory chapter based on the paper I had given. This book was first published in German as *Die erfundene Wirklichkeit* in 1981 and in English as *The Invented Reality* four years later. It became the European Manifesto of radical constructivism and a few months ago, twenty-four years later, it reached its eighteenth German edition. As far as I am able to find out from the Internet, it never went beyond the first edition in the United States. This difference is all the more striking, because in the course of the eighties, Paul Watzlawick had become a leading figure of the flourishing new discipline of family therapy in the United States. The fact that he advocated a method of short therapy, rather than the months- or years-long treatments customary in most branches of psychotherapy, did not endear him to his colleagues. They felt that nothing much could be achieved in a couple of sessions and continued to compete with psychoanalysis in protracting the duration of treatments. Yet, Watzlawick's name did not cease to be cited and he remained one of the pillars of a discipline that had little time for his unorthodox philosophical ideas that formed the basis of his European reputation.

He was reluctant to talk about what he actually did with his patients, but once I managed to get him to describe one of his "short therapies". An attractive middle-aged woman had come to him to find relief from her chronic depression. He quickly discovered that the main source of it was the fact that her husband seemed to have lost his interest in sexual activities.

"How do you have your bedroom arranged?" he asked, "I mean where is the bed?"

The question obviously surprised her, but after a moment she answered:

"Well, its head is against a wall and it faces the windows."

"Which side of the bed is your husband's?"

"He sleeps on my left."

"All right," Watzlawick said, "you have to think of a reason to move the bed. You might say that the light at dawn disturbs you. And then you move the bed so that your husband sleeps along the wall."

"I'll try," she said, and the way she looked at him made him suspect that she had guessed what he foresaw: namely that the husband, who regularly had to get up during the night, would have to climb over her and that this would be enough to remind him of what marriage was about. A few days later she called to say that she didn't need any further appointments.

Watzlawick also had a knack for choosing intriguing titles for his books and using everyday language when writing about intricate problems of philosophy. He illustrated his points with the help of quite ordinary situations and his advice never sounded philosophical but seemed just plain common sense.

Perhaps the simplest powerful statement he made was: "One cannot not communicate." For me, it belongs to the class of Humberto Maturana's "Everything said is said by an observer." The inability to avoid communicating when someone else is about, may give the very naive the idea that communication is easy. Its most profound implication, however, is that communication always involves interpretation. And Paul Watzlawick was thoroughly aware of the fact that interpretation is a highly subjective affair. I think of him every time I watch TV. If the people who deploy their social antics there only knew what they are communicating to me!

It may be surprising that someone who knew all about communication, wrote extremely well, and was both amusing and perfectly uninhibited in his public talks, did not like to mix with people. Several times when we were together at international meetings, he took my arm when we had finished what we had to do and said: "Let's get out of here!" and led the way to the exit before anyone could buttonhole us. It was like a real phobia and he showed some of the signs of pathological anxiety. He did not relax until we sat in some café or restaurant as far as possible away from the congress. In time, I learned to respect this peculiarity and helped him as best I could to avoid the onslaught of admirers.

Watzlawick never spoke about his family. Only once, when we happened to commiserate about the increase of neo-Nazis in Austria, he told me an unexpected detail. During or immediately after the First World War, he said, a branch of his family separated itself and changed their name by omitting the first half. They called themselves "Wick". This sounded thoroughly German—after all there were the Counts of Wickenburg—and it got rid of the Slavic echo. They all turned into enthusiastic Nazis, he said, and I think this may have been the main root of his people phobia.

Mountain Magic 2008

Both my mother and Luggi, who was my mentor when I trained to become a ski instructor, had taught me to respect mountains. Not just because they could be dangerous. Hills and plains and the sea had their attractions, but mountains attained a grandeur that was not to be found elsewhere. When you contemplate a mountain and try to plan your way up, it acquires a personality, a character that is quite specific, and beyond this it shares the formidable power possessed by all mountains, the power that springs from avalanches, from hidden crevasses, and from the uncanny ability to shroud themselves in thick fog at a moment's notice. All good reasons to be respectful. But if you have learned to see them as a special feature of the world you live in, they generate a kind of awe that has nothing to do with the perils they may cause. It determines the style in which you approach them, the way you lay your track into the slopes, and it colors your experiences.

During that winter in Château d'Oex, when I was teaching Isabel to ski, I occasionally took a day off and went up somewhere by myself. On one of these excursions I wanted to explore a mountain I had seen on another trip. I took a bus to the point where I thought I could start my climb. After a couple of hours I reached the tree line at the beginning of a broad slope that led up to rocks and, on the far left, to a shoulder from which, I thought, I might get to the top. The last snow fall had been more than two weeks ago and avalanches were very unlikely. So I imagined a straight line diagonally across and up the slope to the shoulder I wanted to reach and started to make my track. The snow was perfect. Well-settled powder that did not let your skis sink in more then three or four inches. The swishing sound, as I alternately pushed them forward, only accentuated the magnificent silence and the invisible crystals that were raised by the skis' motion gave the air that incomparable smell of purity and sun.

It was easy going and the rhythmical tensing and relaxing of muscles in legs and arms quickly produced the kind of trance one falls into after two or three hours of climbing. Your movements are perfectly adjusted to what you perceive, but the adjustment is automatic and quite unconscious. In fact you do not know where your mind is. Just like after several hours of driving a car—if someone asked you what you have done or where you were during the last hour, you have no immediate answer. All you know is that you were at peace.

I was in that state of blissful oblivion when I reached the shoulder which opened a view into a big cauldron. There was no way to my peak on skis. It was all rocks. But half way across the cauldron there was a little pass in the ridge and some very skiable slopes led up to it. That clearly was where I should go and I worked out how best to lay my track from where I stood. When I focused on the pass, a nick in the skyline I wanted to reach, a little black dot separated itself from it, moved in leisurely circles, staying high above the ground but coming steadily nearer. By the time I recognized it as an eagle, it stopped circling and came towards me in a wide descending curve. When it was within a hundred feet, the eagle swooped up and disappeared over the ridge behind me.

Had I been dreaming? Only once before had I seen a mountain eagle, and that was through binoculars. They are extremely shy. Yet this one had come close enough for me to clearly see his eyes and his beak. I did not think it was a hallucination. But what was it, I wondered, what was it that made this experience so enchanting? In a flash I thought I knew the answer: for a moment, like at the height of an orgasm, there was no split between the experiencer and what was being experienced. For one blessed moment—impossible to say how long it lasted because it was beyond the ticking of time—there was no rift between myself and the world.

It had the quality of a mystical experience. It fitted well into that sublime feeling of oneness, of harmony with a world to which you belong and which accepts you—just as the eagle had accepted me after checking me out.

I believe one can have experiences like this sailing far out in the sea or after several days trudging through the desert. Perhaps they are similar to the inner peace generated by meditation. Hours of climbing a mountain seem to produce a similar magic.

Envoy 2009

Readers of a draft of these reminiscences raised two questions. One, how I explained tragedies in my life when I believed that it was I who constructed the reality I was experiencing. I had had to answer this for myself early on in the constructivist adventure. It is not a question that can be answered in one sentence. The answer derives from fundamental elements of the constructivist way of thinking. I shall try to make it as concise and transparent as possible.

The second question is simple but much more difficult to answer: Why do these reminiscences virtually end in the mid-seventies and why is there not more involving Charlotte. I have thought a lot about this, but did not arrive at a satisfactory answer. In the second part of this envoy I relate some thoughts that came to my mind.

* * *

Vico's path to constructivism was, in I my view, an intuitive one; Kant, half a century later, laid the logical foundations. Our way of experiencing, Kant said, imposes a temporal sequence and a spatial ordering on the sensations our mind picks from an unstructured manifold. Kant considered it "wholly contradictory and impossible" that concepts should be produced by the mind and then refer to external objects. But how concepts actually *should* be thought to arise is one of the most difficult parts of Kant's model of reason. He tries to be explicit about abstract concepts that determine the *form* of our experience, space and time, for instance, and other relational concepts that we apply to experience but do not derive from it. He is not very clear about how we generate the ideas of the objects with which we furnish our experiential reality. Both Piaget and Ceccato did groundwork towards a comprehensive model of that area and many of my efforts were attempts to extend it.

I make three assumptions about what we call "mind". The first two are that it has the still mysterious powers of memory and awareness. This means that it can reflect on experience, both present and remembered. The third is that it tends to attribute values to sensations and what can be developed from them. Wilhelm von Humboldt, at the end of the 18th century, put this into three remarkable aphorisms:

1.   The essence of thinking consists in reflecting, i.e., in distinguishing what thinks from what is being thought.

2.   In order to reflect, the mind must stand still for a moment in its progressive activity, must grasp as a unit what was just presented, and thus posit it as object against itself.

3.   The mind then compares the units, of which several can be created in that way, and separates and connects them according to its needs.

This constructive work begins at birth and probably even earlier. Some of the connections that are made turn out to be repeatable, and the more often they are repeated the "harder" they become. As a result, some early concepts turn into fixtures that are not likely to be modified, especially if they have been used as cornerstones of satisfactory complex conceptual constructions. Language, then, bestows upon them a permanence that makes them seem absolute.

What we experience as the world we live in is built out of concepts and conceptual relations that have served us well in many circumstances. It is they that determine the possibilities of further construction as well as the constraints that limit it. That is why we hurt our shin when we run into the coffee table and why we demolish our car when we crash into a tree. The way we have formed our concepts has consequences that are inevitable and often unforeseeable; and if these consequences are tragic, we are unable to retrace our constructive steps in order to generate more congenial alternatives. In other words, we are caught within a conceptual scaffolding that we could not undo without losing everything that has helped to structure our experience since the day our mind awoke.

* * *

When Charlotte some ten years ago began to lose her way driving home from town, I was struck by the horrifying suspicion that she might be going the way of her sister, who began to develop Alzheimer's when she neared seventy. The suspicion soon turned into certainty.

Almost from one day to another, she lost interest in working in her studio, and this radically changed the climate of our togetherness. She began to forget whatever happened in the present and much of what had happened in the past. When she realized what was going on, she somehow managed to maintain the appearance of equanimity. She kept her rage—which I knew consumed her at times—almost entirely to herself. She could not stand any form of commiseration. Once she burst out and said she was sorry to have become an impediment for me. She knew perfectly well that there was no way to deny it. I took her in my arms and it was the only time she cried.

Our interactions that had been a constant pleasure for twenty-five years, quickly became limited. Conversation is not possible when what is said cannot be linked to what was said before. Any comment you make loses its meaning if the hearer has already forgotten what you are commenting on. What remains are the interactions of caring, tender but hollow, with a person whose mind has bit by bit gone to sleep.

Many of the sketches in this book are the result of a recollection that appeared to me in the middle of the night. Lying in the dark with nothing to see gives free reign to the unconscious. If you have ever been in a forest early in spring, you may have noticed the first sprouts of ferns. They spring from the soil like little question marks, pale and delicately curved, a promise of what may come. In time they straighten out and develop into luxurious fronds. It's an image of how ideas pop out of the dark.

Alzheimer's curse cast a paralyzing fog into the forest of my imagination. The recent past lost all color and nothing sprouted and seemed worth developing into a sketch. The pain of the last decade somehow corroded the memory of the years with Charlotte and my mind escaped into the more distant past. This may be just a comfortable fiction, but I have to leave it at that; it's the only explanation I can offer.

Josef Mitterer

Afterword

1. A few years ago I visited together with Ernst von Glasersfeld St. Anton, the ski resort in the Austrian Alps. This is where he often spent the winter months in his youth and where he was a ski-instructor in the famous ski school of Hannes Schneider. He was going to get the Golden Merit Award of the Ski Club Arlberg of which he became a member seventy-five years ago. We stood in front of a post-card shop and he said that he wouldn't need any cards, he knew "his" St. Anton well enough … and then there was this "Nostalgic Postcard" where he skies the deep snow with his friend Rudi Matt, photographed by Lothar Ruebelt in 1936 …

2. Ernst von Glasersfeld could be a wealthy man today. His family owned several buildings on Wenzels Square in Prague and they were never expropriated, as his parents opted for Czech citizenship after the Austro-Hungarian Empire collapsed at the end of World War I. When restitution became possible some fifteen years ago he told me that he would not do anything in this direction. It could only get a burden and even a hindrance for his work and he would much rather write another book on Radical Constructivism.

3. When Ernst von Glasersfeld retired from the University of Georgia he moved to Amherst, Massachusetts. His friend Jack Lochhead invited him to join the *Scientific Research Reasoning Institute* of the *University of Massachusetts* to which he still belongs. And apart from that there were still "real winters" in New England. He bought a house at the foot of a wooded hill and he cut his own private ski slope into the forest, where he skied until the age of 90.

4. In a recent survey among eighty top researchers in Science Education Ernst von Glasersfeld came out as the most influential philosopher apart from Thomas Kuhn.

Sometimes I get the impression that Ernst von Glasersfeld is so modest that he does not even want to realize the impact he has on so many disciplines of contemporary science, especially in Continental Europe. Perhaps it is difficult for someone who started his work as an outsider, on the periphery of science, to find himself all of a sudden in the center of attention. He is a "thinker" in the best sense of the word — not belonging to any one discipline, not fitting into the traditional academic canon.

His work is discussed and recognized in cognitive science, in communication studies and in media theory, in science education, in economics, in psychology and in psychotherapy. He practised interdisciplinarity or even transdisciplinarity long before it became fashionable.

5. Only in academic philosophy, which is a rather inert discipline when it comes to change and to the reception of new ideas, Ernst von Glasersfeld is still a marginal figure, being criticized if not ignored by its mainstream representatives. Academic philosophers accuse him of denying reality, claim that his model of thought leads into extreme relativism and that his constructivism is incapable of solving problems of everyday life. But then the application of the ideas of Ernst von Glasersfeld turns out to be most successful in such disciplines as education or psychology and psychotherapy.

6. What is Radical Constructivism? In the words of Ernst von Glasersfeld it is an unconventional way to deal with the problems of knowledge. Radical Constructivism is based on the assumption that all knowledge, however it is to be defined, exists only in the heads of people, and that the thinking subject can construct his knowledge only on the basis of his own experience. What we make of our experience — this alone shapes the world in which we live consciously. Knowledge is not passively received by the thinking subject, but is actively constructed. Cognition serves the organization of the world of our experiences and not the discovery of an ontological reality.

The concept of truth as a true picture of an independent reality is replaced by the concept of viability, which simply claims to be a potential thinking model for the only world we can "recognize", namely the world we construct as living beings.

7. It is pointless to aim at describing the world as it really is: Each subject makes different experiences, even when making experiences and world-building is restricted through manifold social interactions.

The goal which unites almost all non-constructivist philosophies is the idea of a successful pursuit of truth and knowledge. Ernst von Glasersfeld repudiates this goal. To attain knowledge of an independent world we would have to compare our knowledge with it. But in order to do so, we would need some kind of direct access to a reality which lies beyond one's own experience and which is not touched by ones own "pictures" and their representations in language. Experiences can only be compared with experiences, descriptions with descriptions and not with a reality beyond our experiences and descriptions.

But there is still a "realist rest" in constructivism. We cannot know what lies beyond the cognitive structures, which we have built up ourselves. The reality beyond the worlds constructed and made by us remains inaccessible. "Nature has thrown its keys away", says von Glasersfeld. But this reality shows up, when our constructions fail. Here is a certain relationship with the Critical Rationalism of Karl Popper, who however still remains within the traditional framework and allows at least for approach and closeness to truth. For the Radical Constructivism of Ernst von Glasersfeld truth as agreement with a reality "beyond" has no hold. Of relevance is the usefulness of our ideas for shaping and forming the world we live in and the failure of a theory only shows the impracticality of this construction for its purpose. In this respect von Glasersfeld is closer to the pragmatism of James, Dewey and Rorty than to Critical Rationalism.

8. A decision of another philosophy is always as well a decision for other problems. Radical Constructivism has led Ernst von Glasersfeld to repudiate a question which is central for most philosophers, namely the relation between language and reality; instead he provides answers to questions which have hardly been asked before.

The growing shift of focus in contemporary philosophy from the object of knowledge to knowledge of the object, to the process of knowledge, is a development where Radical Constructivism takes a leading position.

9. The search for viability, for practical ways, is an alternative for the goal of truth of the realist. A Constructivist too makes decisions, but these decisions don't happen twice: He has no "reality beyond" for anchoring and fundamentalizing his decisions. He has no instance "beyond" to which he could transfer the responsibility for his decisions. Although he makes his decisions from his standpoint, this standpoint is just a footstep on his path of knowledge. And he will proceed on this path only when he leaves it, when he makes a step away from where he is.

The constructivist knows that, when he stays on a standpoint for too long, he gets into danger of getting caught deep in old realistic mud, till the ground of truth in being …

10. Ernst von Glasersfeld does not rest on a standpoint. The given is only a crutch for him, which he throws away, after he has used it to go further. The idea — and the problem — of an independent reality as a referee in a "Beyond" of our experiences has become powerless and cannot be used to decide on our knowledge-claims. We need to take up ourselves the responsibility for our decisions, our actions and our facts.

When we refer in our discourses to reality as an instance, and use phrases like "in reality" or "in truth" or "in fact", then these phrases hold no argumentative power for the radical constructivist. They simply mark one's own conceptions and cannot get depersonalized or even universalized in order to raise and support claims of dominance against other world-conceptions.

Radical Constructivism is an open way of thinking and it is still in a process of differentiation. It is an anti-fundamentalist answer to questions of philosophy — questions which in other contexts served as topics as well for philosophers like Paul Feyerabend or Richard Rorty.

* * *

The impact of the works of Ernst von Glasersfeld is in no small part due to his excellent scientific prose. He developed his Radical Constructivism in half a dozen books and in more than two hundred articles. He has written and published in English, German, Italian and French and he is still answering questions in all these languages on a website (http://www.oikos.org/vonen.htm), which his friend Vincent Kenny has put together.